IMAGES
of America

DIXFIELD

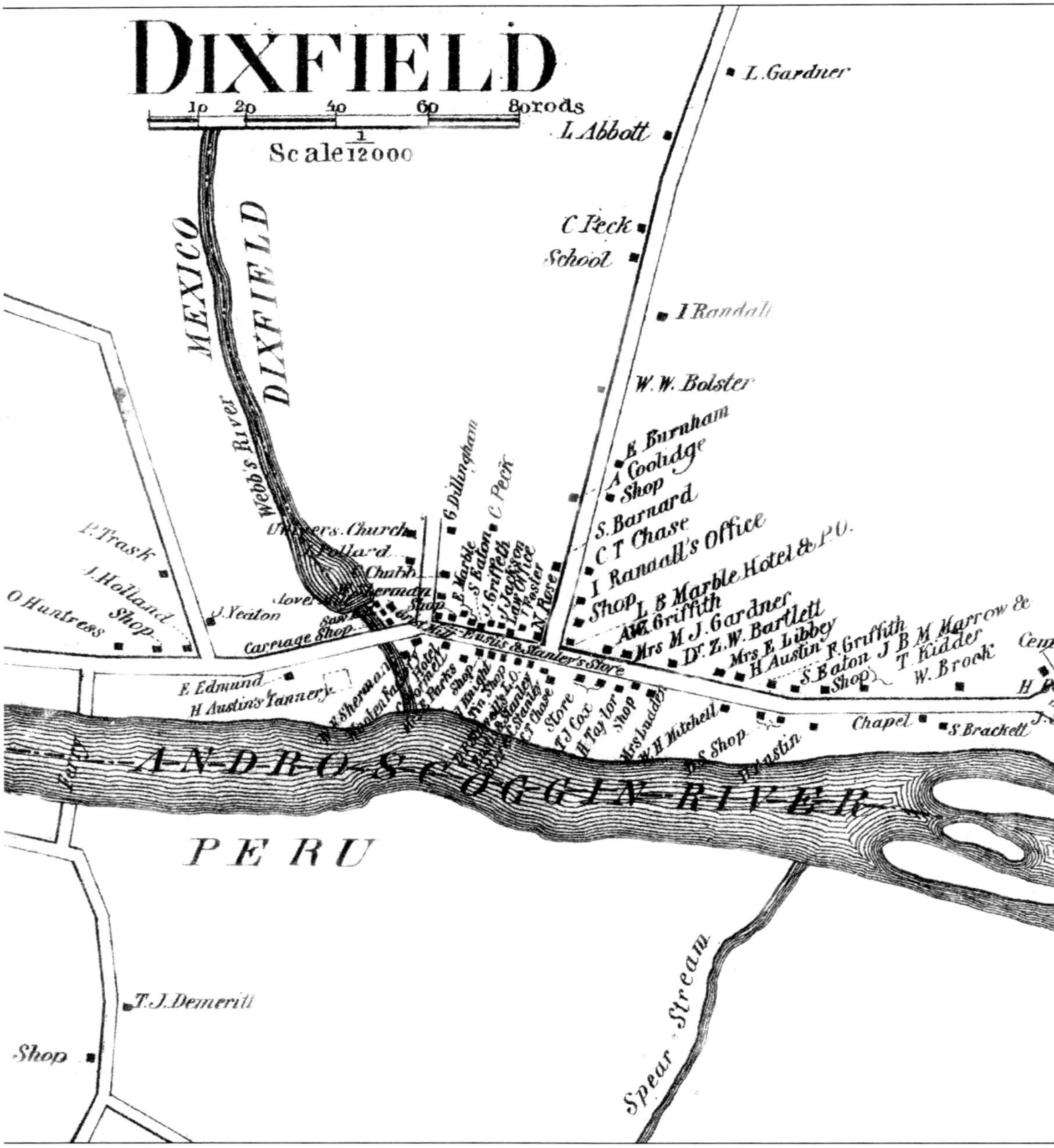

Dixfield Village is shown in this map by the H.F. Walling Company of New York City, published in 1858 by the Gillette and Huntington Company. The village map was one of 54 included on a wall map that measured five feet square. Dixfield Village is formed by its boundary with Mexico and includes many Peru families. (Author's collection.)

On the Cover: The founding family of Dixfield, the Holmans of Dixfield Common, held annual reunions at the old homesteads for many decades. This picture was taken in August 1909 at the Peter Holman farm. Town meetings were once held upstairs in this building, which featured four brick fireplaces. (Dixfield Historical Society.)

IMAGES
of America

DIXFIELD

Peter R. Stowell

ARCADIA
PUBLISHING

ISBN 978-1-4671-2008-1

Published by Arcadia Publishing
Charleston, South Carolina

Printed in the United States of America

Library of Congress Control Number: 2013931530

For all general information, please contact Arcadia Publishing:
Telephone 843-853-2070
Fax 843-853-0044
E-mail sales@arcadiapublishing.com
For customer service and orders:
Toll-Free 1-888-313-2665

Visit us on the Internet at www.arcadiapublishing.com

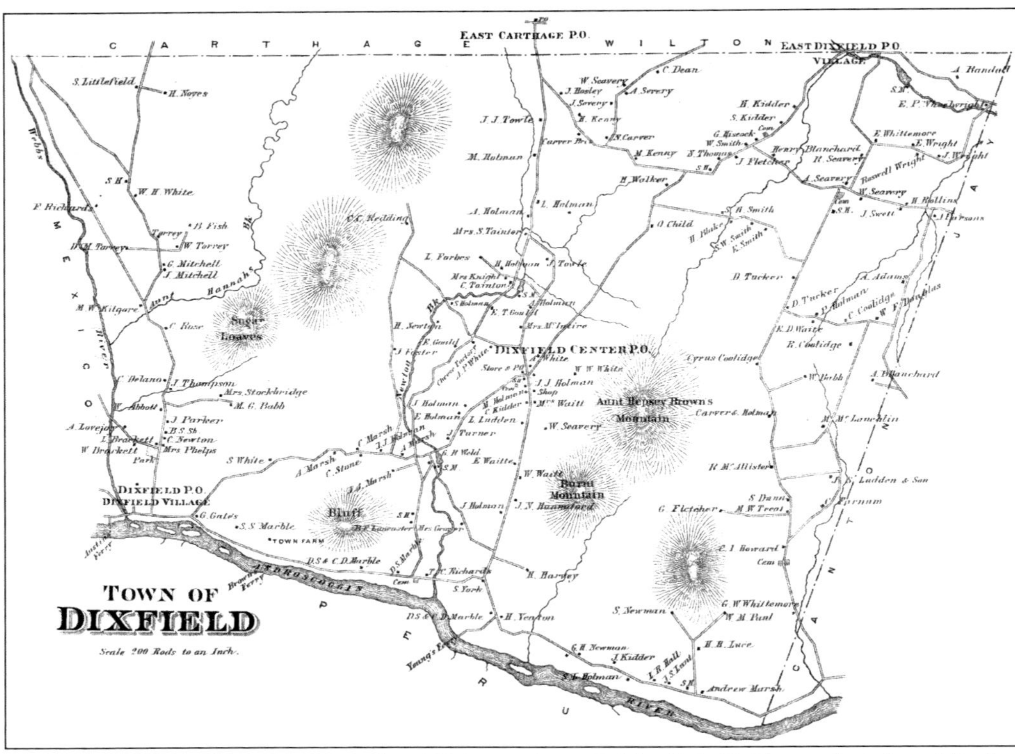

The town of Dixfield is shown in this 1880 map from Caldwell & Halfpenny's Atlas of Oxford County, Maine. Dixfield Village is at the lower left of the map, Dixfield Center is at the center, and East Dixfield is at the upper right. (Author's collection.)

Contents

ACKNOWLEDGMENTS

The author would like to acknowledge the cooperation and involvement of the Dixfield Historical Society for its assistance and unfettered access to its photographs. I would also like to thank Stephen D. Thompson for his photograph of the 1880 Caldwell and Halfpenny map of Dixfield and the photograph of Sophronia Stowell. Thanks go to Palmer Curtis for her review of an early draft, Ben Conant for his photograph collection of early Dixfield families, Albert Spaulding for his valued assistance, Mike Towle for his Stanley-Stowell genealogy, and many others who offered advice and friendship.

Images from the author's collections are indicated by (PRS). Additional contributors include the Dixfield Historical Society (DHS), Nancy D. McReynolds (NDM), the Maine Historic Preservation Commission (MHPC), Teres A. Winter (TAW), the late Dexter M. Stowell (DMS), Paula P. Smith (PPS), William W. Eustis (WWE), Betsey E. Anderson (BEA), Margaret E. Sipple (MES), Joyce Swan (JS), the Mexico Historical Society (MHS), Karen Root Grimm (KRG), Ann T. Kuhns (ATK), Dale R. Harris, (DRH), Peter D. Holman (PDH), Donna C. Towle, (DCT), the late Harriett S. Blake (HSB), Charlotte Collins (CC), Minnie Blodgett (MB), Jane M. Bubar (JMB), the Maine State Archives (MSA), and Lauren A. Hebert (LAH). Others who submitted images were Al Bresette, Tony Martin, and Nelson Coolidge. The author gratefully acknowledges their generosity.

I would also like to acknowledge the work of the following past Dixfield citizens who have helped preserve Dixfield's heritage: Henry W. Park, Hiram A. Randall, Emerson Bartlett, Sybil A. Howe, Ada Murch Smith, Nellie L. Root, Ruth K. Bernard, Winthrop Andrews, Jennie W. Bryant, Rachael Kidder, Roy Hathaway, A. Isabel Russell, Althea W. Fish, Lorraine W. Smith, and Lyman Holman. There are others who have left their marks but not their names. I am grateful to all.

Introduction

There is only one town named Dixfield in the world, and it got its name through a bit of trickery. Originally called Holmanstown after its Sutton, Massachusetts, founder, Col. Jonathan Holman, the name was changed to Dixfield when Dr. Elijah Dix of Boston promised the townspeople a library in return for the favor. They did, but he did not—at least not in the spirit of the promise; he sent along an old trunk filled with medical texts, all of them written in German. Worse, he lost interest in Dixfield and turned his attention to Dixmont, Maine, better suited to his ambition of building a town to rival his native Worcester. In spite of this perfidy, Dixfield prospered and became a leading cultural, educational, and legal center of western Maine. For example, there are governors, congressmen, senators, and judges who can trace their roots or careers to Dixfield. One wag commented that Dixfield had only 400 houses but five attorneys in the 1850s.

Dixfield itself is a township, but within, the following three settlements developed over time: Dixfield Village to the west, East Dixfield to the east, and Dixfield Center in the center of the township. More than 210 years after its founding, these three communities still exist, each with its unique history. Dixfield Center and East Dixfield were primarily agrarian communities while Dixfield Village became the manufacturing center of town.

Unlike many Maine towns, Dixfield has never published a comprehensive early history. Not that they did not try. Indeed, the records indicate that two draft histories were lost while in transit to be published. A 1950s newspaper article cites the loss of the first one while the second, a follow-up to the small volume *The Early History of Dixfield Maine* issued in the bicentennial year of 1976, was lost as well. The present volume is not a substitute for a comprehensive history of the town but rather a reminder to its readers of Dixfield's rich history, which is important to bear in mind perhaps as Dixfield transitions from a manufacturing community to a commuter community with a challenging future.

Over the years, local photograph collections were donated to the Dixfield Historical Society. These were augmented in 2006 through the generosity of the Maine State Library, which graciously developed more than 150 glass-plate negatives in the society's collection. Since 2003, Peter Stowell, who had been assembling his own collection of Dixfield images, has been studying these collections to help reconstruct Dixfield's history. As families left Dixfield to lead their lives elsewhere, additional collections were scattered all over the United States. In 2007, Karen Root Grimm from LaFayette, New York, generously offered her collection of Dixfield area images to the Dixfield Historical Society for its use. Importantly, her images included dozens of neighboring Lake Webb just at the moment Dixfield residents began building their cottages on its shores. Then, Dexter Eustis in Florida steered Stowell onto a Dixfield photograph collection housed by his cousin William Eustis in Rockland, Maine. That collection consisted of more than 300 family portraits, mostly unidentified. Over the next two years, Stowell, with the other collections to aid him, identified dozens of them, bringing back to life people whose names had been lost to time. Soon afterwards, the Nancy Drew McReynolds collection surfaced in Bellevue, Washington.

Because most of the hundreds of photographs were neatly identified and dated, they quickly filled in important gaps in Dixfield's history.

By the time the scores of photographs housed at the Maine Historical Preservation Commission (MHPC) surfaced in 2012, literally hundreds of previously unidentified images could be named and those misnamed could be corrected. The MHPC collection consisted of an assortment of identified photographs and stereoviews, which often cited the name of the photographer, and real-photo postcards, many not previously known. Finally, longtime Dixfield resident Dale Harris had fortuitously bought a dusty old collection of glass-plate negatives at auction in the mid-1960s. He left them unexamined for years before finally discovering that they preserved priceless images of Dixfield around the turn of the 19th century. Sufficient documentation was included with them to attribute them to local druggist James P. Johnston, who sold the images from his store on Main Street. In 2012, Harris made them available to Stowell for use in the present work.

Integrating the history captured by these collections has yielded a plethora of previously unknown historical structures. The location of John S. Harlow's wood conveyor, the Henry Thayer Lumber Mill, the A.L. Coburn Mill Lumber Company, and the original home of Maine Supreme Court justice Charles W. Walton had been hiding in plain sight—we just did not know it. Ida Adair, the mother of silent film actor John Gilbert had Dixfield connections unearthed by a photograph in a private collection and another in the Dixfield Historical Society's collection, both related to Dixfield and both taken by the same Los Angeles studio. Linking these photographs to local legends and news accounts firmly established that John Gilbert visited Dixfield when just a lad. The location of Jefferson Davis's 1858 speech in Dixfield became identified, and two previously unknown photographs of Susan Trask Stanley, the matriarch of the Stanley family in Dixfield, surfaced both in Rockland, Maine, and Bellevue, Washington—the first confirmed such images of her, taken two decades apart. Luckily, her identity in these two images led to identifying her in others.

Over the last few years, Stowell has published some of these photographs in the quarterly newsletter of the Dixfield Historical Society, the *Dixfield Star*; each image is chosen to inform its readers of newly discovered aspects of the town's history. More photographs were posted on the society's website at Dixfieldhistory.com. Still more have appeared on the Maine Historical Society's *Maine Memory Network*. Do not think for a moment, however, that any of the valuable images in this book have been commonly available; they have not been. Indeed, it is safe to say that scores of them are being seen for the first time outside their collections. This is true as well for virtually all the family photographs tucked away in bureau draws or back rooms—they are being seen here beyond their family confines for the first time. It is our hope that they will serve to bring pleasure to those who read *Dixfield*, engendering appreciation for a small town in western Maine who lived life the way it used to be.

—Albert Spaulding, charter member and former president
Dixfield Historical Society

One

Lower Main Street

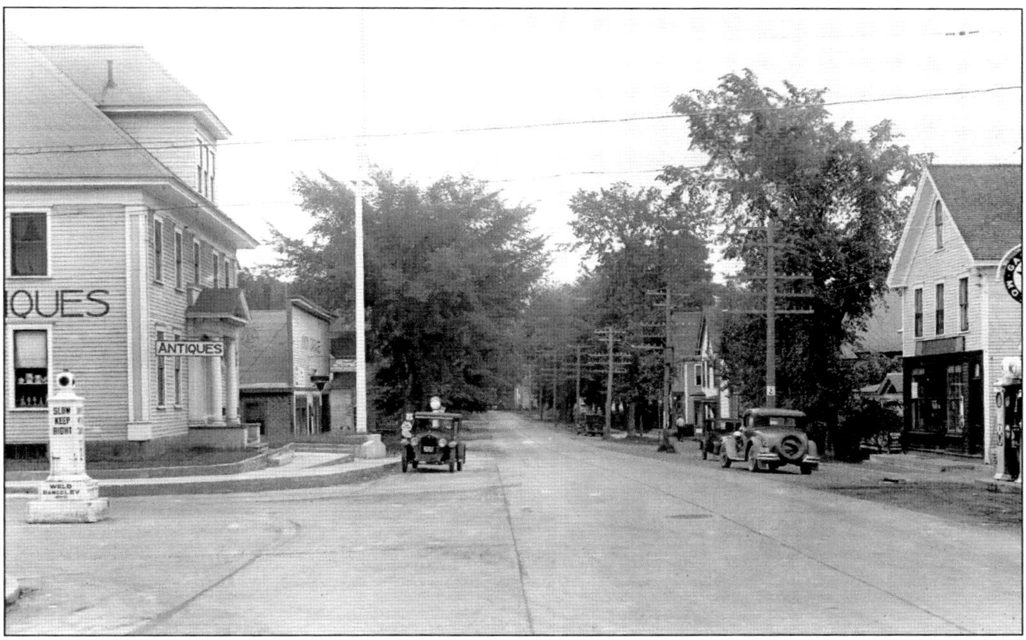

Dixfield Square is where lower Main Street and upper Main Street intersect with Weld Street, shown to the left. This is how the square looked in 1934; the cement streets had been laid down in 1926. Ione Harlow operated her antiques store from the Harlow Block on the left, and the Knox Garage sold Ford automobiles just beyond. Across Main Street, Guy O. Gardner served customers at his drugstore, and Texaco gasoline was sold at the Don Gates Garage, just out of sight behind the gas pumps. The National House, a five-story hotel, tavern, and community center, previously stood on the Harlow Block site. (DHS.)

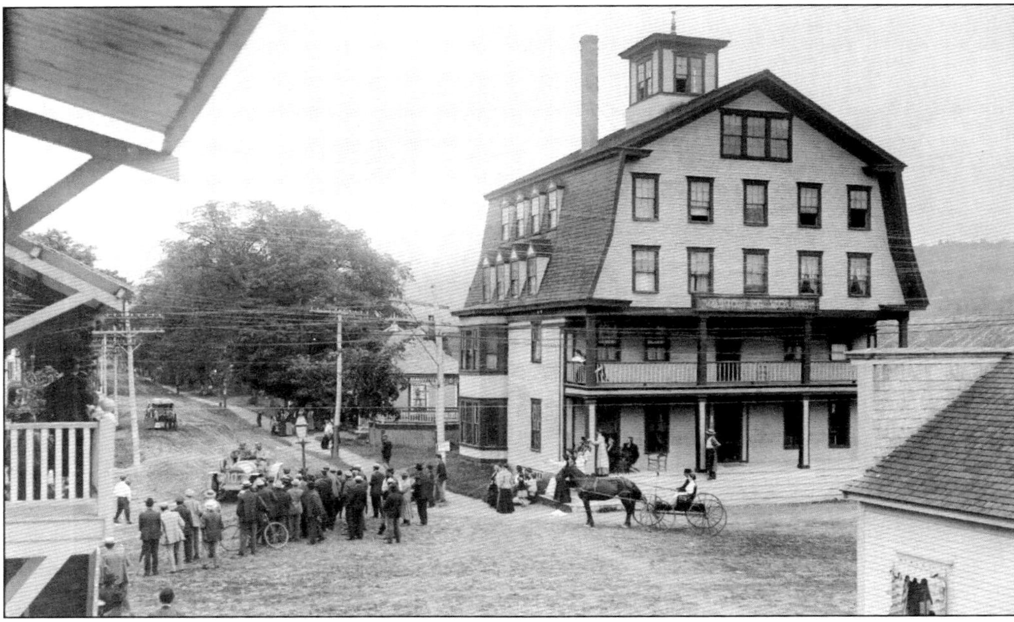

The National House, built in 1858 by Baldwin L. Marble, offered rooms and refreshments to its patrons. Dances and public suppers were held there during the winter months, serving extravagant courses until the wee hours of the morning. In this c. 1910 picture, a crowd of people is watching early cars race on Weld Street. A few years later, the hotel would be remodeled into a modern office building. (DHS.)

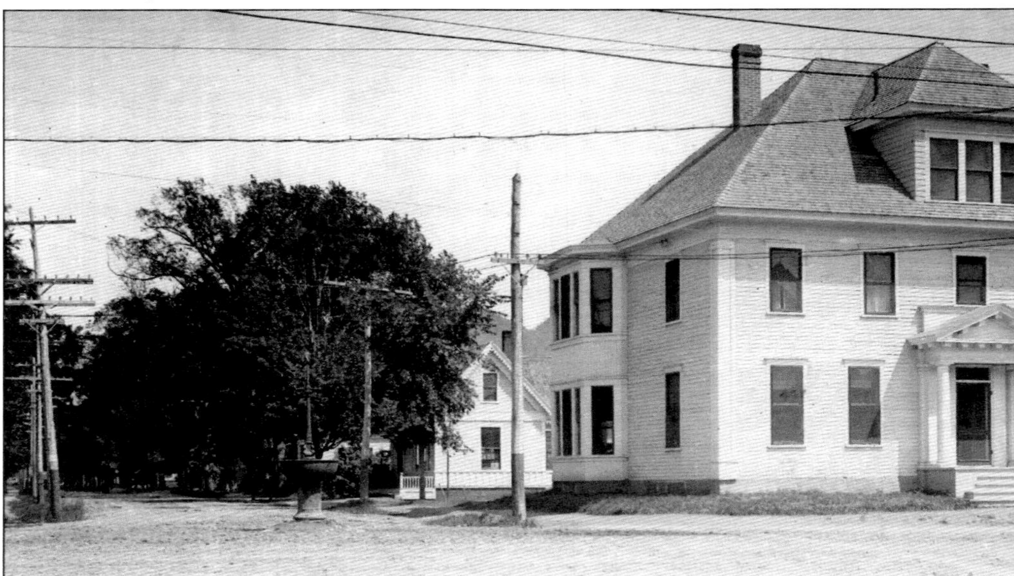

After its remodeling, the National House became known as the Harlow Building, after its owner, attorney John S. Harlow, Dixfield's leading citizen and businessman. His younger sister Ione soon established an antique shop in the back rooms, and the public library soon located upstairs as did the New England Telephone and Telegraph Company and offices of the Forster toothpick mill. (PRS.)

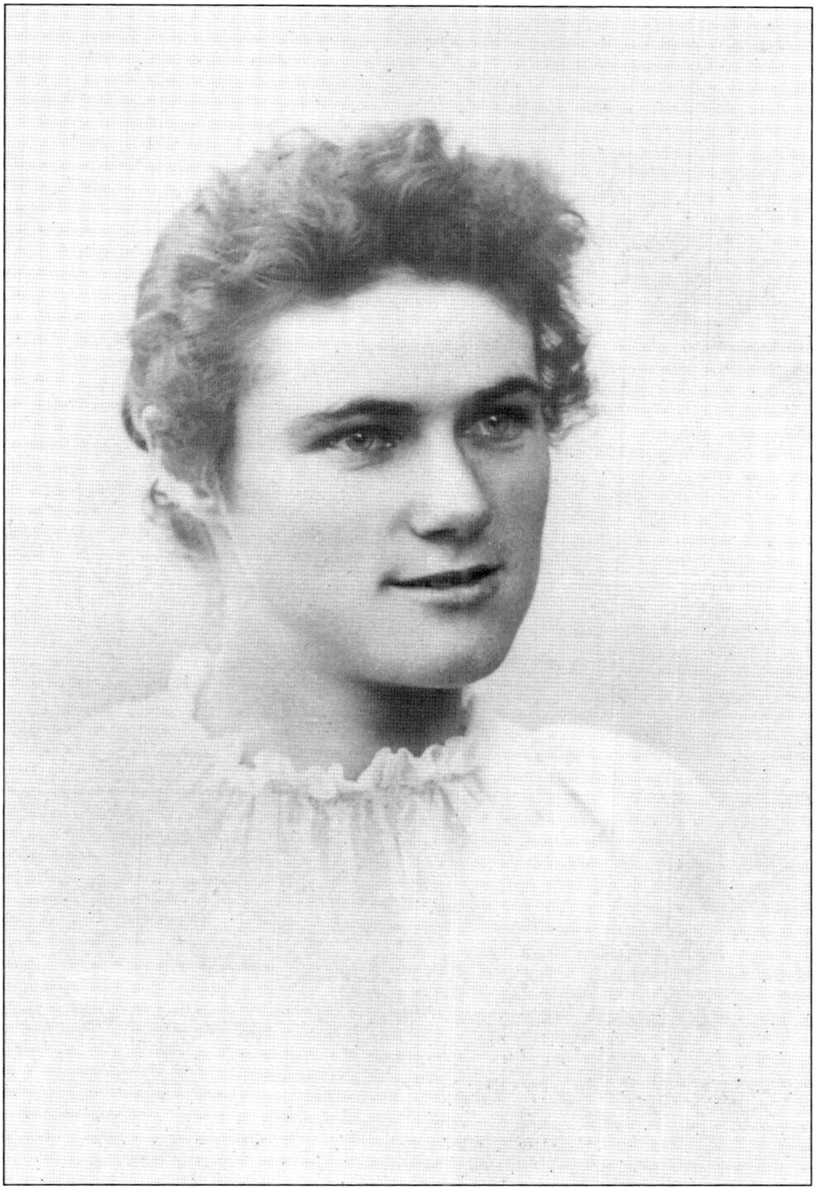

Ione Harlow (1870–1968) was the fifth child of Elbridge Gerry and Rosella Harlow. She operated a millinery store on Main Street and then opened an antiques store in the new Harlow Block. Widely recognized throughout New England as an expert on early American antiques, she owned several pieces of furniture handed down from the village founders. In 1948, she moved her antique business into her home in the 1820 House on Weld Street. Upon her death, Harlow bequeathed a large sum of money to the people of Dixfield to be used for community betterment and scholarships. To this day, the Ione Harlow Scholarship Committee meets to determine how it can help use Harlow's gift to best aid local students. She was a descendant of Amos Trask, who founded Dixfield Village after the original proprietor, Dr. Elijah Dix, abandoned Dixfield for Dixmont, Maine. Trask bought Dix's village holdings, and in 1816, "the year without a summer," generously assured that his neighbors had seed for the next season's planting. (NDM.)

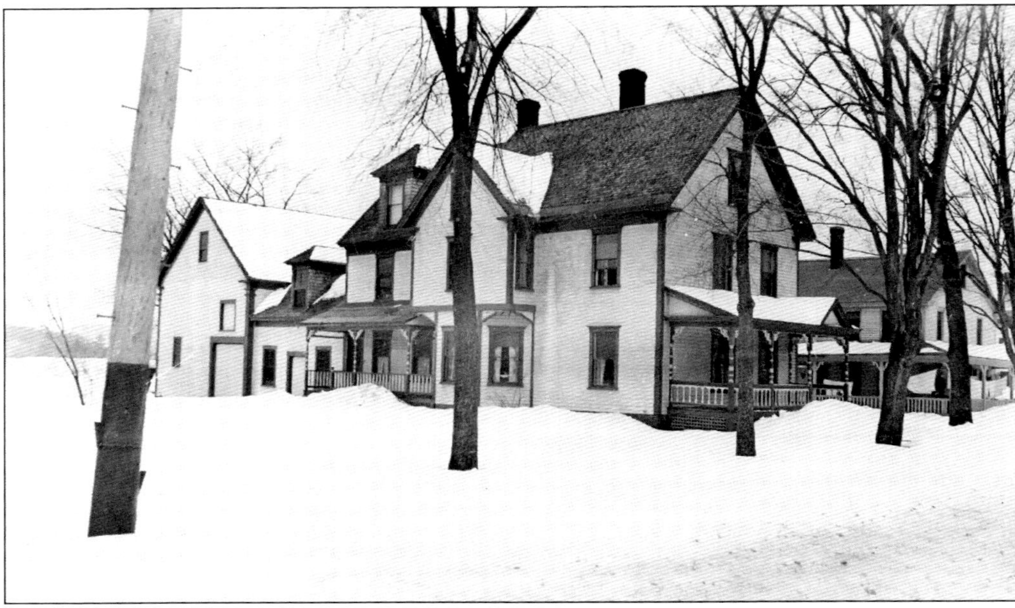

The John Jackson Towle home (left) on lower Main Street was built in 1899 on land once belonging to William Mitchell, a blacksmith, who also owned the house on the right. The Dixfield Historical Society purchased the building in 1997 to serve as the headquarters for it top-notch tool museum, period exhibits, and archives. Its meetings are held in the connecting space between the house and the barn. (DHS.)

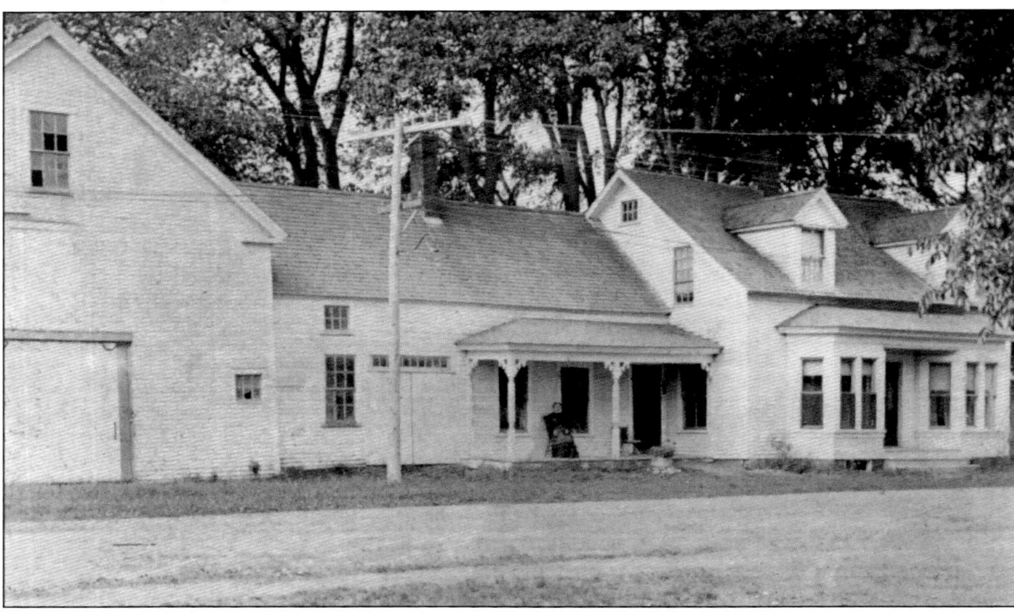

Charles W. Walton built this house in the 1850s. Born in Mexico, Maine, Walton studied law with Isaac Randall on Weld Street in the 1840s and later served as a congressman during Pres. Abraham Lincoln's administration, resigning to accept an appointment to the Maine Supreme Court, where he served for the next 35 years. Shown in the picture is Hattie Kilgore, wife of Marcus Kilgore, a later owner. Still standing, the Walton home has been greatly modified. (DHS.)

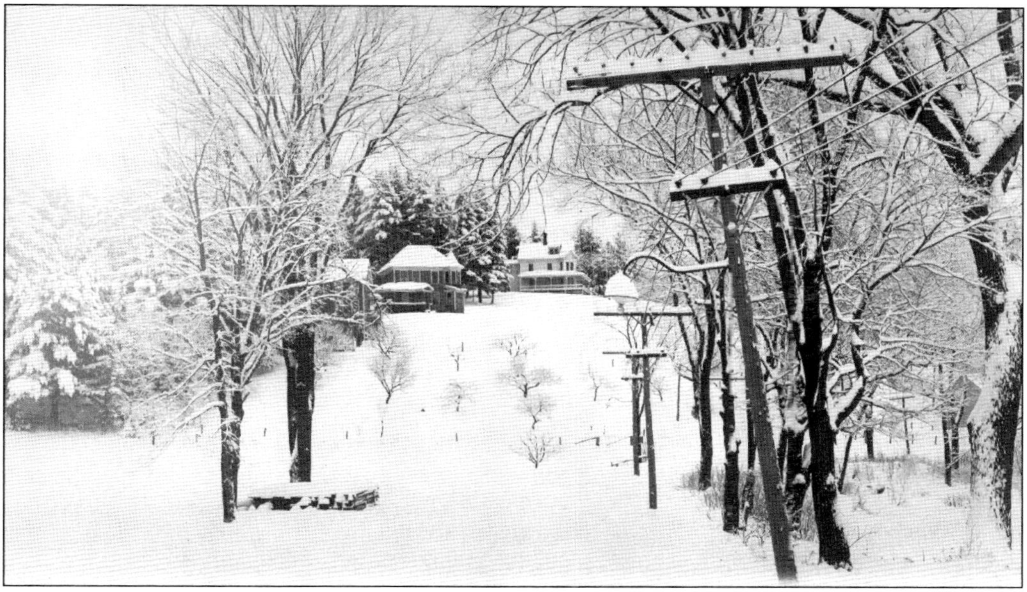

Shown in this c. 1910 image is a view of Abbott Hill from lower Main Street. The home of William W. Abbot crowns the hill, while lumber dealer William F. Putnam's residence sits above the orchard of fruit trees. (PRS.)

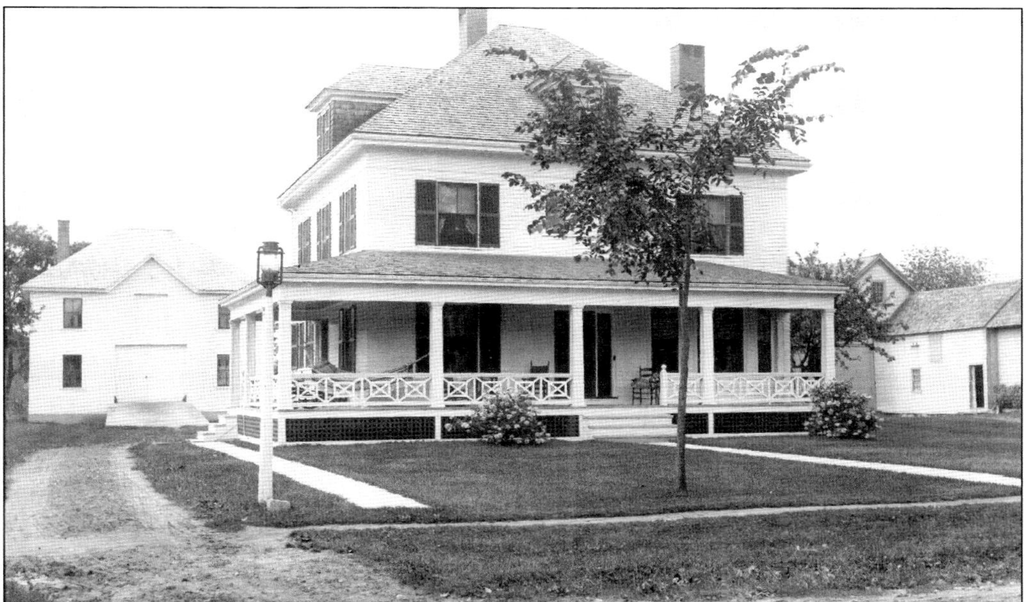

Prevented by the terms of his father's will from inheriting the Forster toothpick mills in Dixfield and Strong, Maine, Maurice W. Forster went into business with attorney John S. Harlow, who had played an important role in developing the spool industry in town. By late 1907, when this picture was taken, Forster had prospered enough to enjoy this new home. Subsequent owners included Guy O. Gardner, who ran a popular drugstore in town, and Newton S. Stowell, who built the world's largest spool-manufacturing business. (MHPC.)

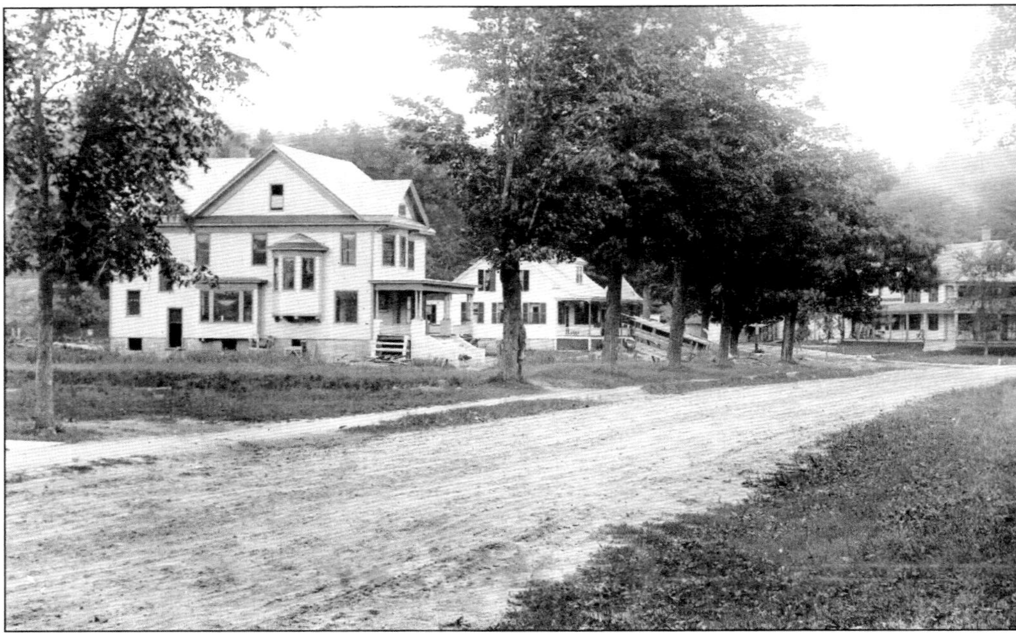

Arthur Newton Stowell built the house on the left in 1911. He was the eldest son of spool mill baron Newton Stanley Stowell, who gained control of the town's three spool mills in 1903. Soon after returning from his studies at Westbrook Seminary, Arthur helped his father in the management of the mills. Charles Lyman Eustis built the middle house in the 1820s. And Deacon Joseph Wheeler built the house on the right, again in the 1820s. (DHS.)

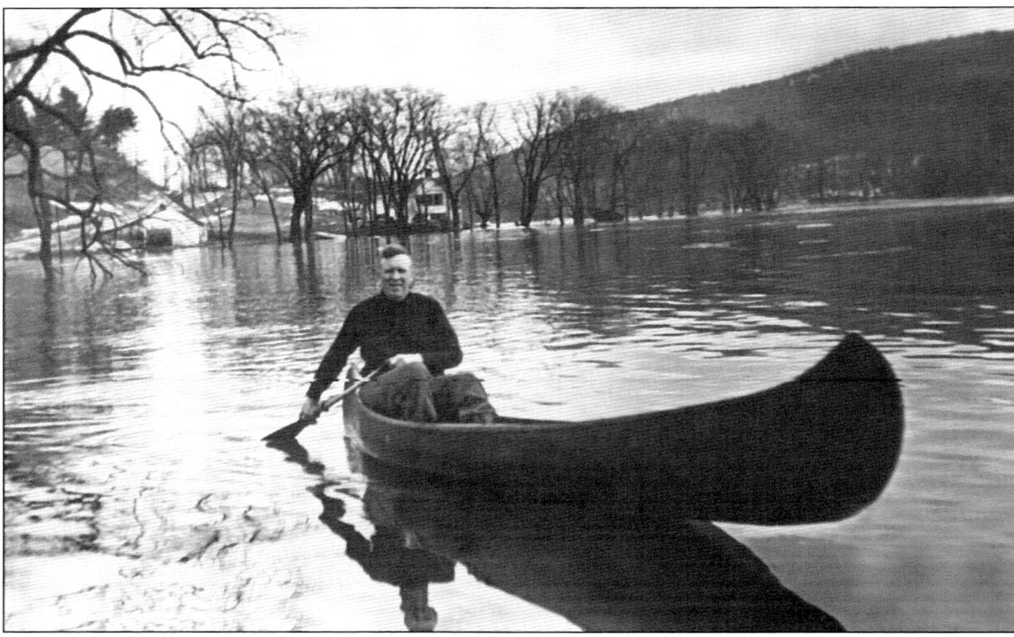

The flooding of the Androscoggin River in March 1936 was one of the worst ever recorded. In this picture, Arthur Stowell paddles his canoe, exploring the extent of the damage. He lived just a few hundred feet away on US Route 2, which can be seen ascending the hill to the left. (TAW.)

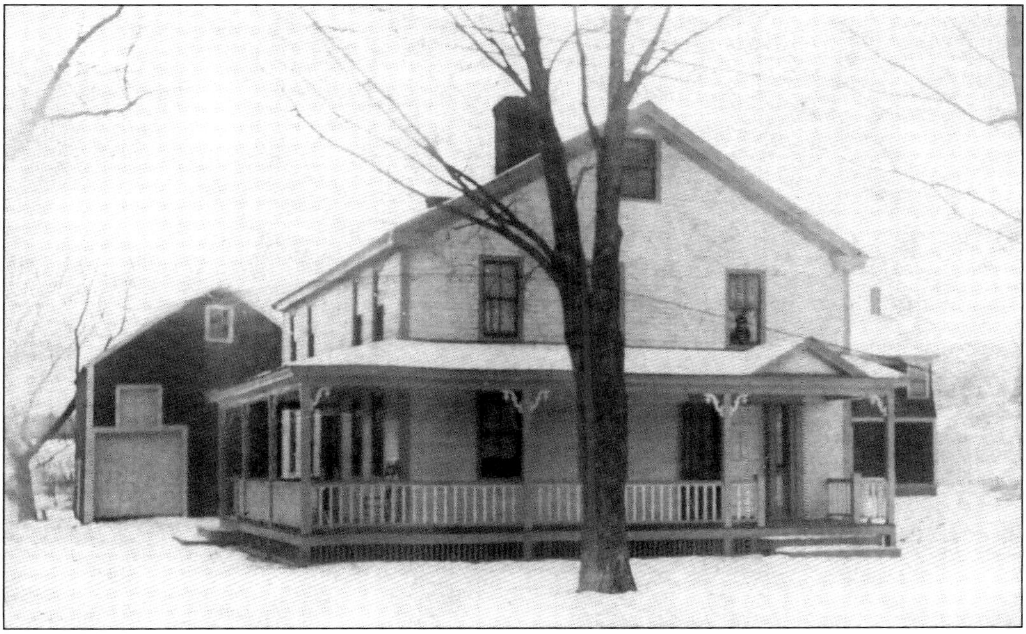

No existing records show when the William W. Mitchell home was built, but it was most likely shortly after his marriage to Sara Mason Eustis in 1859. The Mitchell family had come to Dixfield from Freeport, Maine. Mitchell was a blacksmith. Later in life, he moved to Massachusetts. His home was later owned by Charles H. Towle and, finally, removed in 1996 to make room for the Dixfield Village Green. (DHS.)

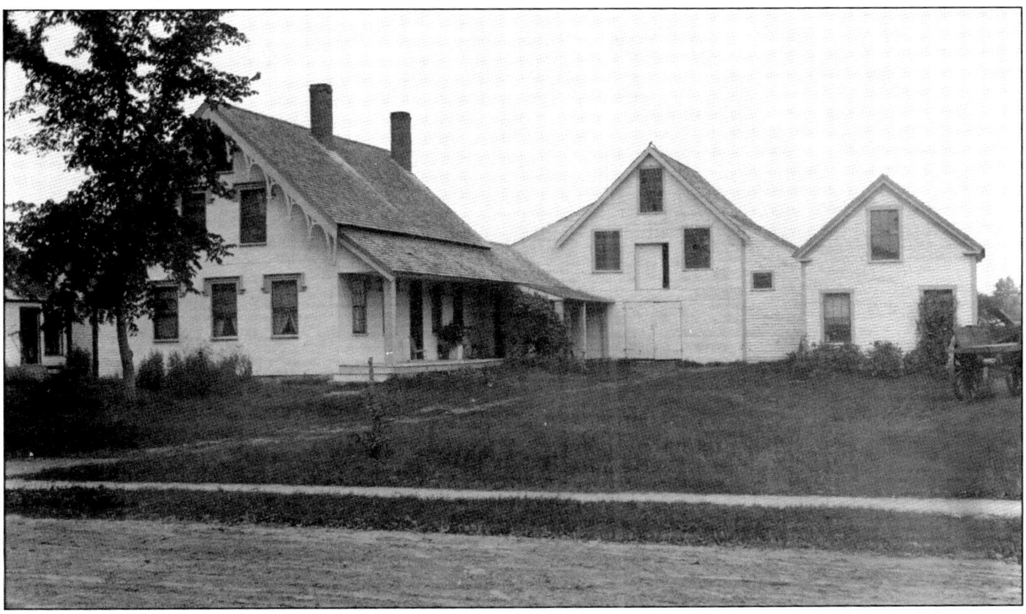

The Edwin T. Merrill homestead on lower Main Street in Dixfield consisted of a small house, a small barn, and outbuildings. The house burned flat in 1925. Merrill rebuilt, and the replacement home still stands today, owned by E.T. Merrill's descendants. The gingerbread treatment to the eves was a fairly common decoration in Dixfield homes. (MHPC.)

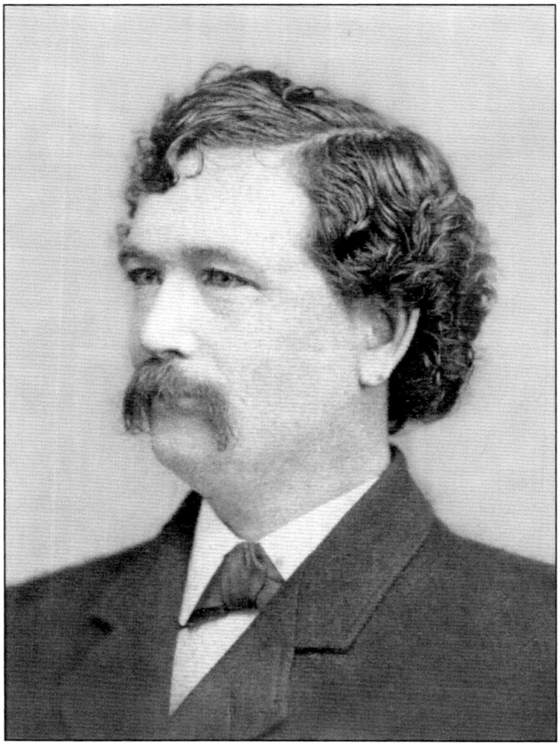

In the mid-1880s, George A. Marsh came to Dixfield from South Paris, Maine, where he worked for the Burnham and Morrill Company canning corn. He repeated that work in Dixfield. He built a large house on Main Street where the Ludden Library is now located. His influence on Dixfield lasted many years and provided employment to dozens of people. He received several patents for making improvements in the corn-canning process. (NDM.)

George and Josephine Marsh lived in this fine home on the north side of lower Main Street, raising their three daughters—Alice, Netta, and Josie. They married the following three men who contributed to Dixfield's economy: Maurice Keith, George Stanley, and Adolph Walters, respectively. Later, the Welch family owned the house. Lorraine Welch Smith became a local newspaper reporter and historian, donating thousands of documents to the Dixfield Historical Society. (NDM.)

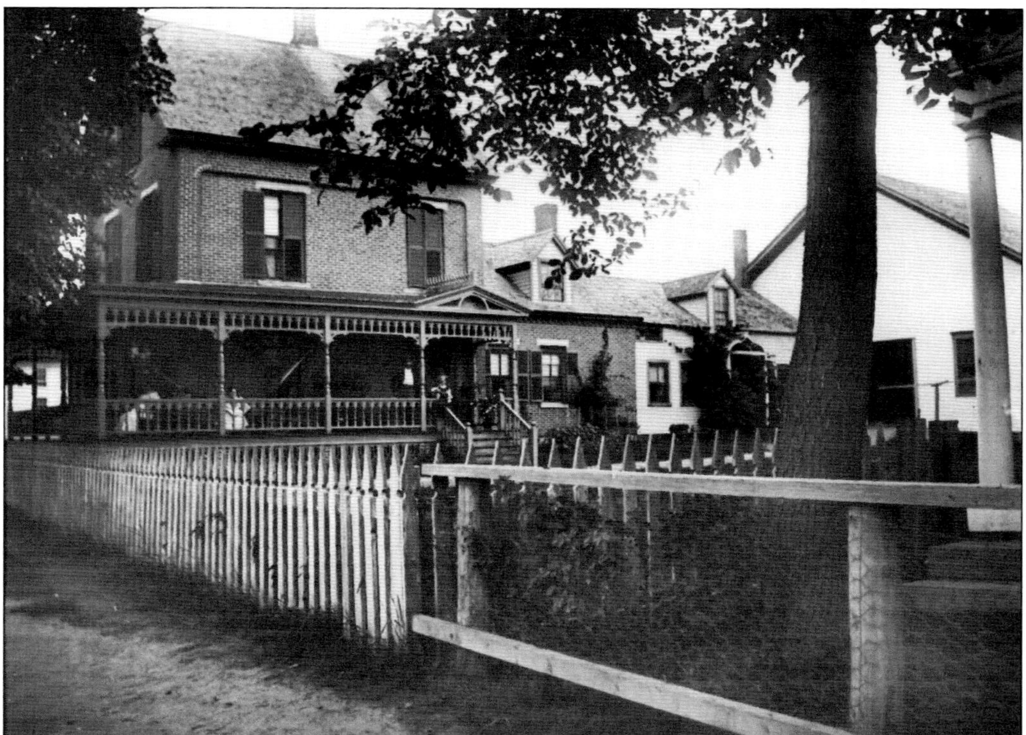

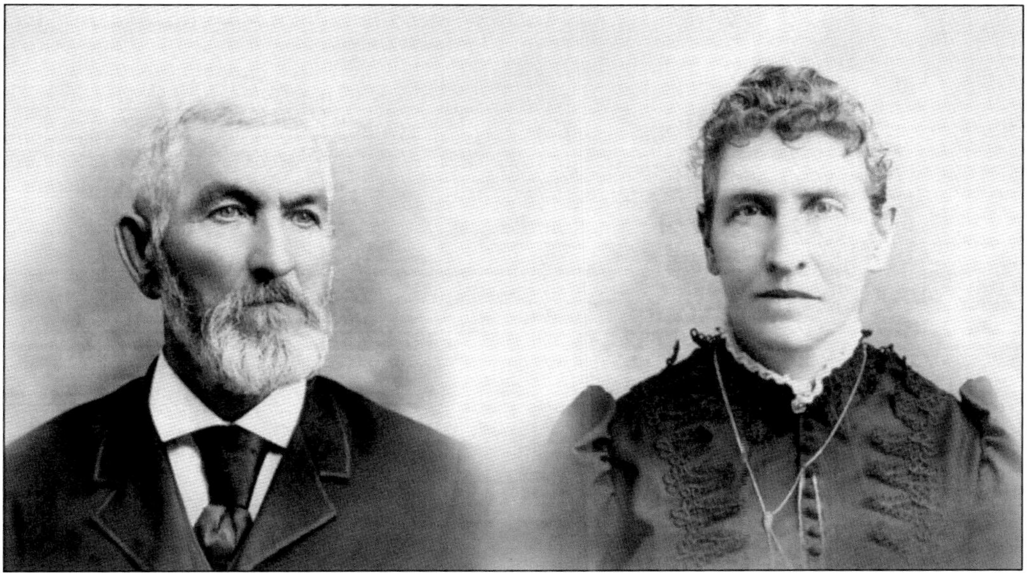

George and Dorcas Evans Gates came to Dixfield from Milan, New Hampshire, in 1872, settling on the farm built in the 1820s. It was originally constructed by deacon Joseph Wheeler and later, after being torched by a state ward living with the Wheeler family, rebuilt by his son Sumner in the 1860s. George Gates became a charter member of the IOOF in Dixfield. His son Don opened one of the first auto dealerships in Dixfield, selling Reos and Hupmobiles. (DMS)

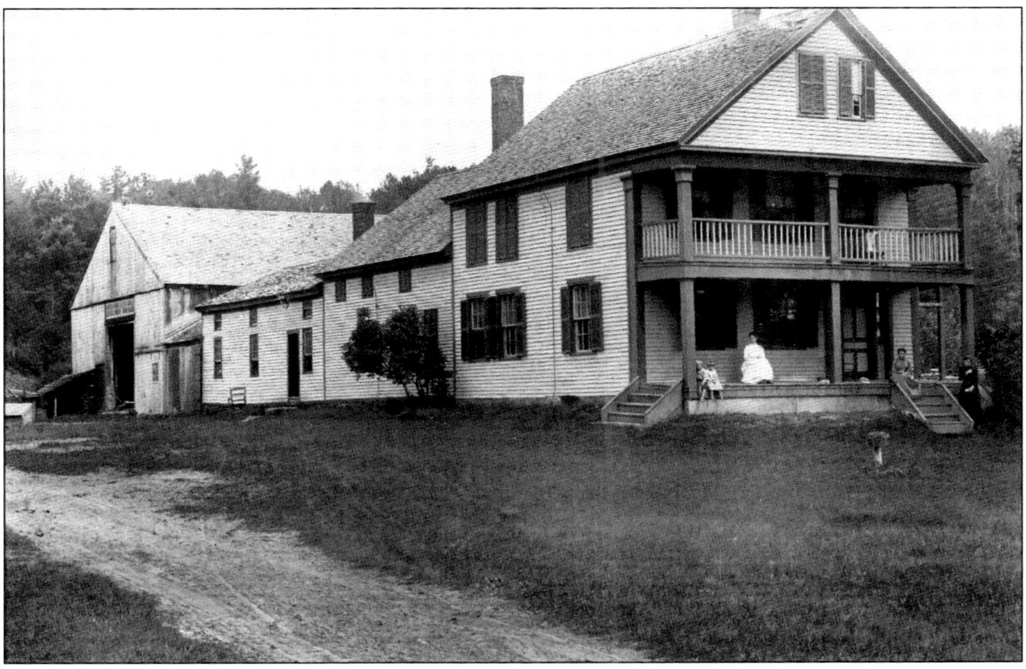

George and Dorcas Gates added the large front portion of the house. Gates was a farmer and a sportsman who spent much time fishing and hunting at the Rangeley Lakes. Their daughter Edith married Newton S. Stowell on January 1, 1881. Stowell had recently moved to Dixfield from Canton, Maine. (DHS.)

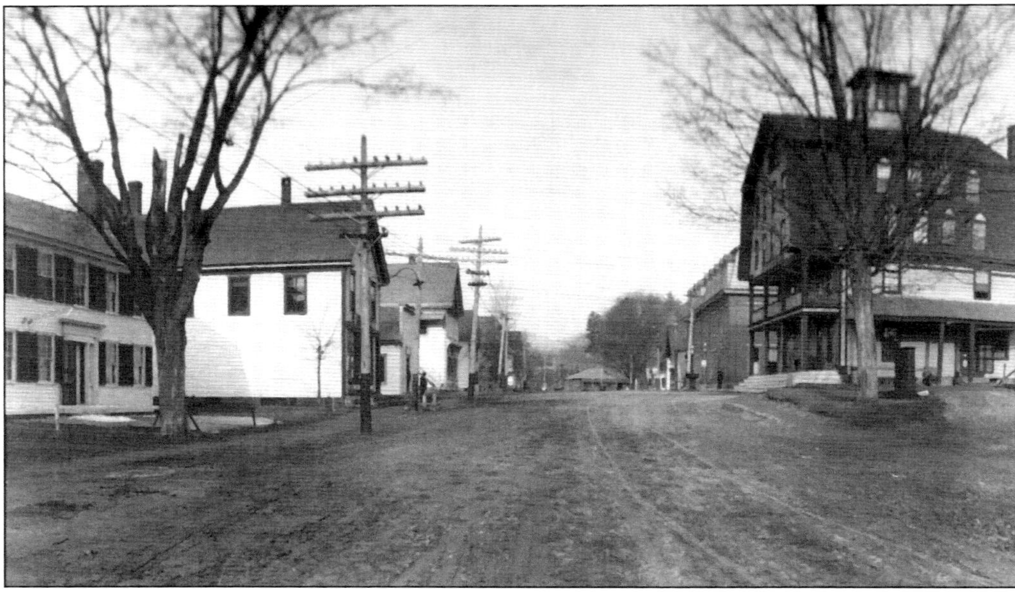

This c. 1910 view of lower Main Street looks west toward the center of the village. On the left is the Thomas Jefferson Cox house, one of the first built in early Dixfield. On the right is the National House, shown during the last few years of its existence. The brick building next to it is the Hotel Stanley, built in 1879, more than a score of years later than the National House. In the battle for overnight guests, the Hotel Stanley would prevail. (PRS.)

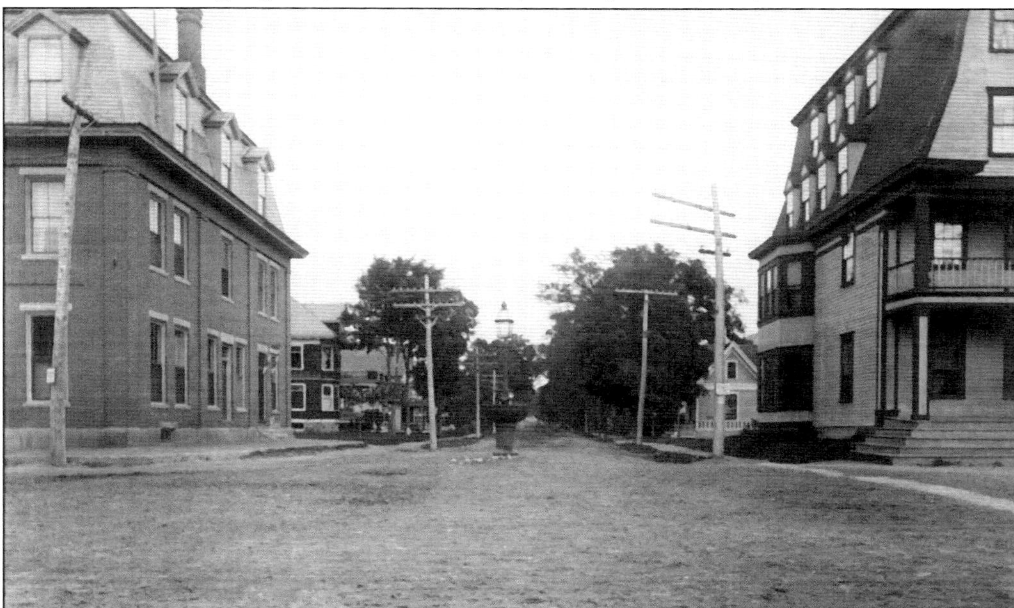

Looking up Weld Street from the intersection with Main Street, one can see the Hotel Stanley (left) in this 1910 view. Next to it is the new home of William Gerry Harlow, erected in the fall of 1906. Harlow ran a dry goods store in the hotel. Across the street on the corner is the National House, and behind it is the hardware store of Almon Stockbridge. Items sold there included blacksmith supplies, stoves and ranges, saddlery hardware, and horseshoes. (DHS.)

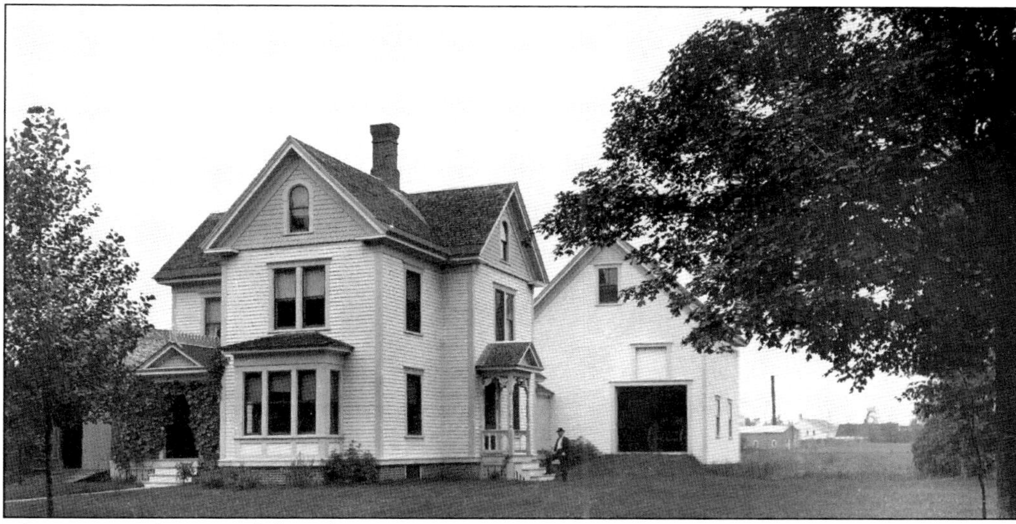

This is an early view of the Christine Masterman house, constructed in 1900. The front walk distinguishes it from a nearby neighbor. Later occupants included Walter and Emma Small. Walter was a spool-maker, and Emma served for many years as secretary of the Advance Club, a civic group dedicated to the advancement of women. The stack in the background belongs to the spool mill, and the white building behind it is the Burnham and Morrill corn shop. (MHPC.)

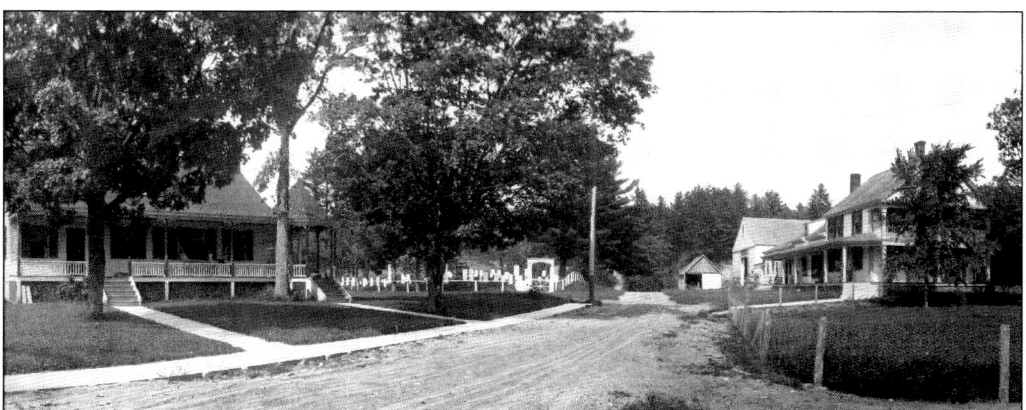

Both the Charles L. Eustis (left) and the Deacon Joseph Wheeler houses are shown in this panoramic view of Hall Hill Road as it joins lower Main Street. Eustis boldly purchased vast tracts of Maine land when only 19 years old, selling them off to earn money to build the house on the left. Deacon Wheeler fared poorly in Dixfield for many years but eventually prospered enough to build the fine house on the right. (DHS.)

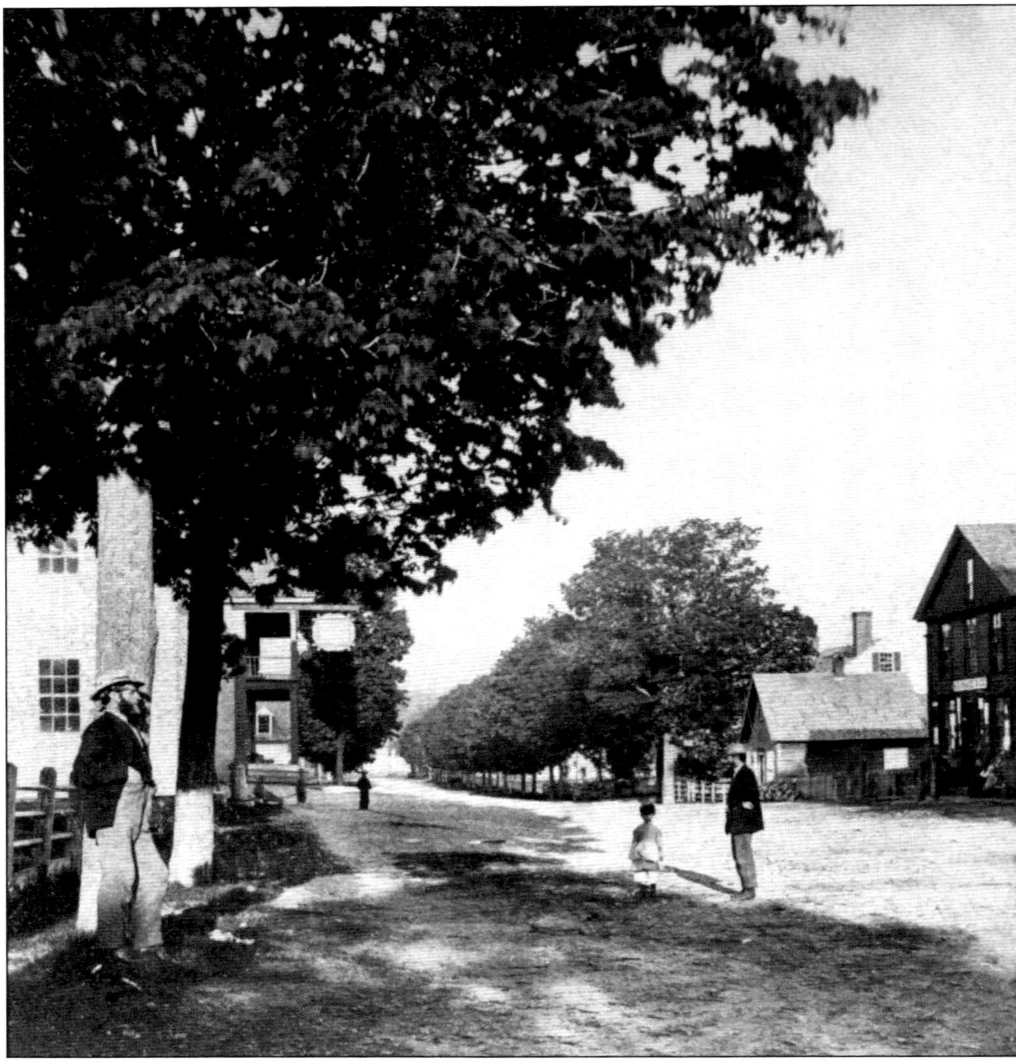

An 1872 view of Main Street looking east is shown in this picture. The man leaning against the tree is Stephen E. Griffith, a harness-maker. The girl standing in the middle of the street is Nellie Stanley, seven-year-old daughter of Henry O. and Mary Stanley. She is with her cousin Walter Scott Chase, owner of the general store shown at the right. (MHPC.)

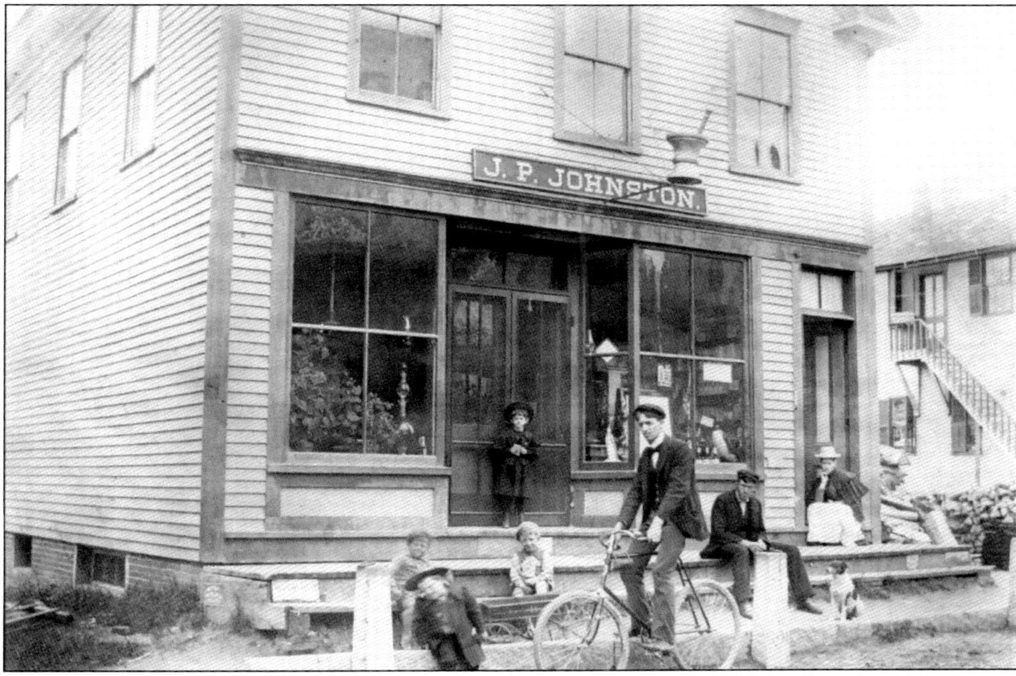

James P. Johnston's drugstore serves as a gathering place for Dixfield residents in this c. 1898 photograph. Johnston had been one of the community's druggists for more than 20 years. His building was erected in the 1880s. Josephine Stanley is shown in the doorway, and Walter Cole is on the bicycle. The W.S. Chase store is shown on the right. (NDM.)

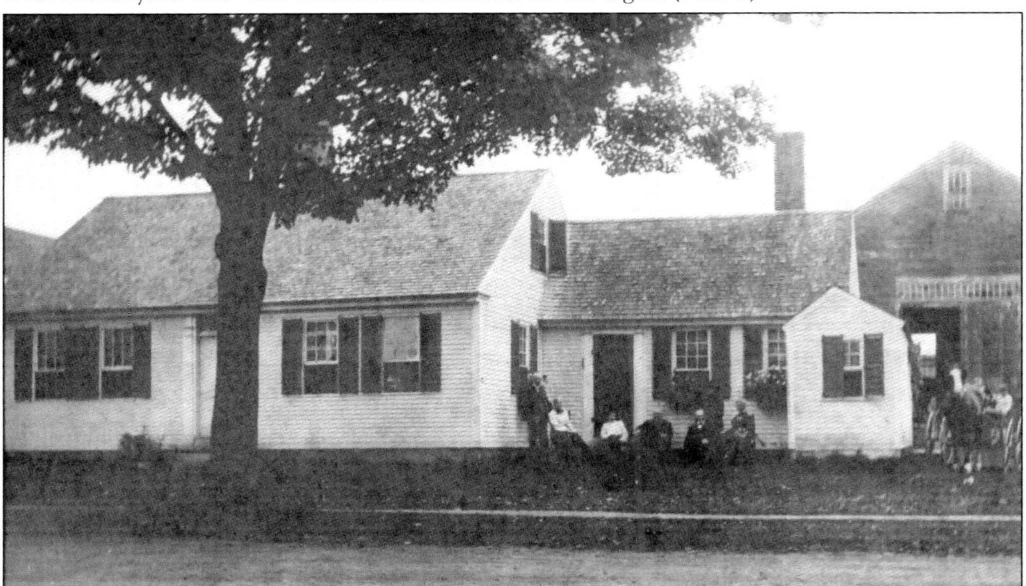

William W. Wait owned this lower Main Street home in the 1880s, as did his family both before and after. One of its features is a large semispherical metal tub built near the main chimney to insure a constant supply of hot water. Wait served in the Maine legislature, representing Dixfield and surrounding towns. (DHS.)

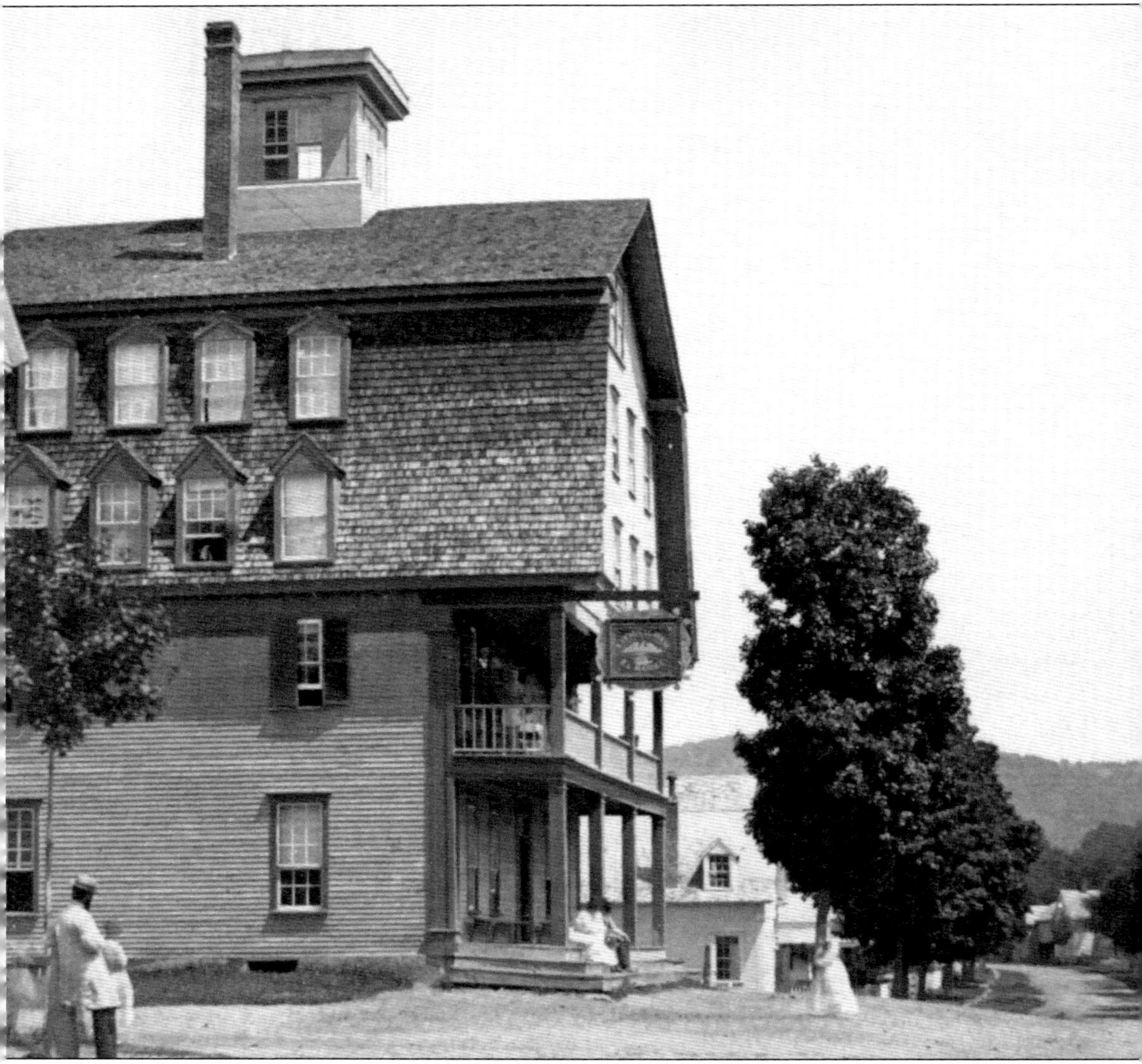

This early-1870s view of the National House at Dixfield Square clearly shows its sign out front. Guests are enjoying the day from both the lower and upper porches. A man observes the scene from the opposite corner. The National House in Dixfield Village was long a significant landmark, greatly increasing its capacity to host out-of-town visitors. Historian Henry W. Park was one of the many people contributing to its construction, and he played in a band there, providing entertainment for suppers and dances. Builder Baldwin L. Marble was an ardent supporter of Sen. Jefferson Davis of Mississippi and persuaded him to speak in Dixfield in 1858 while Davis was in Maine for his health. Local tradition holds that when the National House was remodeled around 1910, many of the upper-story windows were used in other buildings on Weld Street. (DHS.)

Two

Upper Main Street

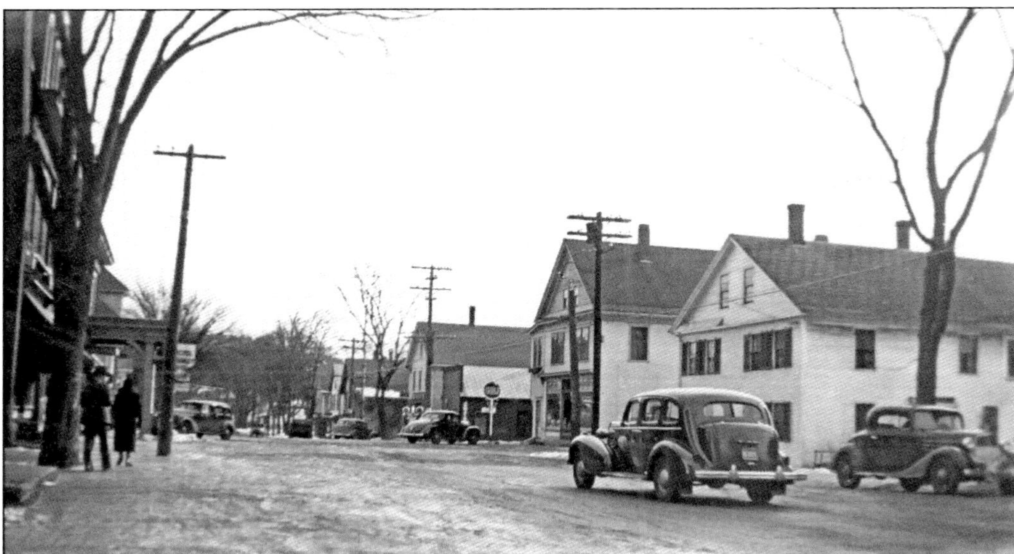

A car drives on upper Main Street in the 1940s and is about to pass in front of the house built in the 1830s by Isaac Newton (1804–1881) and Susan Trask Stanley (1809–1901). Stanley was a selectman in town, a surveyor, a storekeeper, a fulling mill operator, and a county commissioner during his lifetime as well as a trial justice. Beyond the house is the Charles Stanley's Sons store (later Holmes Market), built after 1905 when the Fred Keene Store burned. The Stanley home burned in 1959 but at the time was known as the Tainter Building. (DHS.)

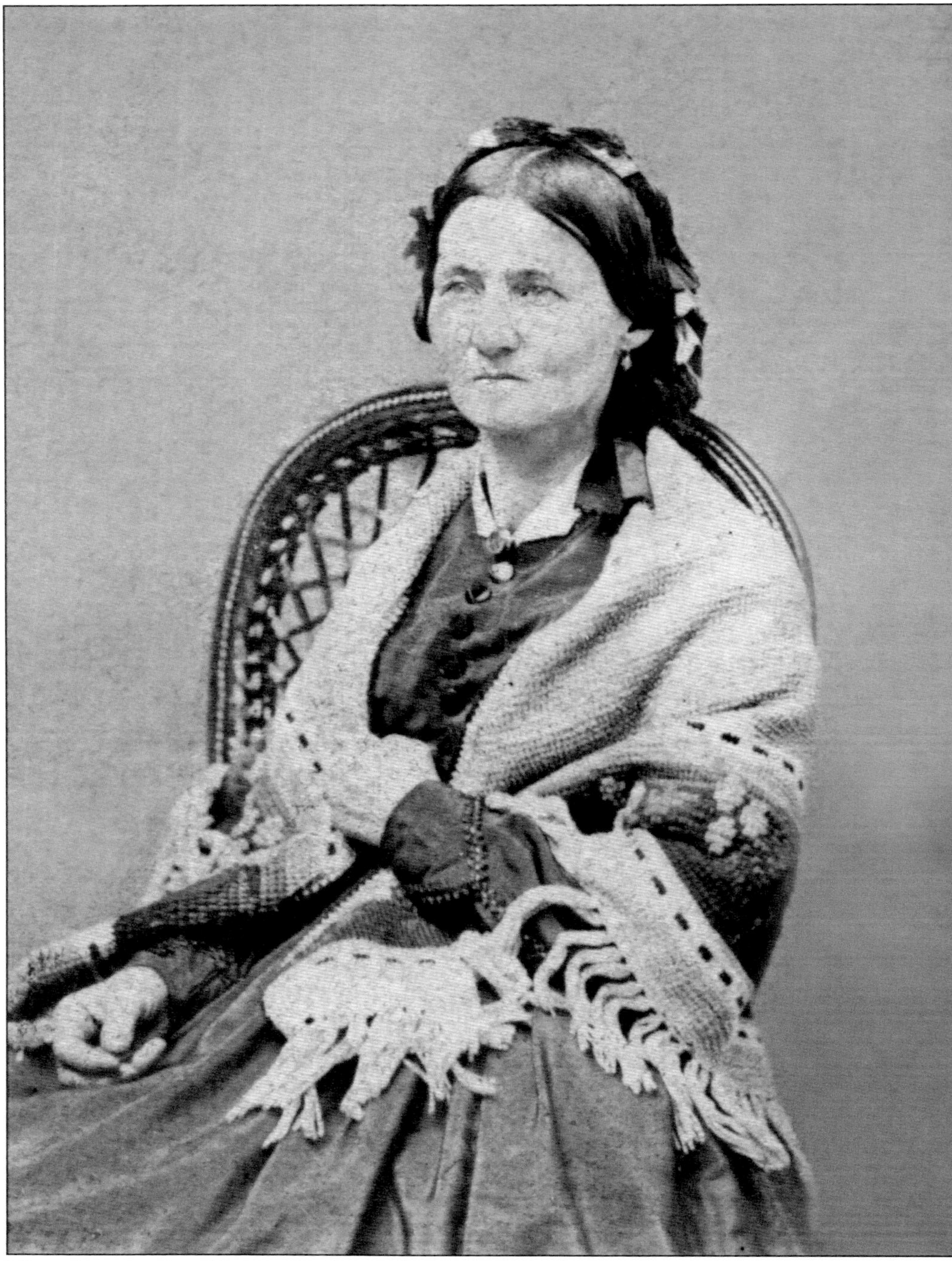

This photograph of Susan Trask Stanley was taken about 1870 by photographer Horatio N. Robinson, who had moved to Dixfield from Hartford, Maine, that year. Stanley had just turned 60 years old. The youngest of five sisters and omitted from their social affairs, Susan once mounted the family workhorse, caught up with them on an outing with their dates, and embarrassed them by telling all their family secrets. (WWE.)

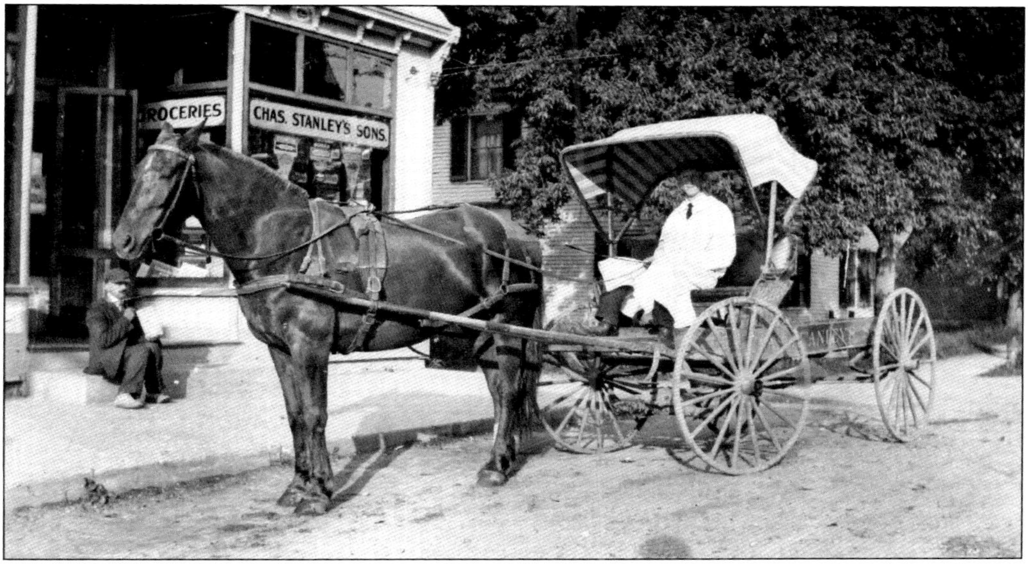

Conie Masterman poses with his horse and buggy in front of the Charles Stanley's Sons market. Charles descended from Isaac Newton's younger brother Calvin, both coming to Dixfield from Winthrop, Maine. Isaac married Dixfield native Susan Trask. Calvin came to help run Isaac's businesses in Dixfield while he was surveying upcountry. The Dixfield Historical Society recently transcribed an 1854 survey notebook written by Isaac. (DHS.)

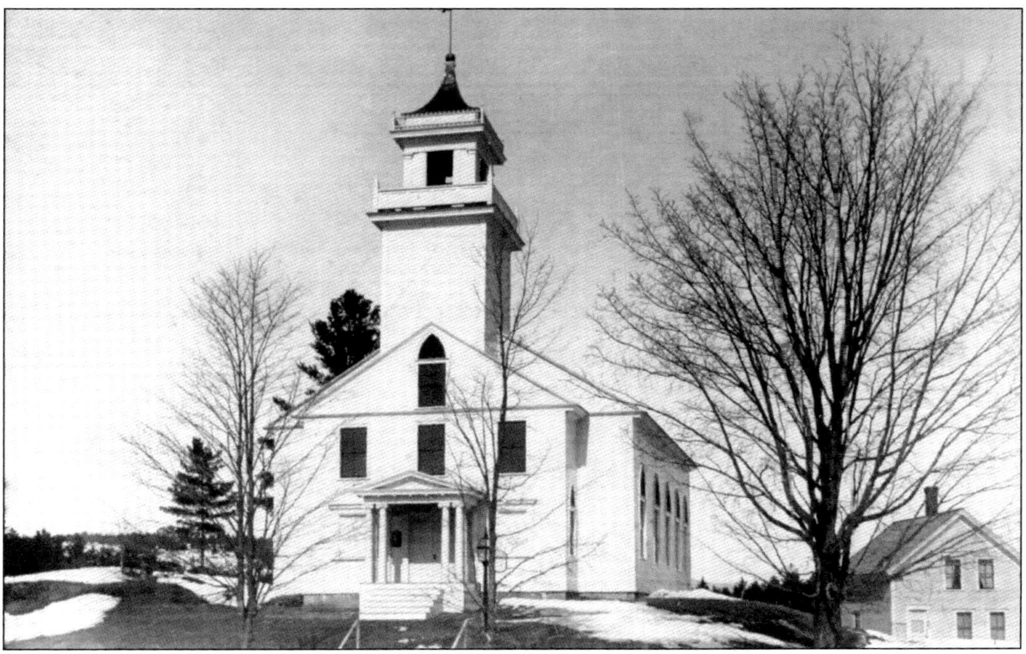
The Church on the Hill dates to 1836, although the church was organized 30 years previously. The location of the church was embroiled in controversy until a group of unidentified local partisans moved the foundation stones from lower Main Street to the present location in the dead of night, settling the matter once and for all. Early church members were primarily Universalists, but by 1912, the Congregationalists owned it. (MHPC.)

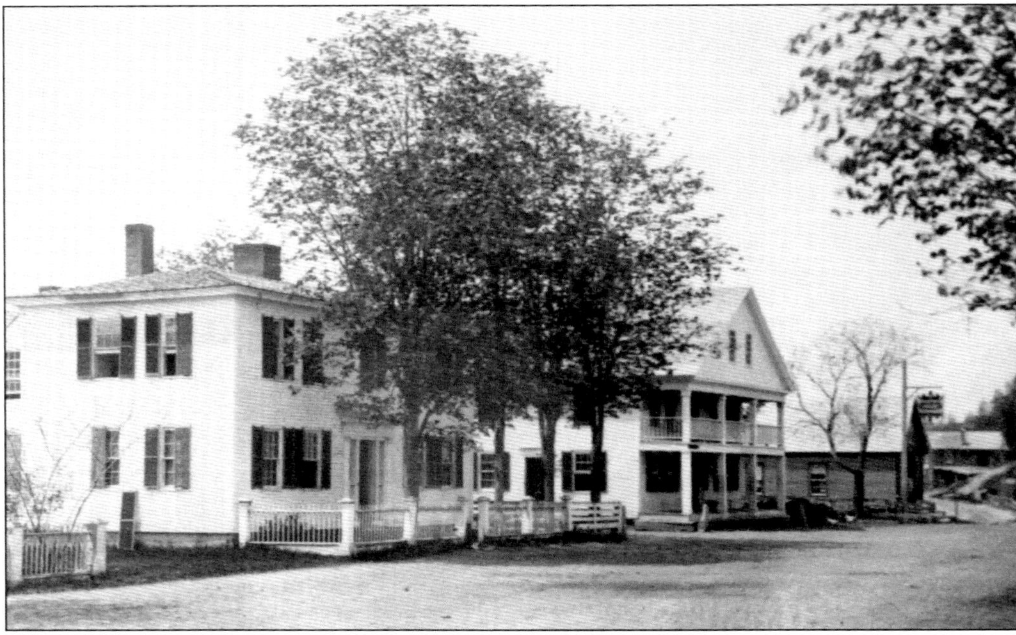

The Isaac Park boardinghouse and the Morrill Tavern both burned about 1975. Park built many of the houses in Dixfield, and many carpenters learned their trade from him, offering board to several of them. The Morrill Tavern, called the Androscoggin House by later owners, was the site of one of the first schools in Dixfield Village, with sessions held in the tavern's meeting rooms. (DHS.)

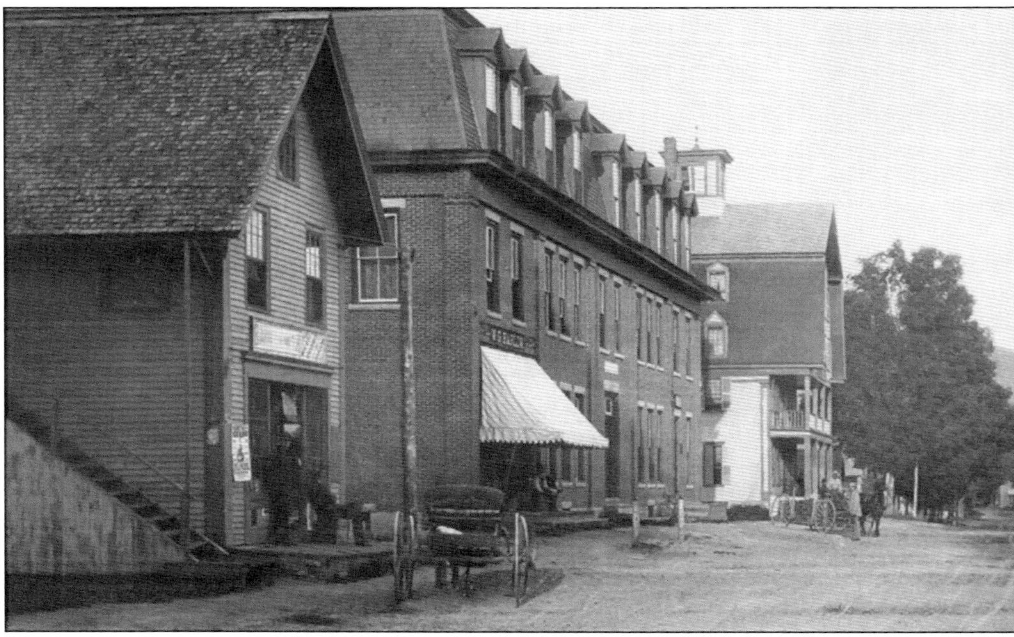

This is a view the north side of upper Main Street looking east, about 1895. The first building is the Barrett and Smith store, purveyor of meats, groceries, and provisions. Next is the Hotel Stanley with William G. Harlow's awning shading the entrance to his men's store. Across Weld Street, men are talking among themselves near the National House. (DHS.)

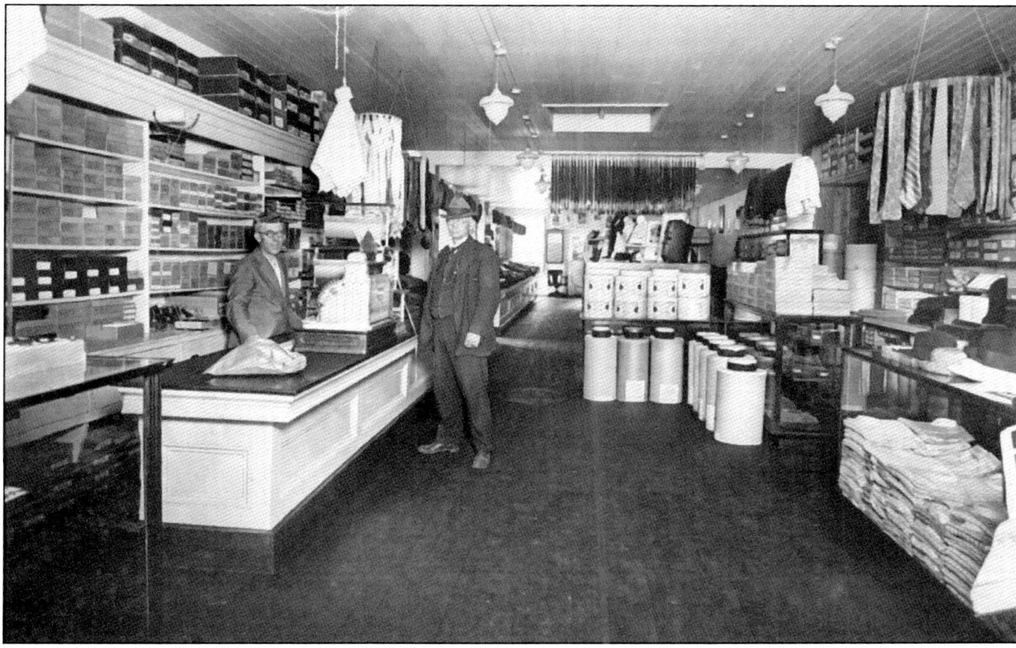

Businessman Don Gates (right) is shown in this 1920s picture with William G. Harlow in Harlow's store in the Stanley Hotel. For many years, Gates was in the wood-processing business with John S. Harlow, harvesting thousands of cords of pulpwood and birch wood for spools and toothpicks in the Dixfield area. (DHS.)

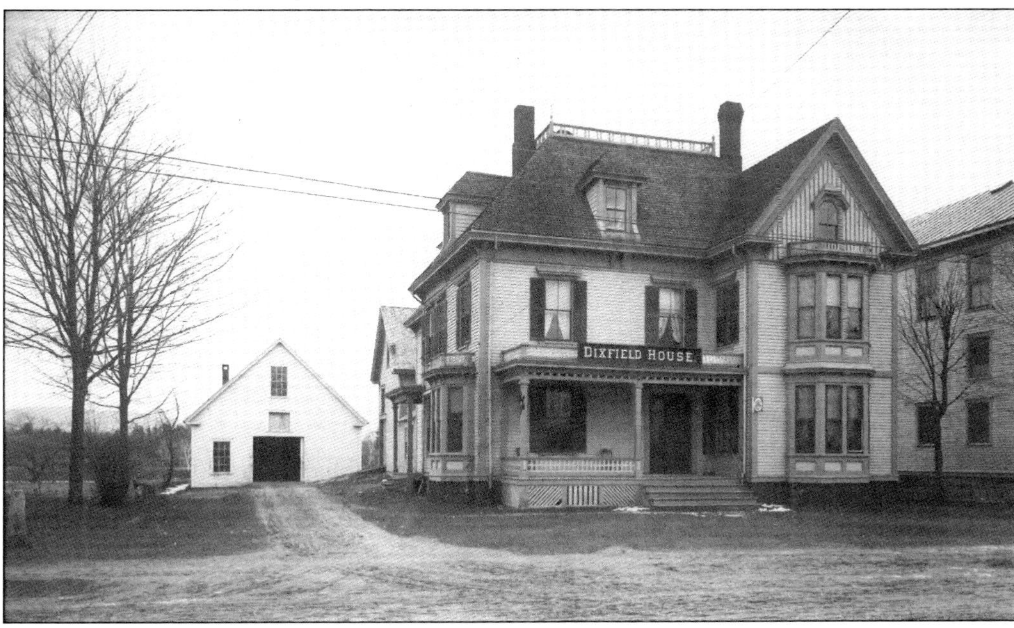

Lodging was often hard to come by in Dixfield according to local accounts. The Dixfield House emerged from the ashes of the Androscoggin House to provide public accommodations. Local tradition holds that the outbuilding to the left was originally the first town meetinghouse at Dixfield Common. (DHS.)

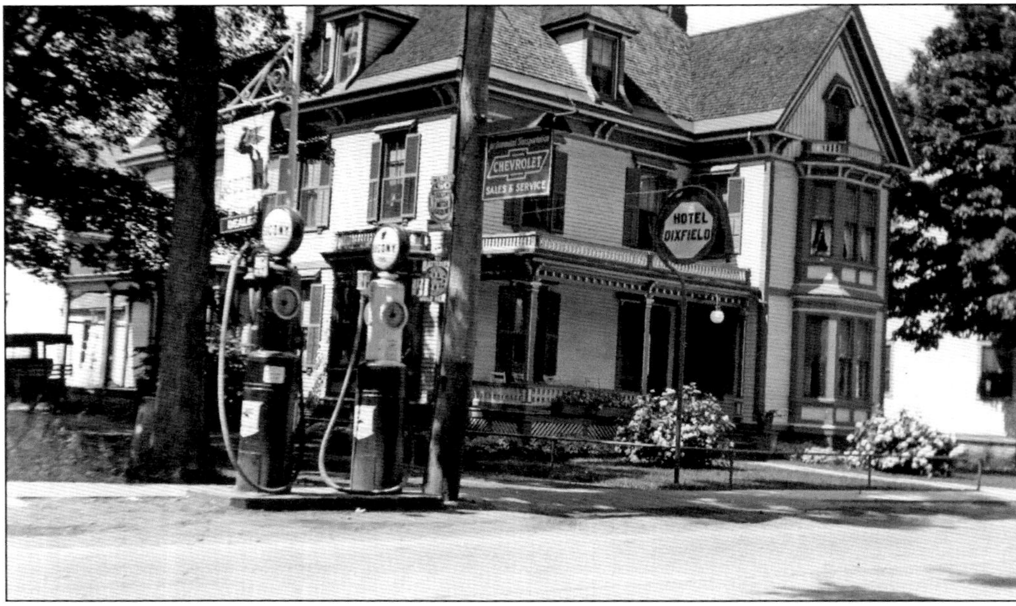

Changing with the demands of a changing public, the Dixfield House became Hotel Dixfield and significantly upgraded its offerings. One could purchase not only a night's lodging here but also a Chevrolet automobile complete with a tank full of Socony gasoline. Since this building was badly damaged in a 1936 fire, the photograph must date from the early 1930s. (DHS.)

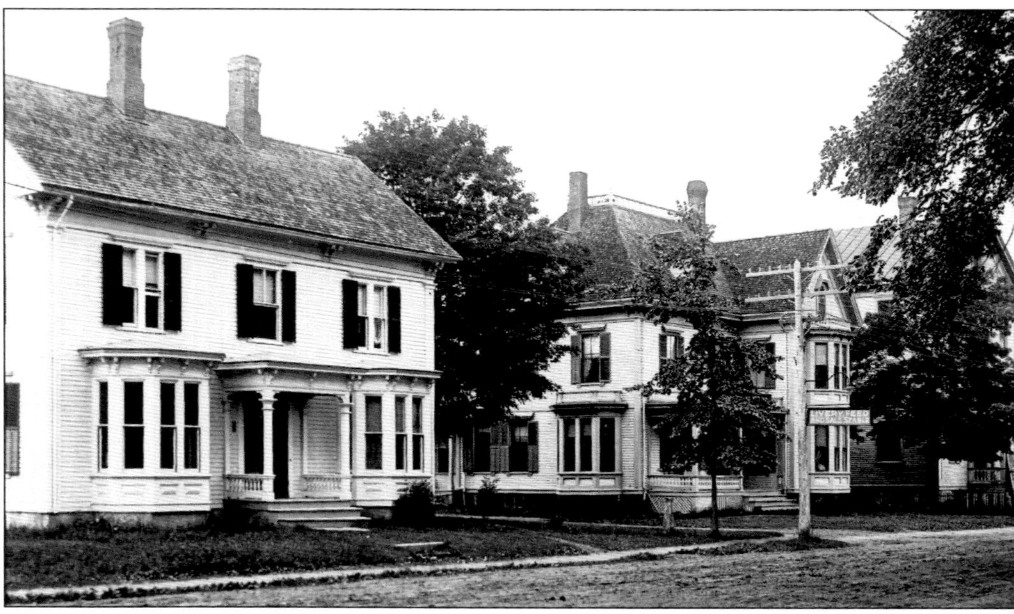

The Wallace Eustis house on the left was built on the spot of the Isaac Park house in the 1870s and housed various Eustis families until the 1930s, when it was sold to Dr. Dexter and Lucile Elsemore who lived here until his retirement in 1977. To the right are the Dixfield House and the Tuscan Opera House. (DHS.)

Civil War veteran and gubernatorial candidate William Tappan Eustis, his wife, Elizabeth, and their five children lived in the Eustis House for several decades. Elizabeth Eustis is shown here in a c. 1902 photograph with her three sons—from left to right, Albert, Stowell, and William. (WWE.)

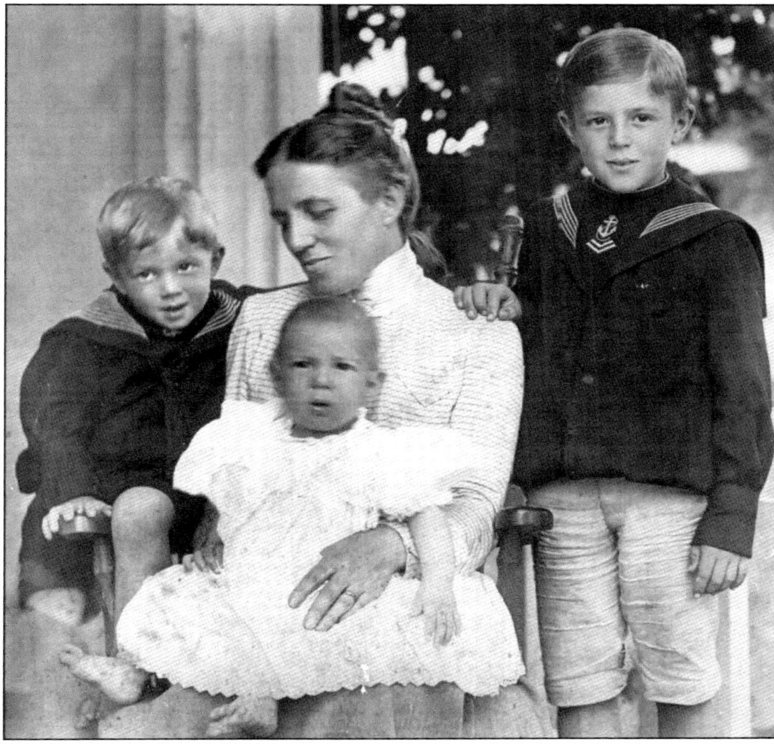

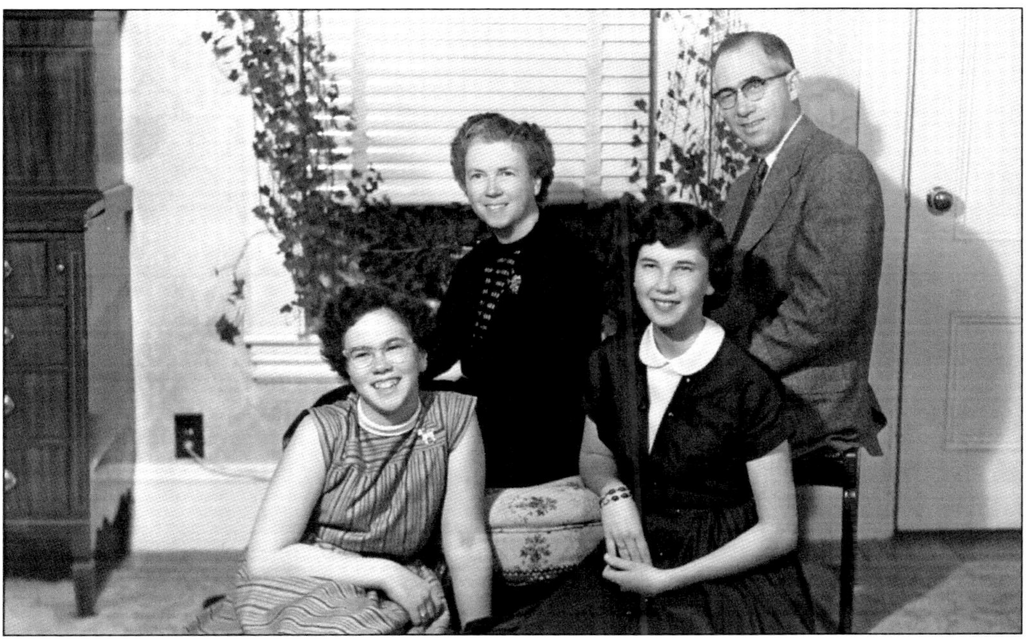

Dr. Dexter Elsemore and his family are shown in this picture. The Elsemores lived in the Eustis house from the mid-1930s to 1977 when Dr. Elsemore retired. The family was given a special retirement week by area communities in recognition of the high esteem accorded them. Pictured, from left to right, are Margaret, Lucile, Betsy, and Dr. Dexter Elsemore. (BEA.)

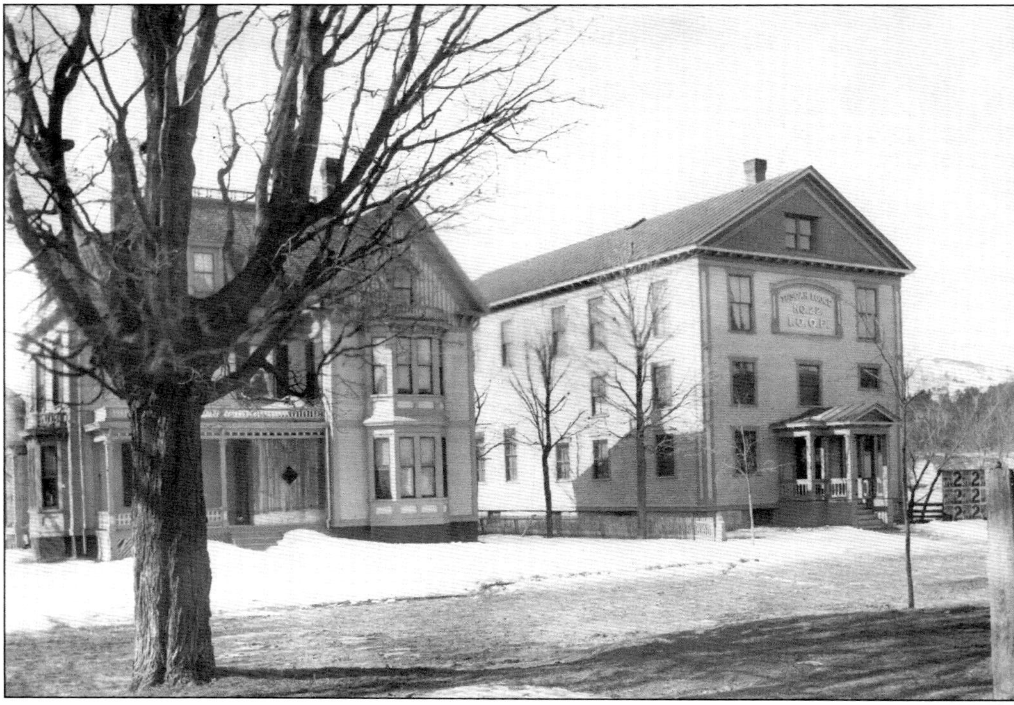

This is another picture of the Dixfield House, taken in the early 1900s. To its right is the IOOF Building, commonly called the opera house and built about 1905 by William F. Putnam to replace a similar structure that burned in January 1901. Both buildings pictured proudly stand today near the banks of both the Androscoggin and Webb Rivers. (DHS.)

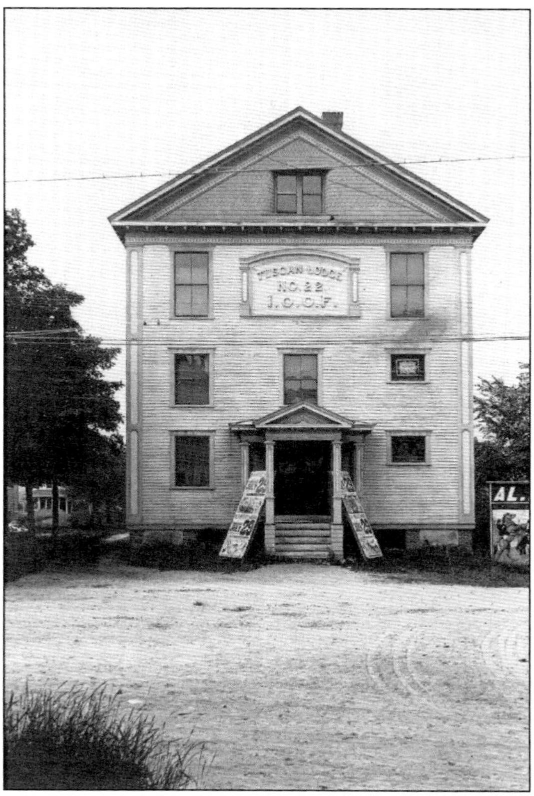

The opera house witnessed countless community functions during its use as a meeting place for Dixfield Village. From graduations to dance recitals, the opera house was home to all. When motion pictures came into vogue, Frank Stanley outfitted the opera house to show them there. (PRS.)

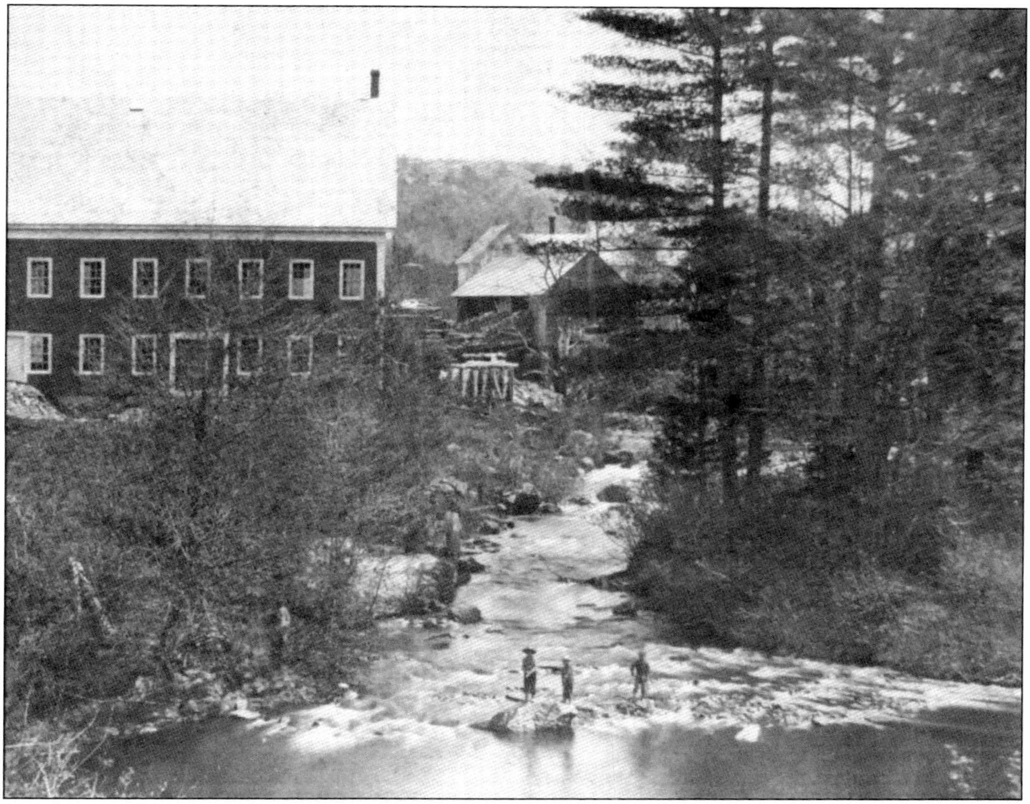

Across the Webb River from Dixfield lies Mexico, once part of Dixfield but incorporated as a separate town in 1818. Shown here is an early view of the Forster Toothpick Company in Mexico, Maine, established in 1873, utilizing the buildings of the old Hosea Austin Tannery. Three boys test their fishing skills at the juncture of the Webb and Androscoggin Rivers. (MHPC.)

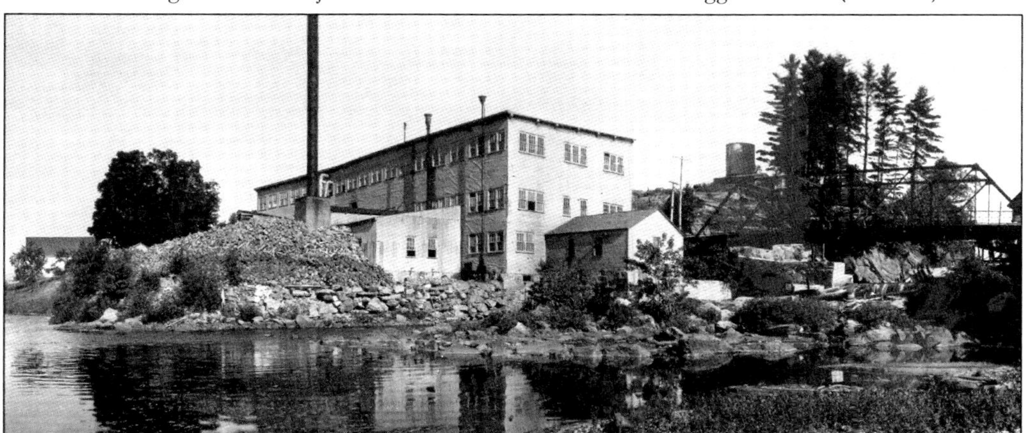

Charles W. Forster's original toothpick mill burned in 1904 and was replaced by this mill, erected under the watchful eyes of the estate of Charles W. Forster and his son Maurice Forster, who soon entered into partnership with George L. Merrill and John S. Harlow, among others, to build still another toothpick mill less than a mile from this one. (DHS.)

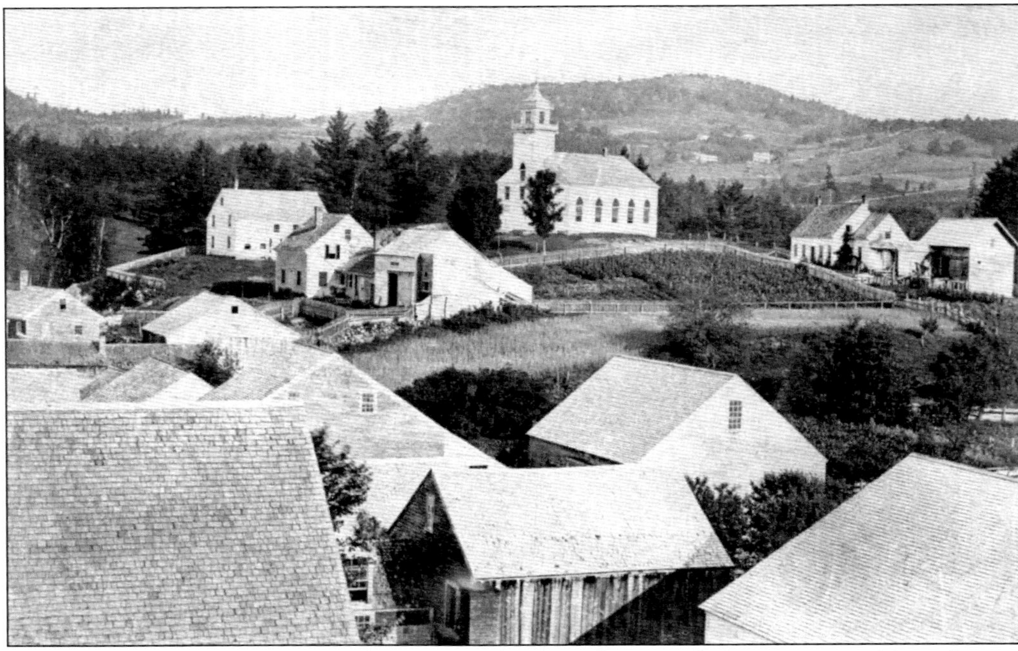

Photographer H.N. Robinson lived in Dixfield for about five years before moving to Massachusetts to continue his career. Robinson took this picture of Dixfield Village near its border with Mexico. The Church on the Hill forms the centerpiece of the image, with houses lining upper Main Street prominent in the foreground. (DHS.)

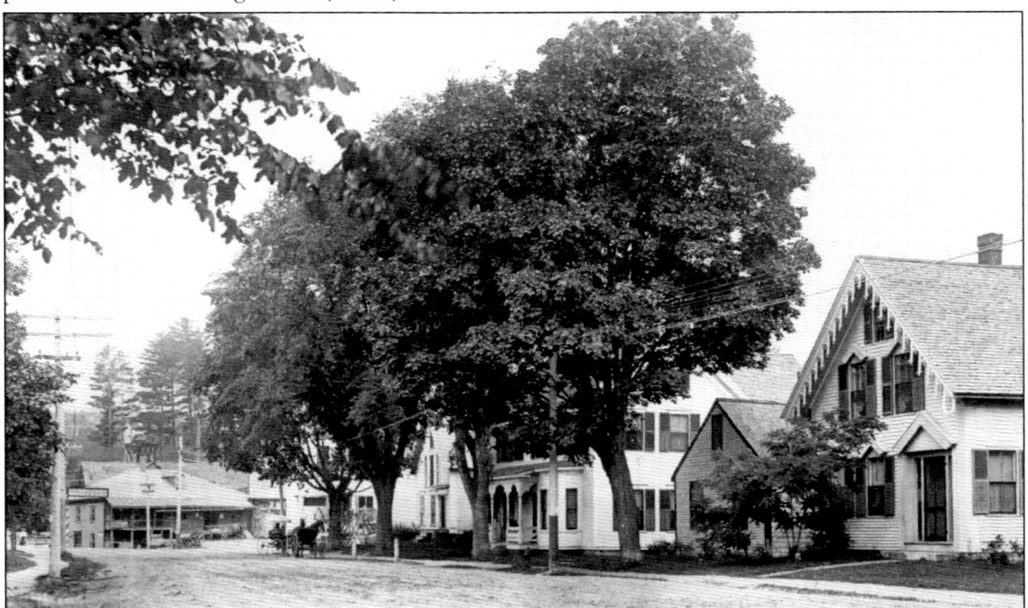

Before the house on the right became the parsonage for the Congregationalist church (also called the Church on the Hill), Joseph P. and Emma Edmunds lived here, raising their daughters, Edna and Ina. Edmunds was a blacksmith and town treasurer and owned racehorses, which he ran at the old Dixfield Trotting Park. (DHS.)

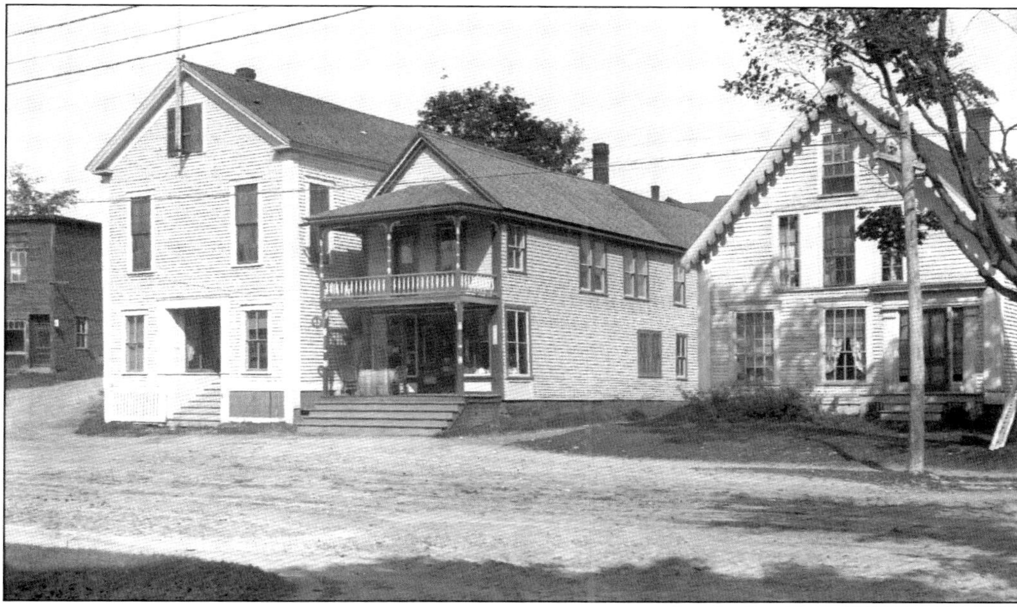

Shown here are three buildings significant in Dixfield Village history; all of them exist today. They are, from left to right, Henry O. Stanley's general store, the millinery shop of Ellen Toothaker, and the harness shop of L.M. Hodsdon. The sign for Hodsdon's business can be seen leaning against the tree. Toothaker's shop operated in the house once inhabited by Sebastian Streeter Marble, who became governor of Maine in the 1880s. (DHS.)

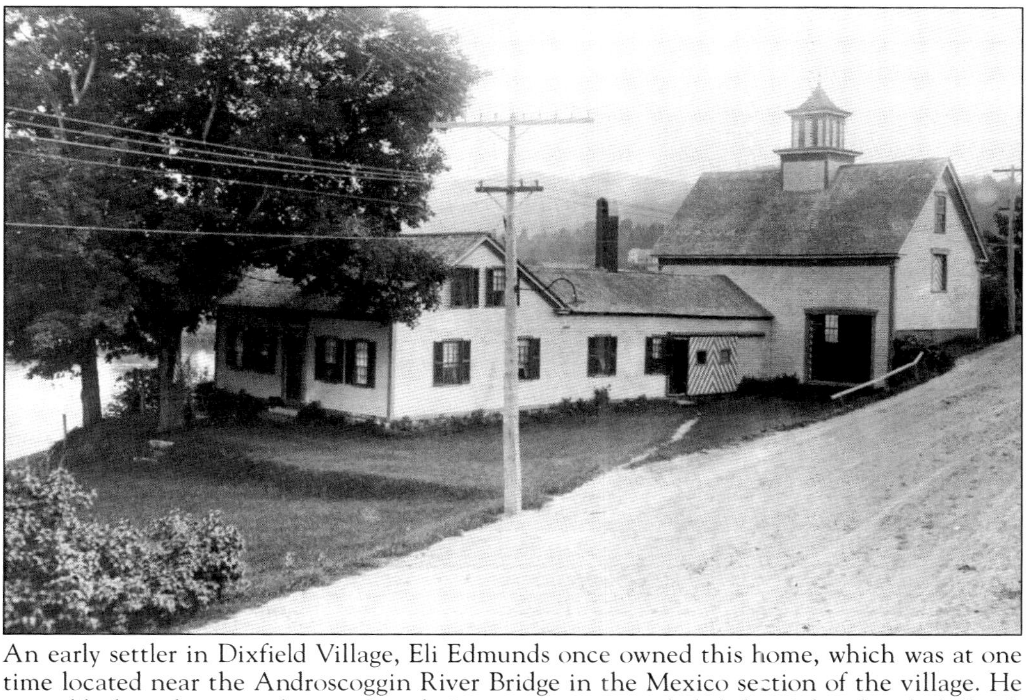

An early settler in Dixfield Village, Eli Edmunds once owned this home, which was at one time located near the Androscoggin River Bridge in the Mexico section of the village. He was a blacksmith, as was his son Joseph. Later occupants included the Holland and Philbrick families. (DHS.)

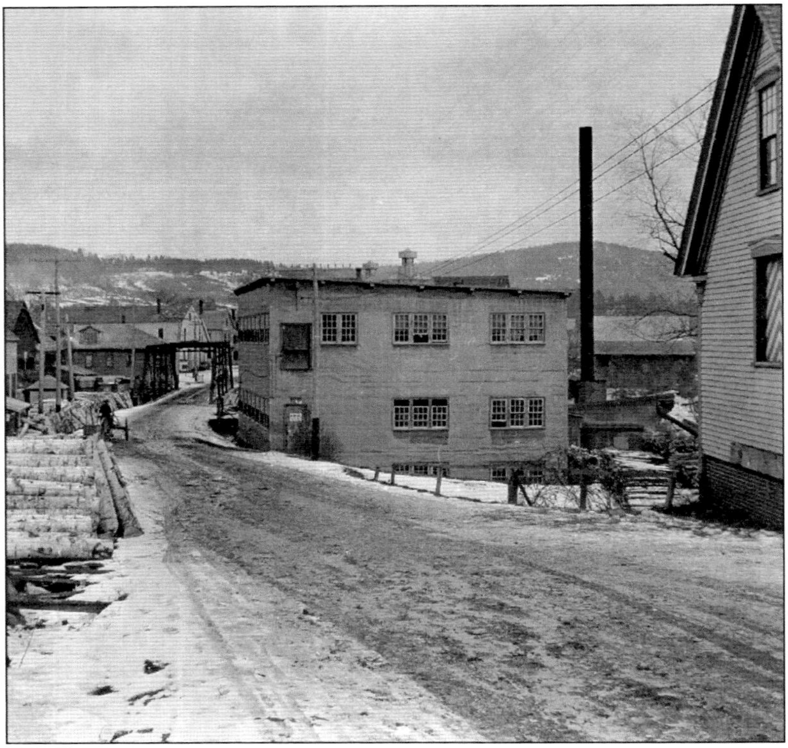

The second Forster toothpick mill dominated the scene leading from Mexico to Dixfield, as shown in this early-1900s photograph. Bolts of white birch destined to become toothpicks line the side of the road awaiting their turns at being shaved into thin veneer to be cut into toothpicks. Dixfield proper is at the farther end of the Webb River Bridge. (MHPC.)

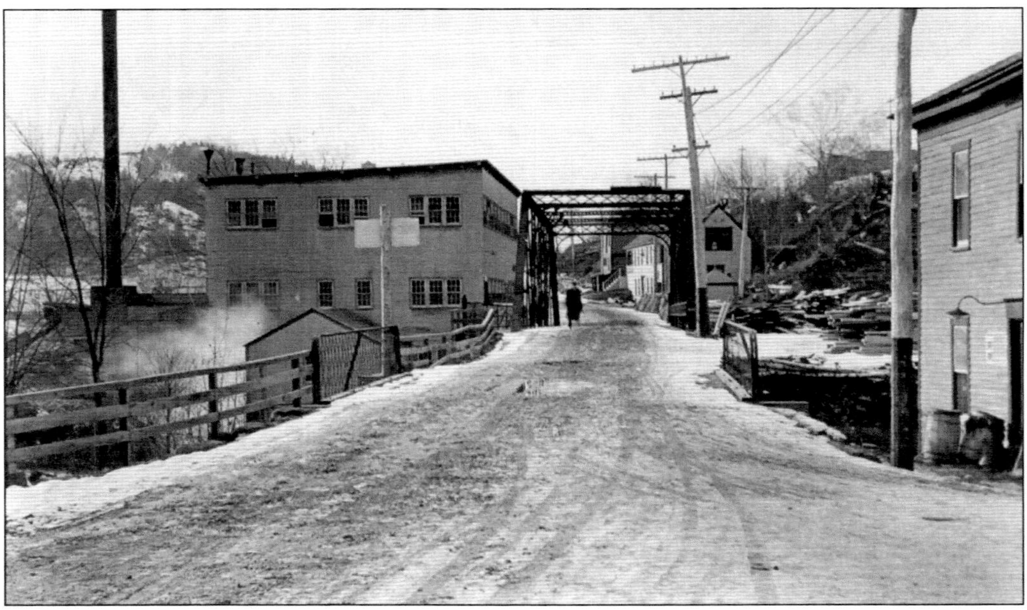

This is much the same view as the previous picture, only taken from the Dixfield side of the Webb River. Historically, competition was keen for waterpower, so deeds firmly established which mill had priority use of it. Called privileges, these rights provided a civil approach to preventing disputes over water rights. This photograph shows a smaller lower bridge over the first chasm in the river and a box girder bridge over the second. (MHPC.)

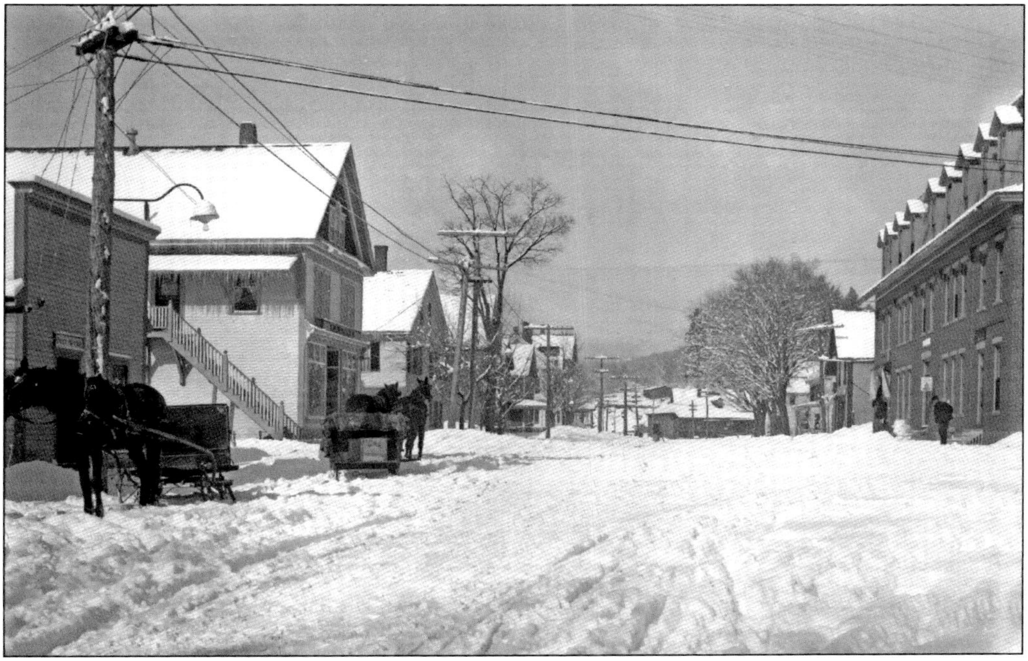

Life on Main Street in Dixfield gets back to normal following a snowstorm. The post office on the left provides a resting place for one horse while a team whose owner appears to be shopping at Stanley's Market next door awaits his return. Across the street at the Hotel Stanley, a man is clearing snow from the sidewalks. The year is about 1910. (DRH.)

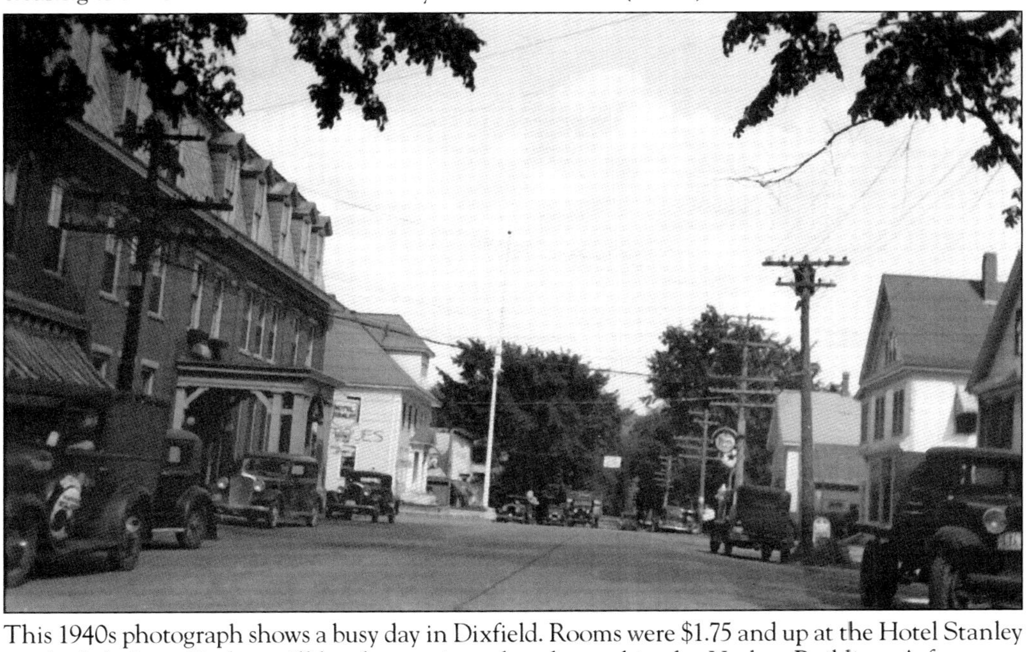

This 1940s photograph shows a busy day in Dixfield. Rooms were $1.75 and up at the Hotel Stanley on the left. Ione Harlow still has her antique shop located in the Harlow Building. A few years later, she would move to the 1820 House on Weld Street. Tydol and Texaco gasoline are sold next to each other near the Stanley Market on the right. (PRS.)

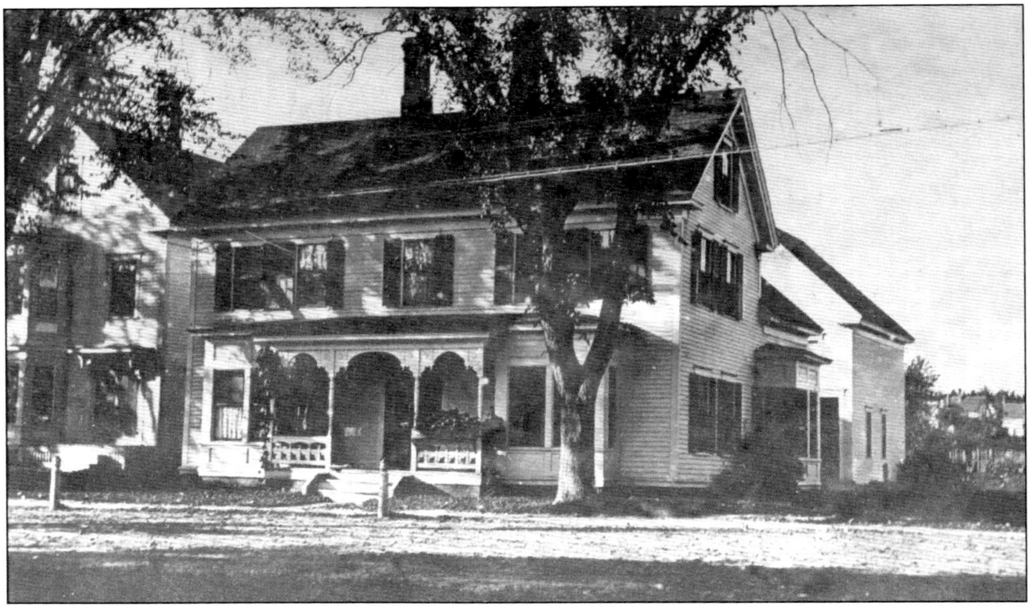

Was this upper Main Street home built by a member of the famous Washburn family of Livermore, Maine? An early-1900s newspaper article suggests so, but proof is lacking. Davis Washburn, who died in 1832, ran a store in Dixfield Village in the 1820s with his brother-in-law James Williams. In the 1840s, there was a law firm called Andrews and Washburn in town. Early in the 20th century, Dr. William Mabry Pease lived here followed by Dr. Garfield G. DeFoe. (JS.)

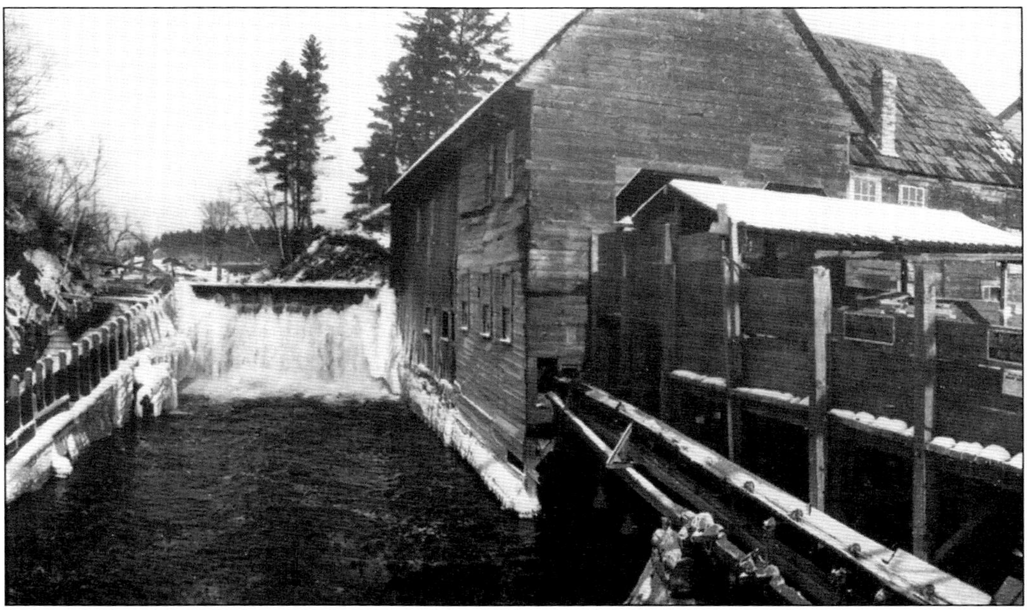

The Webb River was the site of the earliest sawmill and gristmill in Dixfield, built by Dr. Elijah Dix and later owned by Amos Trask. Over the years, mills too numerous to count were working on the river, including lumber mills, a carding mill, and more gristmills and sawmills. Dixfield had nearly a score of such mills operating simultaneously in the early 1900s. (DHS.)

Three

WELD STREET

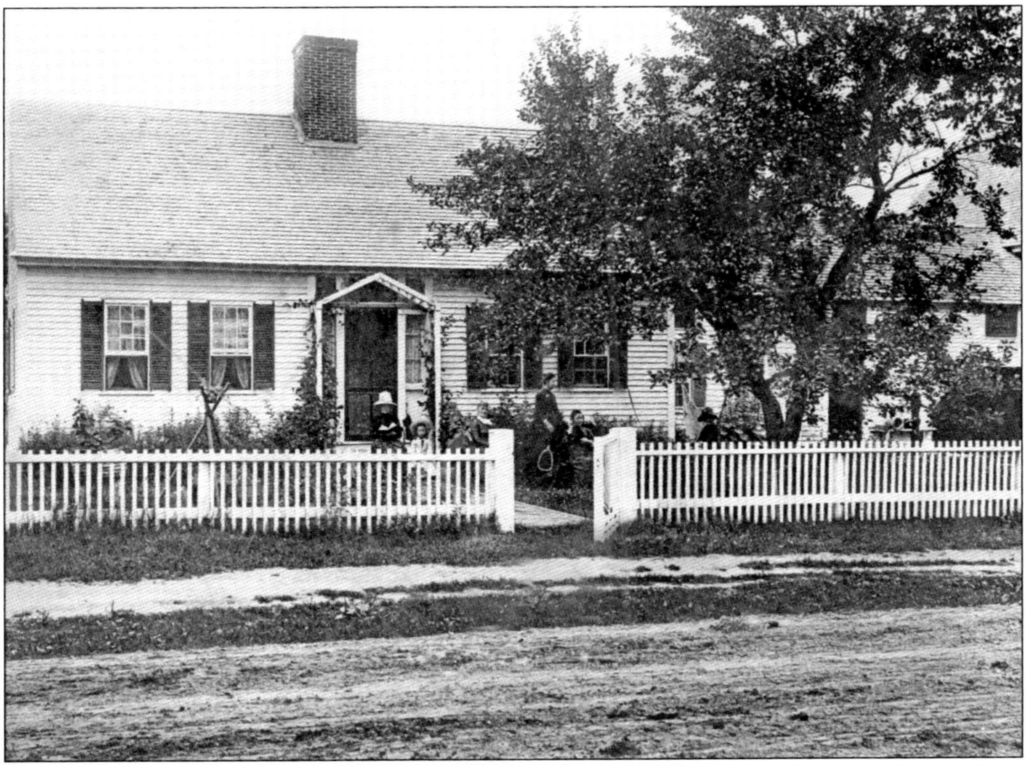

Amos Trask is credited with building this 1820 House for his daughter Lucy Barnard. Her daughter Mahala was born here in 1822 and kept school here at age 14. Her granddaughter Melissa Wheeler was born here in 1845. Melissa planted the apple tree shown in the picture. Emily Knight (left) and Annie Chase are on the steps. Next, to the right, is Delphine Root; Mary Dillingham is standing; Arvilla White is in a chair; Aunt Lucy Barnard is in the hammock. (MHS.)

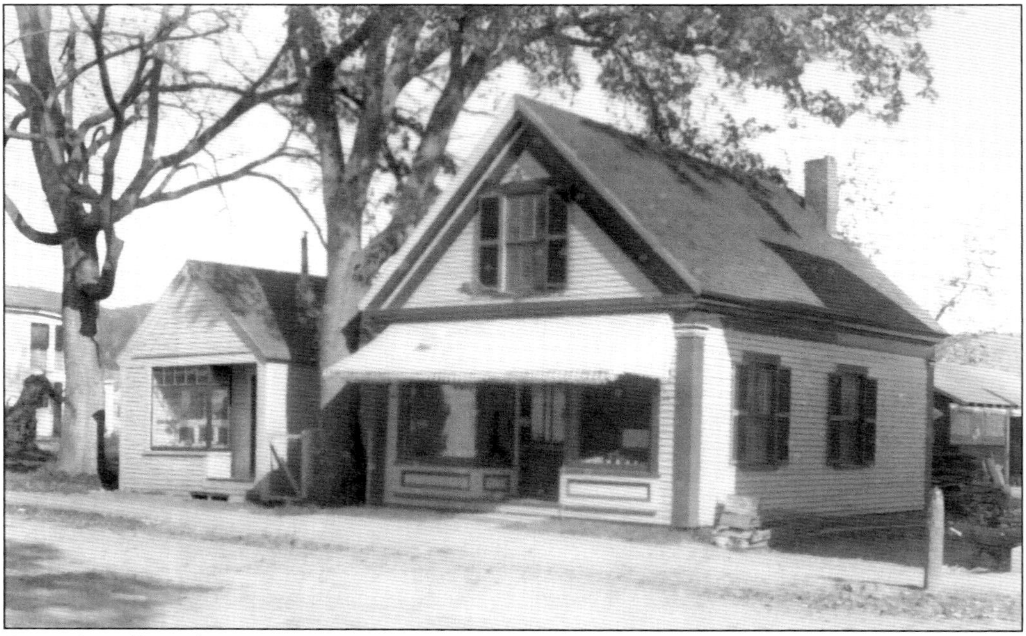

Once the office of noted Dixfield attorney Isaac Randall, the building on the right became Mel Bishop's jewelry store many years later. Other jewelers had business here, as well, like Cleon Corrow in the mid-1920s. Millie Russell also had a millinery shop here. The small building on the right was known as the "light store," where lamps and small electrical items were sold. (DHS.)

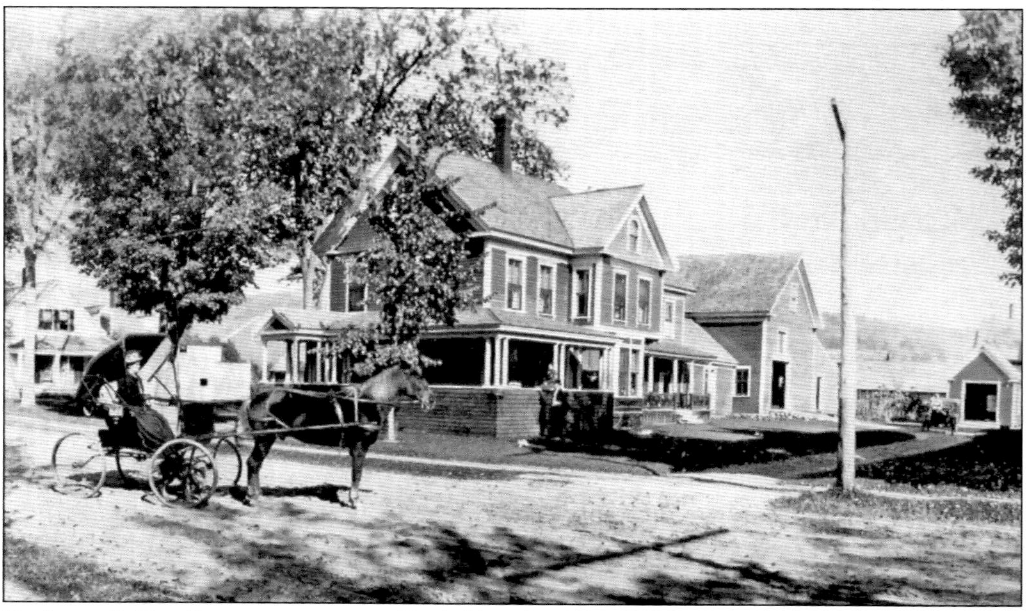

Dr. James Selden Sturtevant came to Dixfield in the 1890s following his brother-in-law's decision to relocate his Dixfield practice to Southern California. Dr. Sturtevant was widely admired in his medical practice while simultaneously serving on local, county, and state medical boards. Also shown in this photograph is his wife, Celia Wing Sturtevant. She was prominent in her own right, at one time serving as president of the Maine Writer's Research Club. (PRS.)

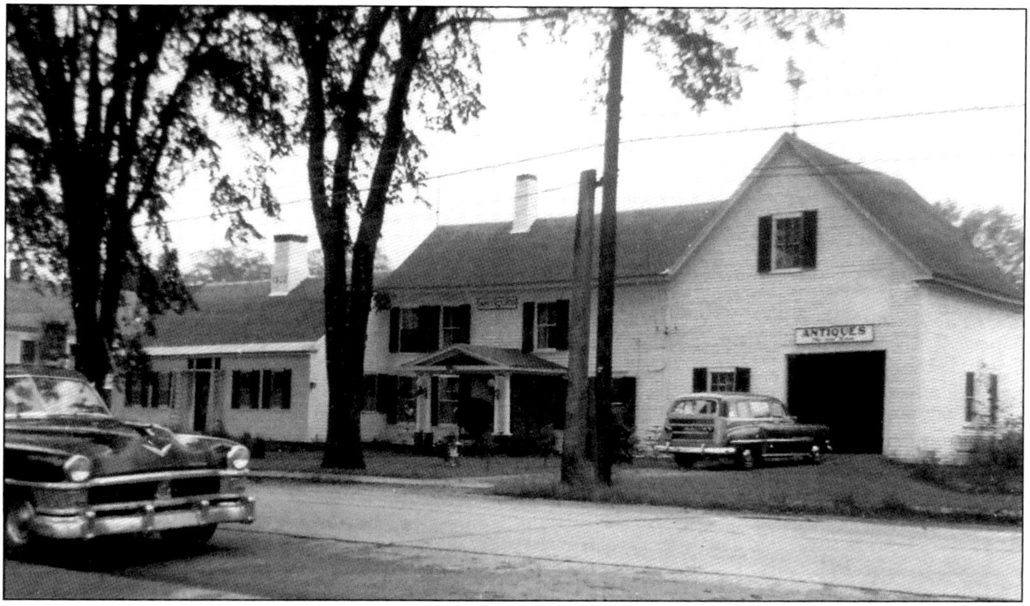

Ione Harlow's cousin Albert Root suggested the antiques business to her shortly after his return to Dixfield in 1923. She displayed a few items in her millinery store, and they sold quickly. By the late 1940s, she had moved her business to the 1820 House, pictured here, the same house Root had used for his own antiques shop. (KRG.)

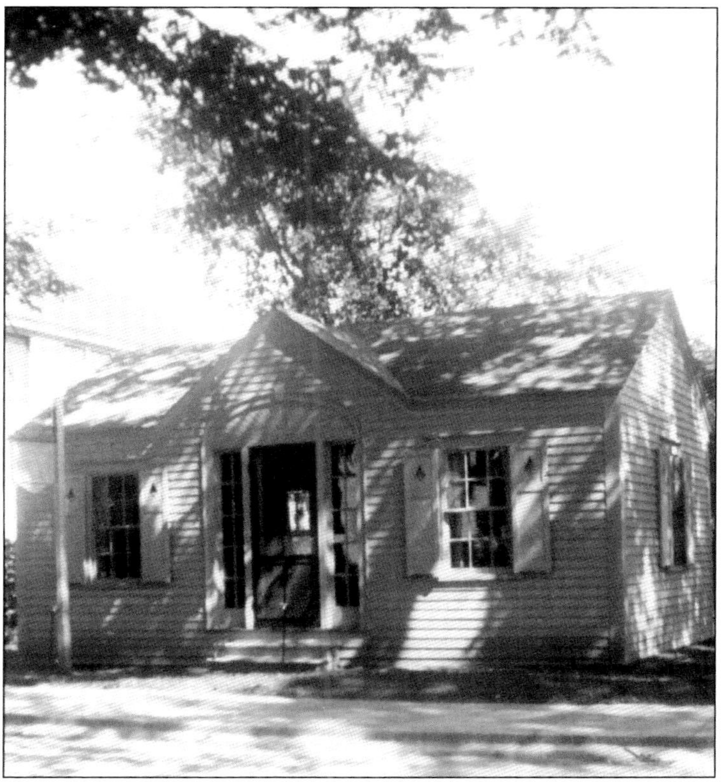

Marion Tribou opened the Blue Door gift shop, designed by her cousin architect Hamilton Harlow, in the 1930s and catered to the afternoon social trade, featuring bridge cards, napkins, serving dishes, and the like. Tribou was the daughter of Dixfield business leader John S. Harlow. In later years, the building became the Blue Bird Diner, operated by the Ames family. (ATK.)

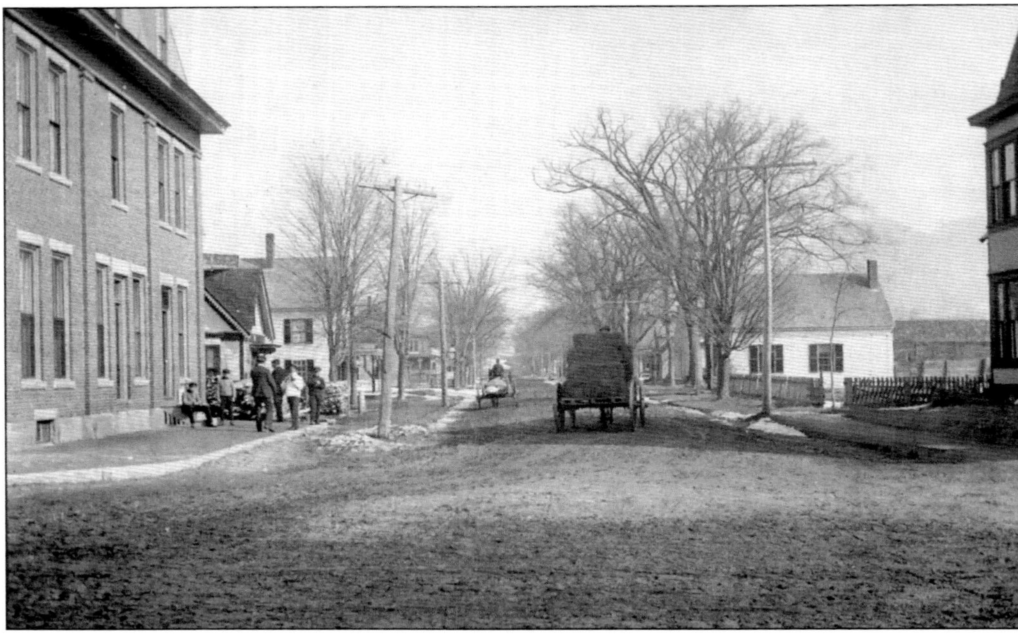

Taken before 1906, this photograph shows how Weld Street looked more than a century ago. The Hotel Stanley is on the left, with Henry O. Stanley's sporting goods store behind it. Erected in 1879 by businessman Elbridge Gerry Harlow, the hotel was named in honor of the Stanleys, the family of his wife, Rosella. (NDM.)

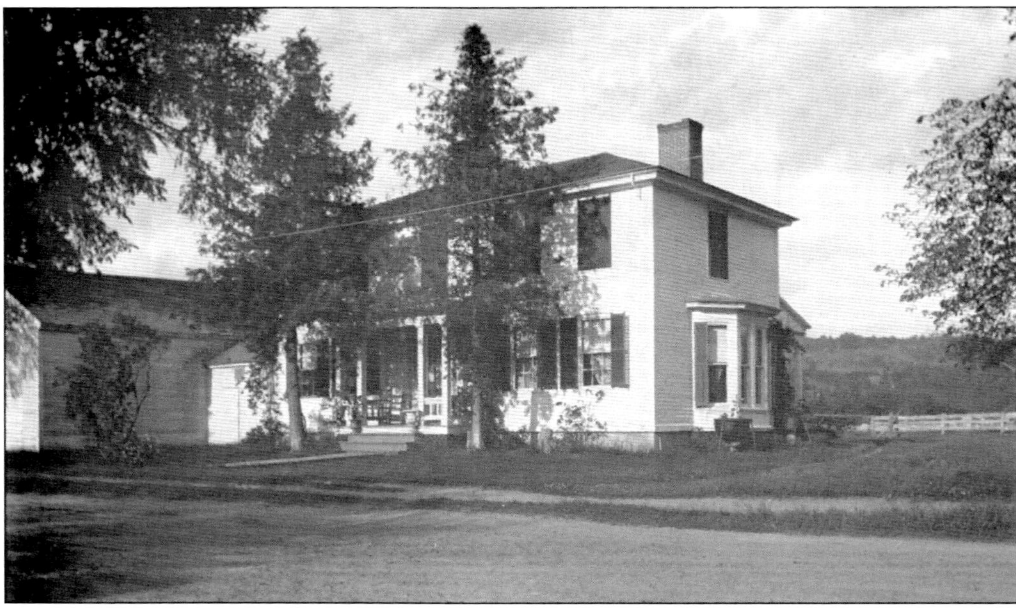

The Charles T. Chase house was one of the earliest on Weld Street in the 1820s. Chase was a storekeeper who married Louisa, a daughter of Amos Trask. His sister-in-law Lucina gave free food to men who bought liquor from him. When he protested the loss of business, she reportedly said to him, "Mr. Chase, just as long as you dispense liquor to these men, just so long shall I dispense provisions." (NDM.)

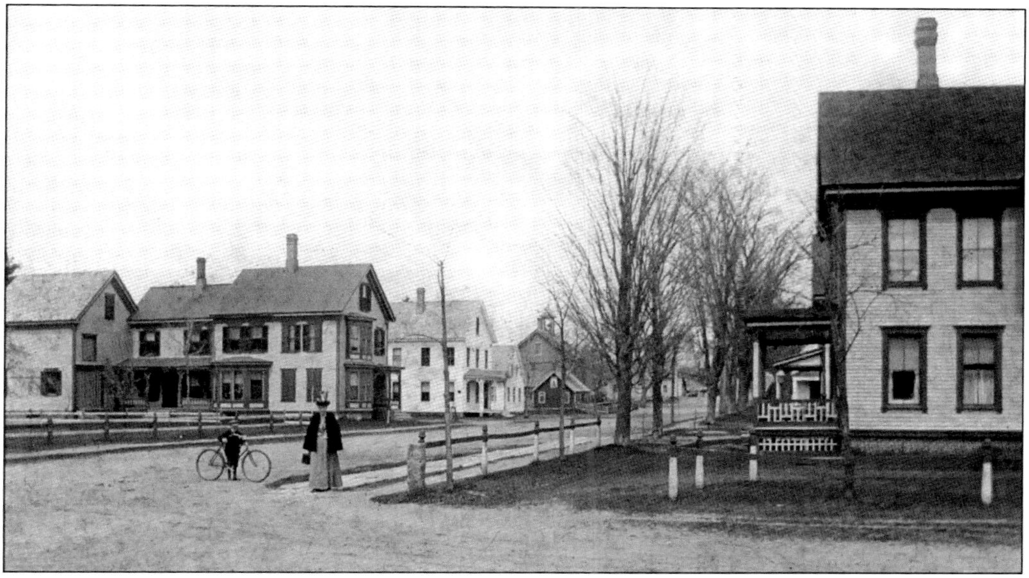

A boy and his bicycle and a hatted woman with a handbag stand at the corner of Mill and Weld Streets around 1900. In the center of the picture, the building with the cupola is the second brick schoolhouse on Weld Street. Many noted people, including future governors, senators, and congressmen, either taught or were taught at the various schools that occupied this site. (DHS.)

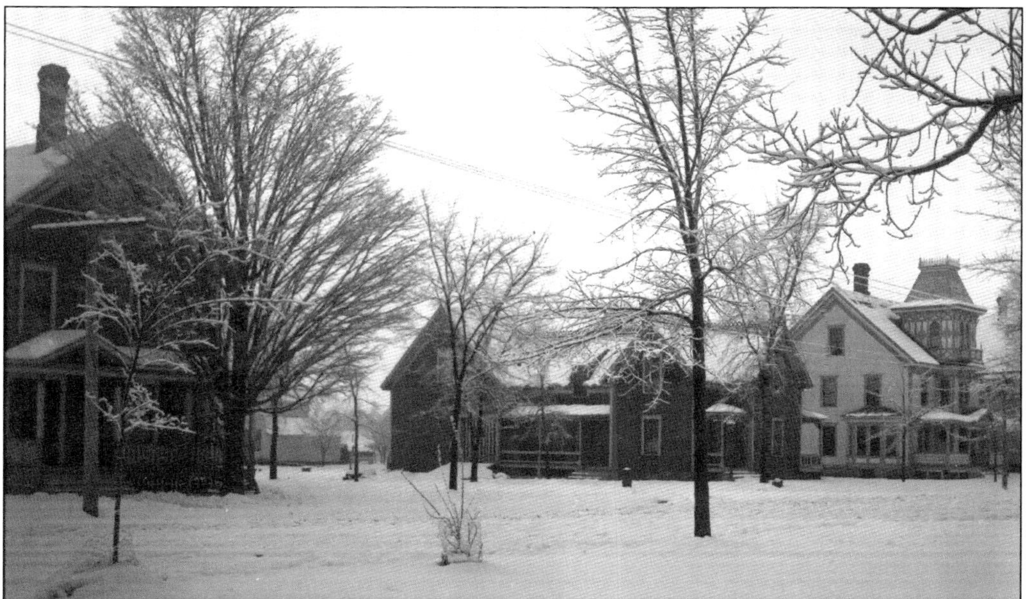

A snowstorm has left its mark on these Weld Street homes. The house on the right belongs to Frank Stanley and was built in 1887. Simultaneously, he was building the Dixfield Spool Company with spool machinery brought from the Searsport Block and Spool Company. Later, the top portion of the decorative tower at the front of the house was remodeled into a more practical style. (PRS.)

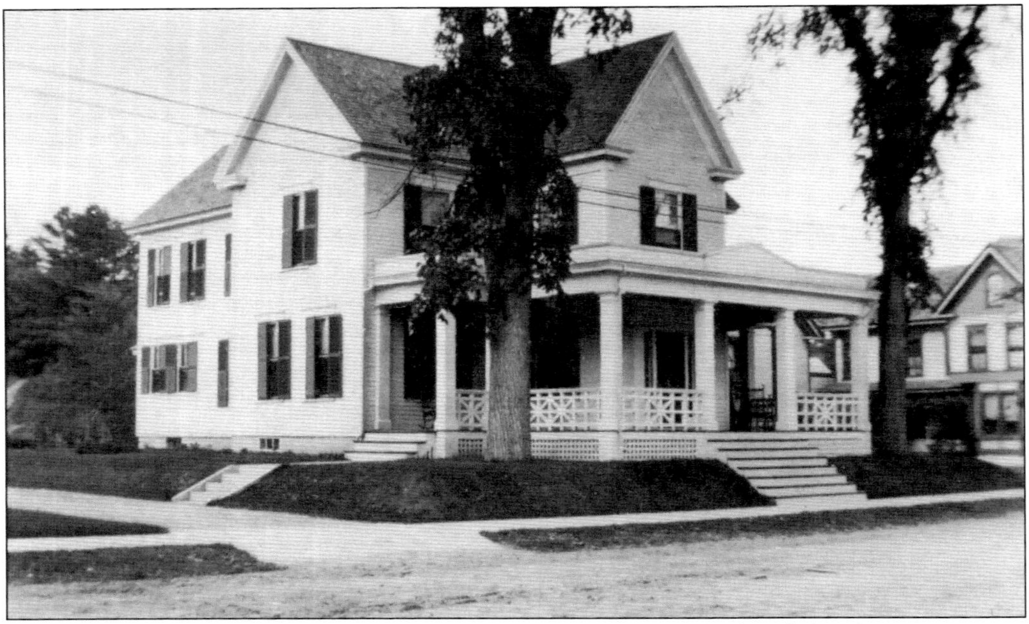

William W. Bolster was one of the many law students who studied with local attorney Isaac Randall. Bolster, from nearby Rumford, built this house on Weld Street during the score of years he practiced in Dixfield. He later became city manager in Auburn, Maine. Dixfield attorney and businessman John S. Harlow lived in this home for many years. (ATK.)

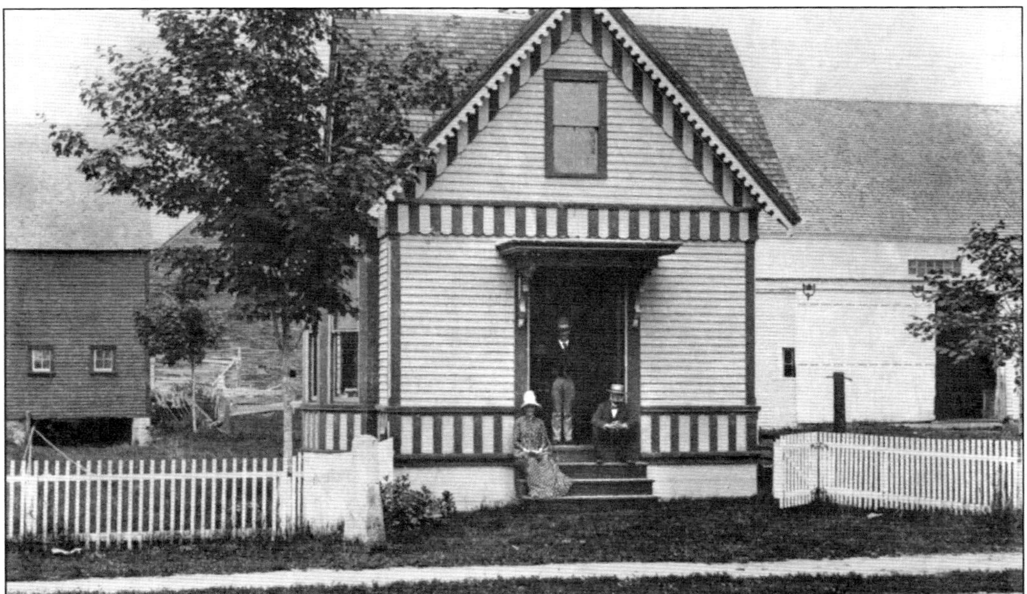

Henry O. Stanley's sporting goods store featured fishing tackle and bicycles as specialties. Stanley was also a fisheries and game commissioner for the State of Maine for more than 30 years—shaping the Maine Warden Service, conducting a statewide survey of fishways, and initiating some of the nation's first conservation programs. An avid fisherman, he is often credited with helping to open the Androscoggin Lakes to the fishing trade. Stanley is seen at the right. (NDM.)

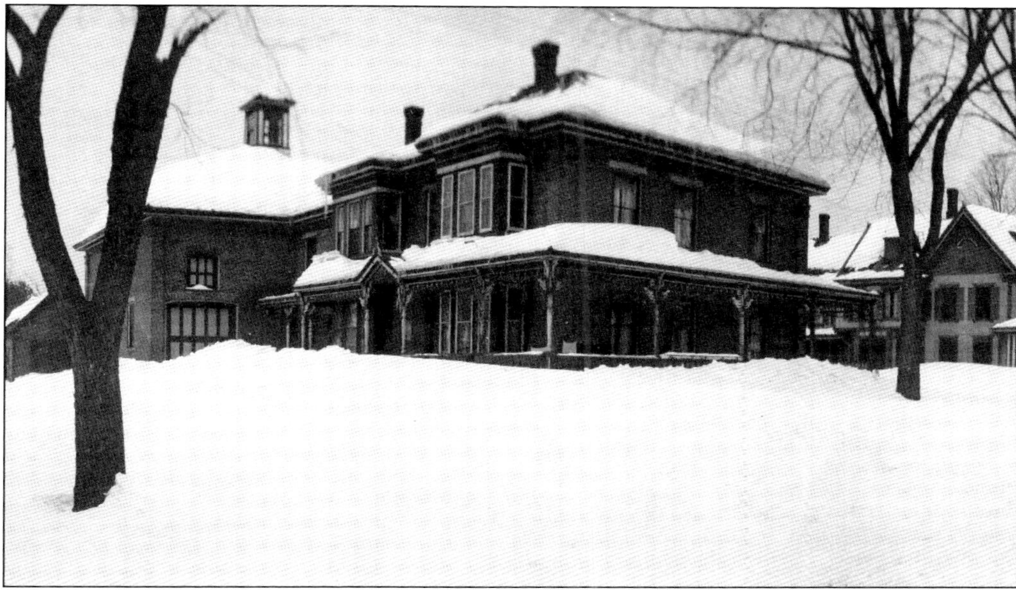

In the 1890s, Albion Marsh, with business ties to Portland, Maine, and Cleveland, Ohio, owned this house built by E.G. Harlow. His brother David Munroe Marsh had done well in the chemical business. Albion was responsible for bringing electricity to Dixfield in the 1880s but was adversely affected by the financial panic of 1893 and never fully recovered. (PRS.)

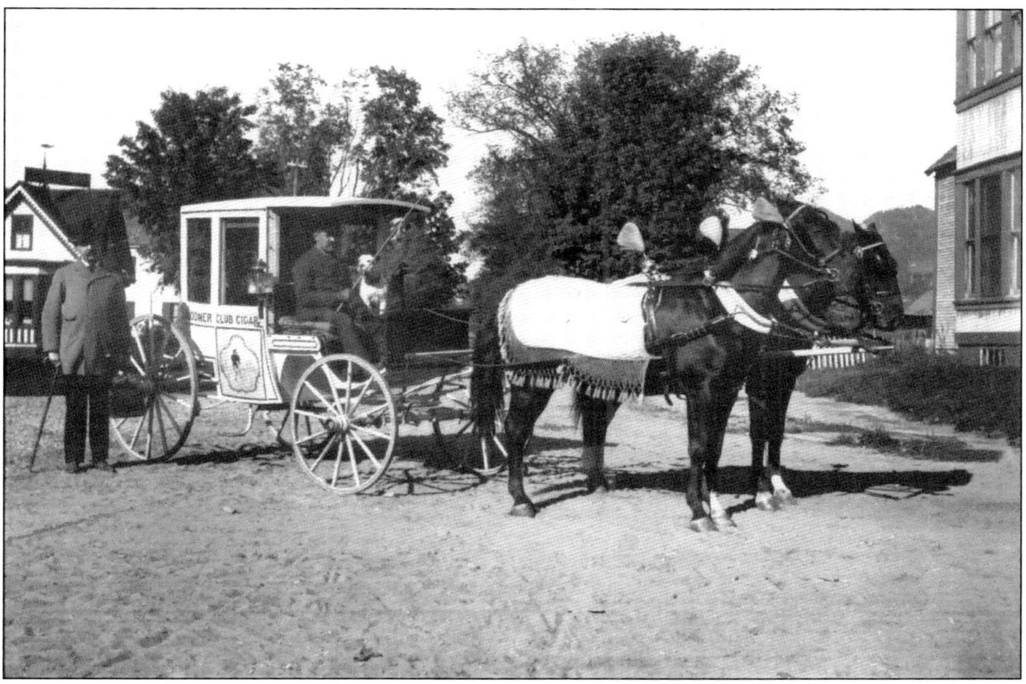

Traveling salesmen were common in Dixfield Village. This pair sold Bloomer Club Cigars near the National House around the turn of the century. The fly netting covering the horse was probably made by seine-makers in Vinalhaven, Maine. The fish-shaped weather vane at the left sits atop the sporting goods store of Henry O. Stanley. (DRH.)

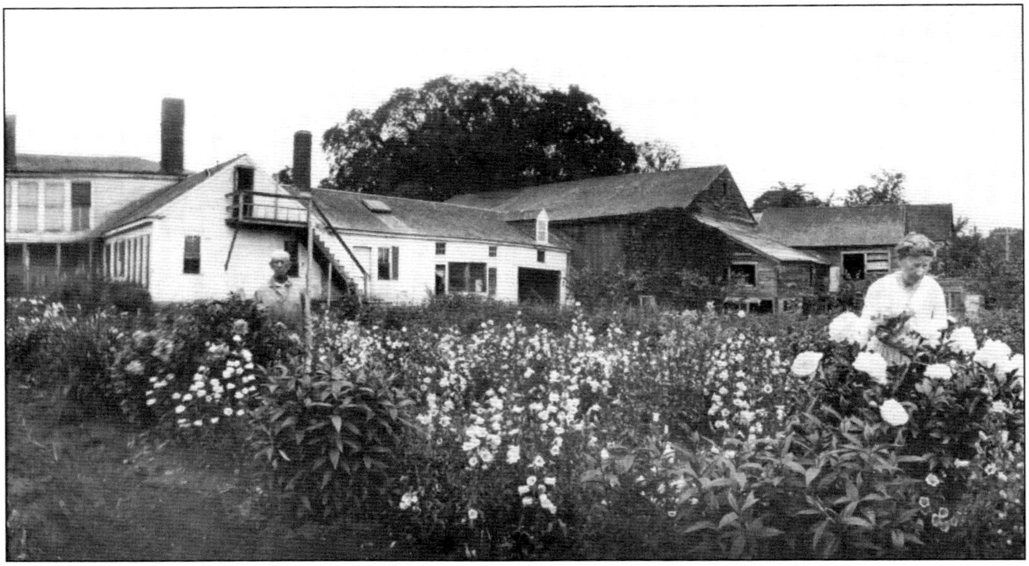

Wilder Chase and his wife, Clara Hooper, tend their massive flower garden behind the Chase house on Weld Street in this 1920s view. Chase descended directly from the builder of the house, Charles T. Chase, who came to Dixfield from Livermore, Maine, and married Louisa, a daughter of Amos Trask. This property has been incorporated into a storage yard for Towle's Hardware. (DHS.)

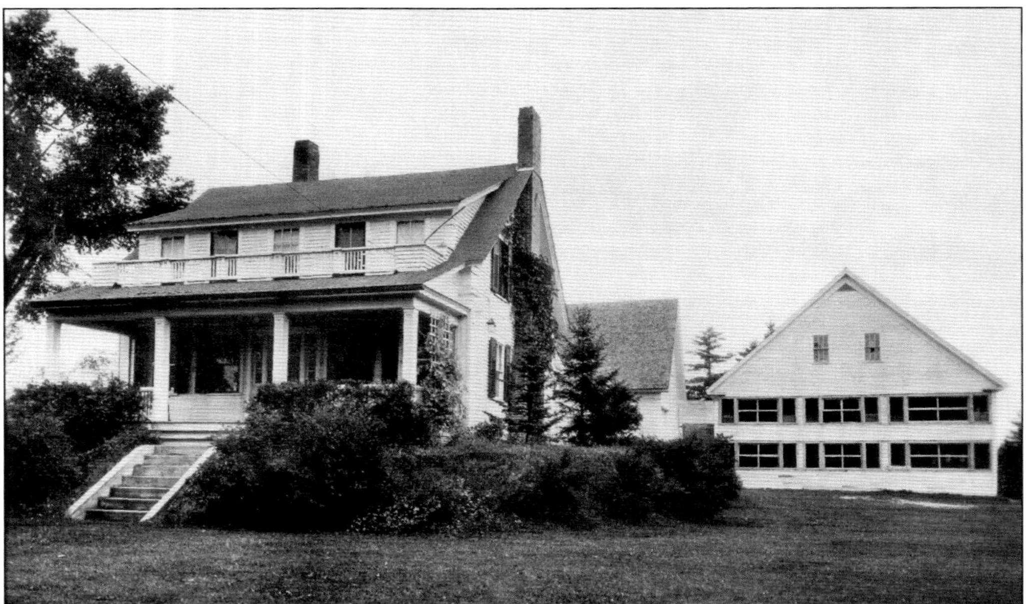

In 1924, Sherburn and Helen (née DeCoster) Leslie and her mother, Edith, acquired an old cattle barn on the Weld Road near Aunt Hannah Brook and converted it into a chicken barn. For about 18 years, they conducted a thriving egg business, ending the operation shortly after Sherburn's death in 1952. The barn began to deteriorate and eventually was sold as salvage lumber. (PRS.)

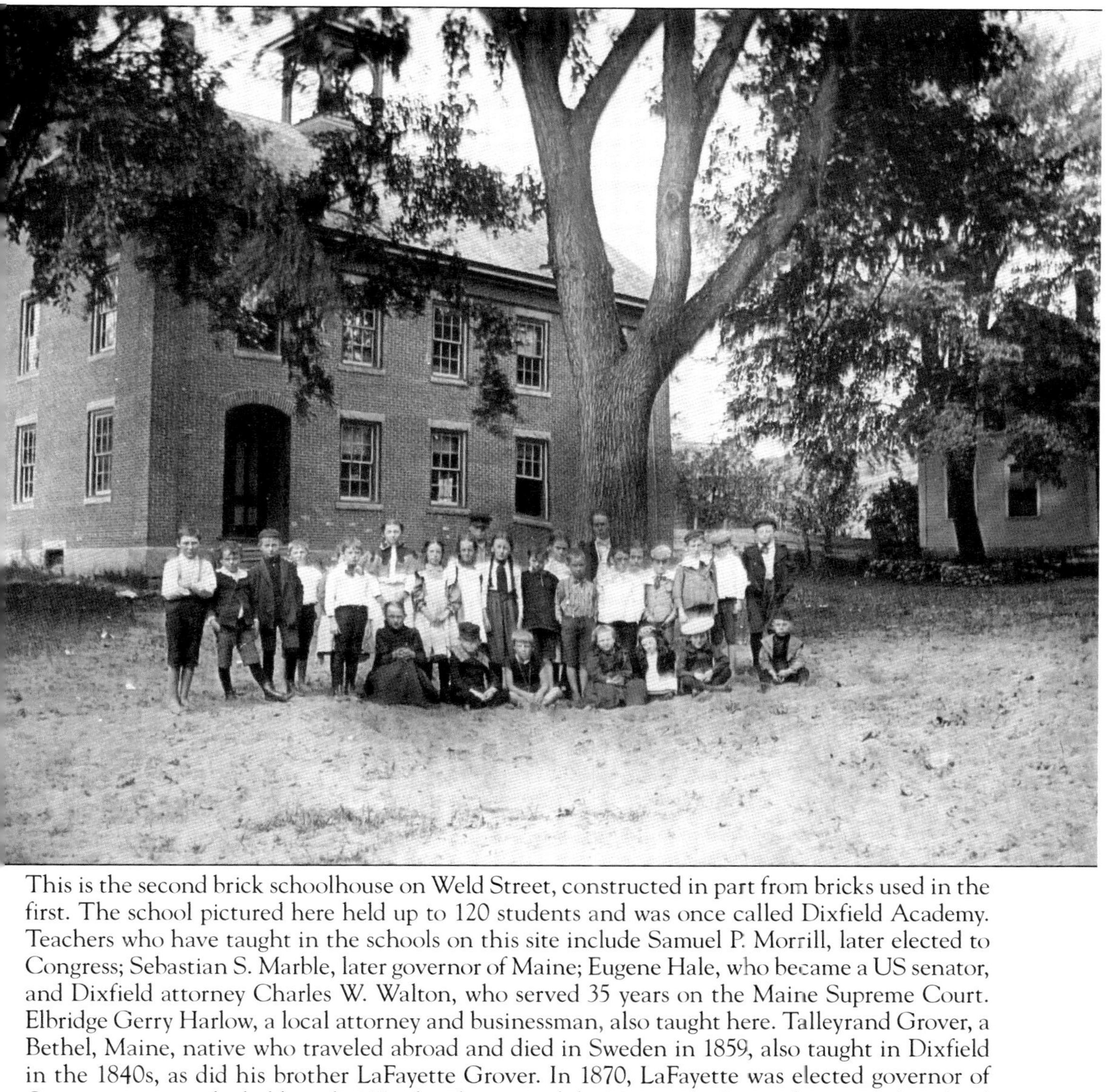

This is the second brick schoolhouse on Weld Street, constructed in part from bricks used in the first. The school pictured here held up to 120 students and was once called Dixfield Academy. Teachers who have taught in the schools on this site include Samuel P. Morrill, later elected to Congress; Sebastian S. Marble, later governor of Maine; Eugene Hale, who became a US senator, and Dixfield attorney Charles W. Walton, who served 35 years on the Maine Supreme Court. Elbridge Gerry Harlow, a local attorney and businessman, also taught here. Talleyrand Grover, a Bethel, Maine, native who traveled abroad and died in Sweden in 1859, also taught in Dixfield in the 1840s, as did his brother LaFayette Grover. In 1870, LaFayette was elected governor of Oregon, a position he held until 1877, when he entered the US Senate. Erected in 1883, the school building is still in use today as an apartment building. (NDM.)

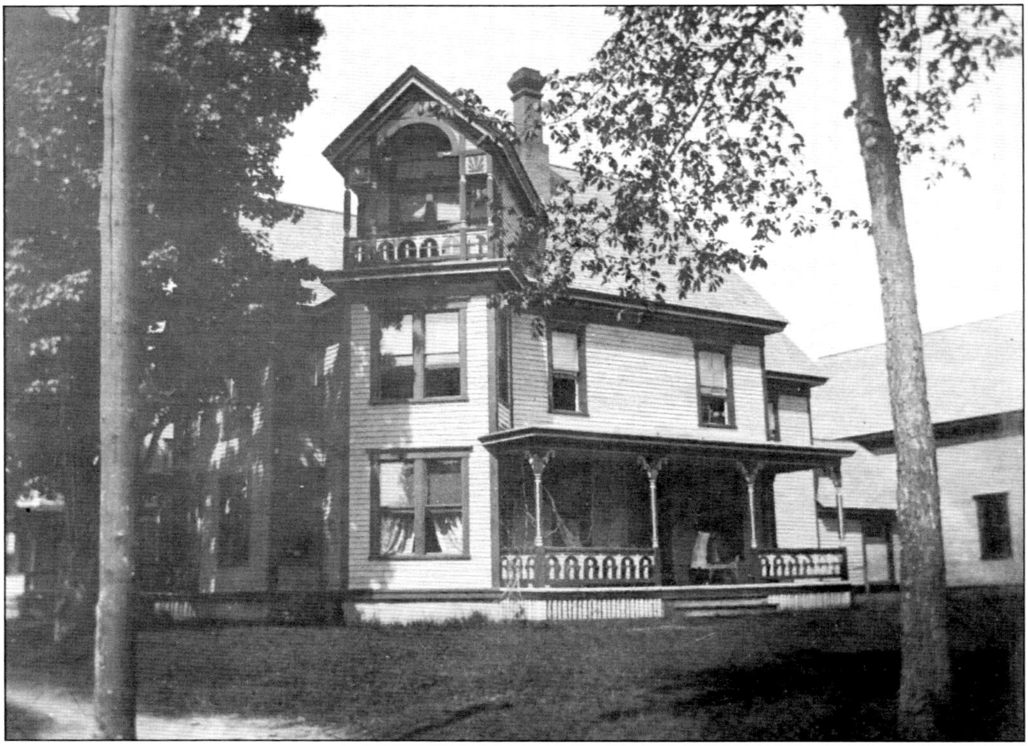

John Ward Howe of Canton, Maine, moved to this home in 1892. His son Carroll was in the grain business and also sold coal and wood. His daughters Cora and Sybil lived here in their later years. Sybil had previously lived in Portland and Augusta. Later owners of this house include the Carletons, Turbides, and Parises. (DHS.)

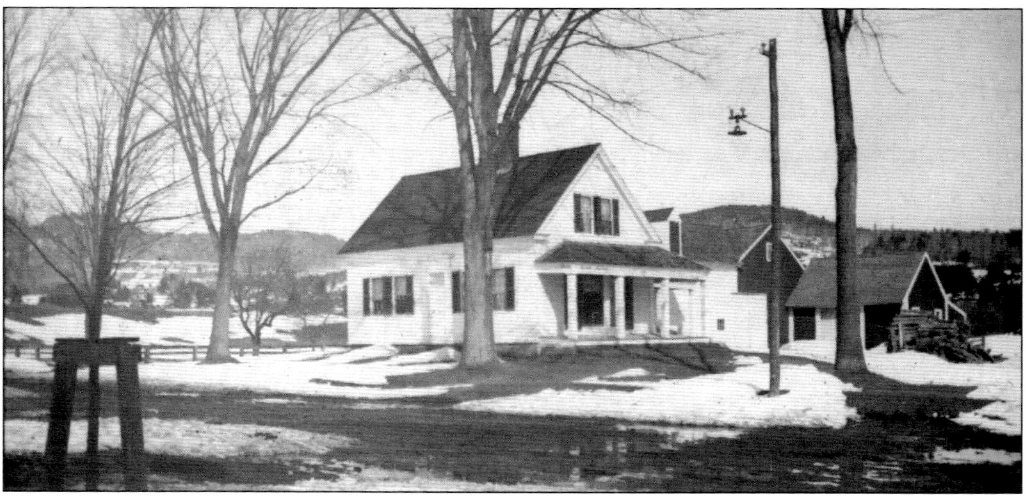

Isaac Randall from Livermore, Maine, studied law at Bowdoin, graduating in 1836. Following a brief stint as headmaster of Gould Academy in Bethel, Maine, Randall set up his law practice in Dixfield Village. He lived in this house on Weld Street, built for him by Humphrey Merrill Eaton. When Eaton died soon after his marriage to Melissa White, Randall married his widow, who was called Aunt Melissa by the townspeople. (DRH.)

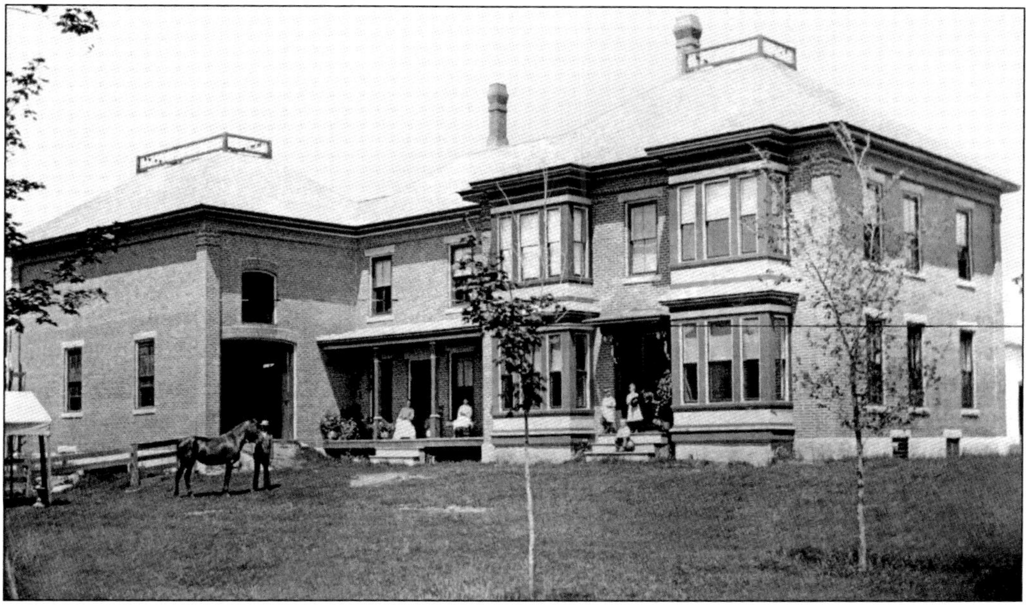

Elbridge Gerry Harlow (1825–1883) built this brick house on Weld Street in 1879. He was at the peak of his influence on Dixfield when his health rapidly declined, and he died a few years later, leaving nine children. His wife, Rosella Stanley (1836–1882), had died the year before. His son William was old enough to fend for himself, and sons John and Frank left for law school in Minnesota. Rosella's brother Frank and his wife, Mary, helped raise the younger children. (DHS.)

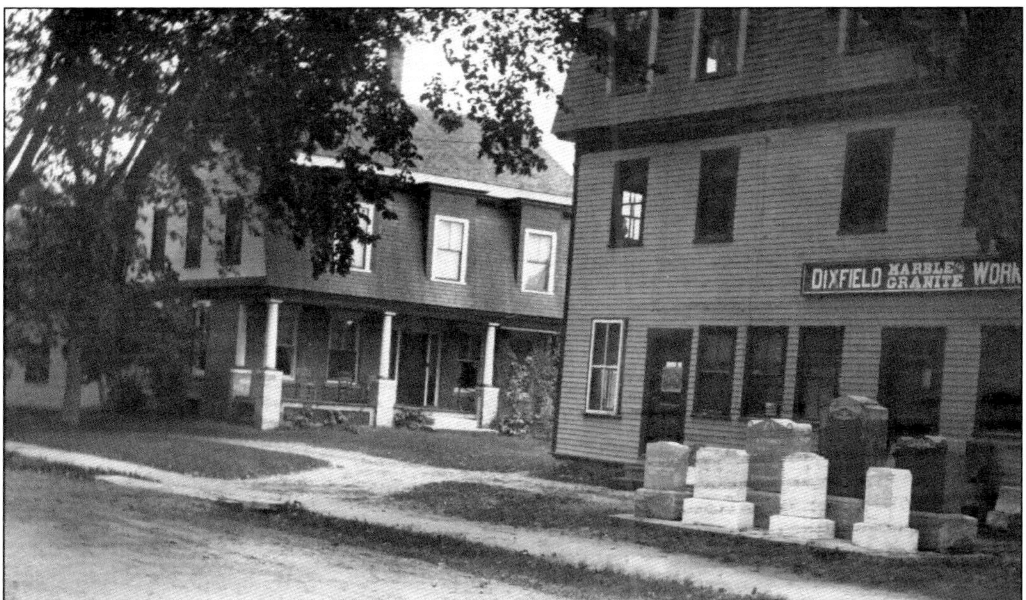

George Holt, a disabled Civil War veteran, came to Dixfield from Bangor to take over Henry Trask's marble works in the late 1860s. With his sons Herschel, Dana, and Thomas, he expanded into printing, turning wooden novelties, selling jewelry, and Cameron automobiles. Dana and Thomas Holt were accomplished musicians; both played with the John Philip Sousa band. (DHS.)

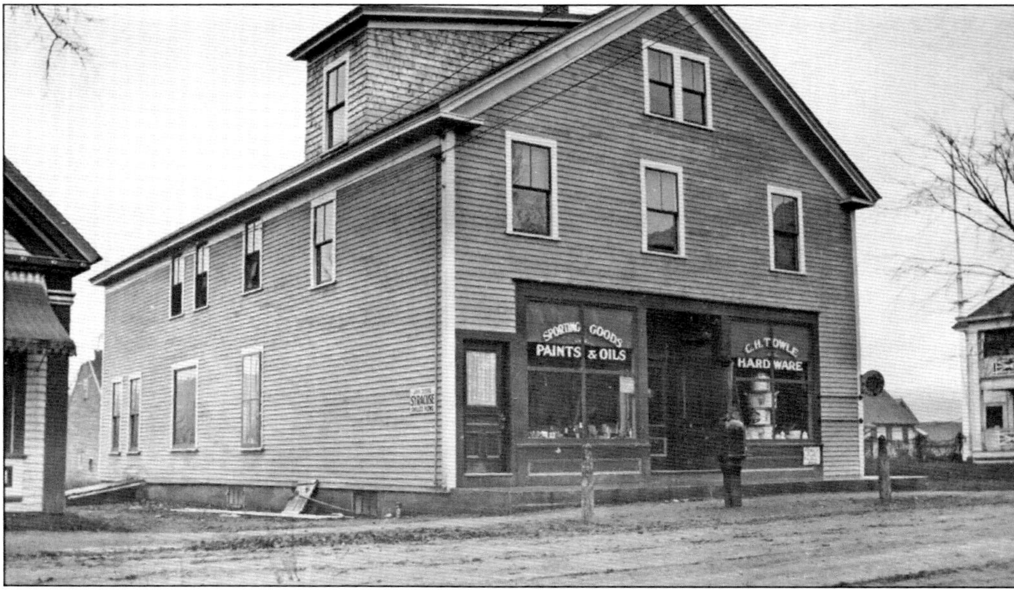

Charles H. Towle purchased and remodeled the old Almon Stockbridge hardware store in 1911 and sold a wide variety of goods, including glass, dog food, paint, lumber, Stanley tools, John Deere tractors, stoves, and gasoline. Turpentine was sold from a large drum, each customer bringing his own container. It was the only building in town to boast an elevator. (DHS.)

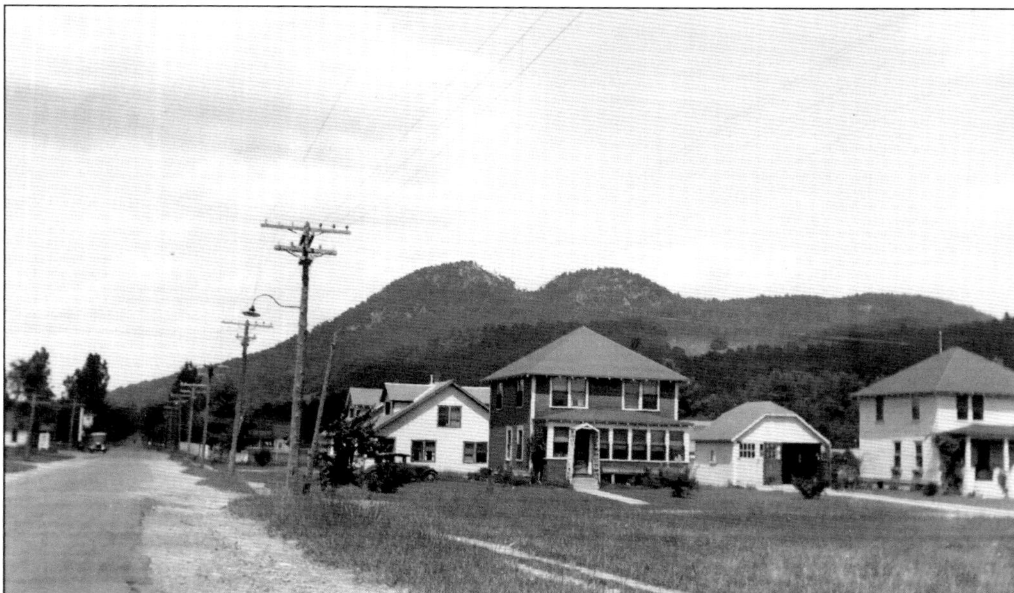

The mountains in the background, called the Sugar Loaves, are Dixfield's most recognizable landmark and attract many people to the area. The darker house at the center was owned by LaForest Collins, and the lighter house to its right belongs to Roland Dennett in this 1920s Weld Street view. (DHS.)

Four

Out and About

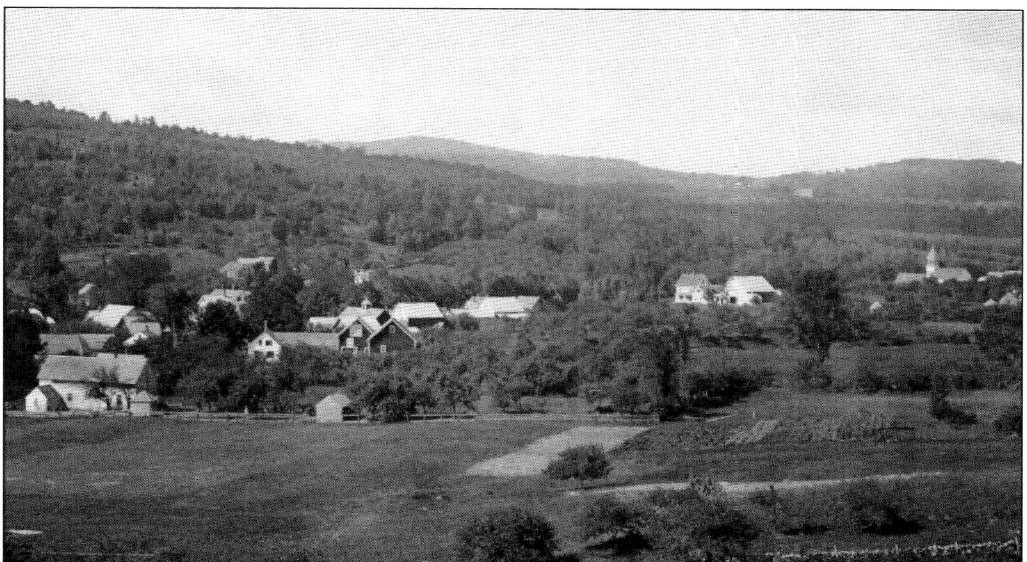

As Dixfield Village is closely identified with Mexico and Peru, so East Dixfield is aligned with the towns of Wilton, Carthage, and Jay in Franklin County. In this 1920s bird's-eye view, the top of the Baptist church is at the center with the steeple of the Universalist church at the right. The town and county lines virtually divide the main street in the village. Many of Dixfield's pioneer families settled here first, including the Severys, Coolidges, Walkers, Kings, Lelands, and Townsends. Severy Hill cemetery contains the gravestones of many early families. (PRS.)

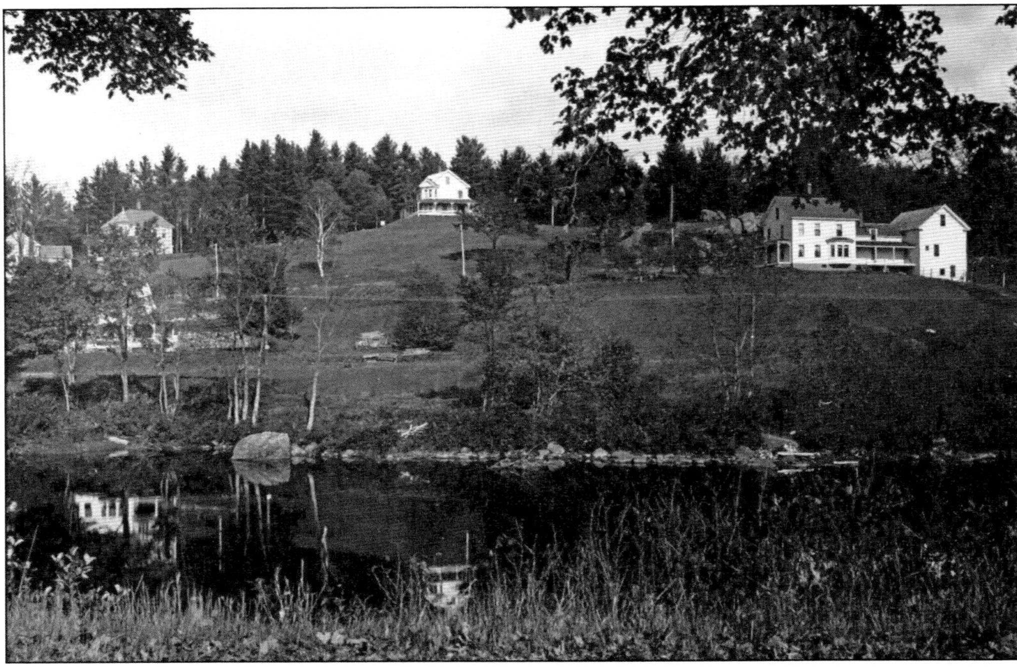

Abbott Hill is seen without trees in this early-1900s picture, quite different than today's shroud of pine trees hiding the homes there. William W. Abbott owned the house at the very top of the hill. At the right is the home of Lewis Humphrey, father of well-known resident Hilda Humphrey Mendes. Down the hill to the left of the Abbott home is the home of lumber dealer William F. Putnam, and closest to the river is the home of deputy sheriff George Dockham. The photograph was taken by photographer Lee Abbott of Rumford, Maine. (DHS.)

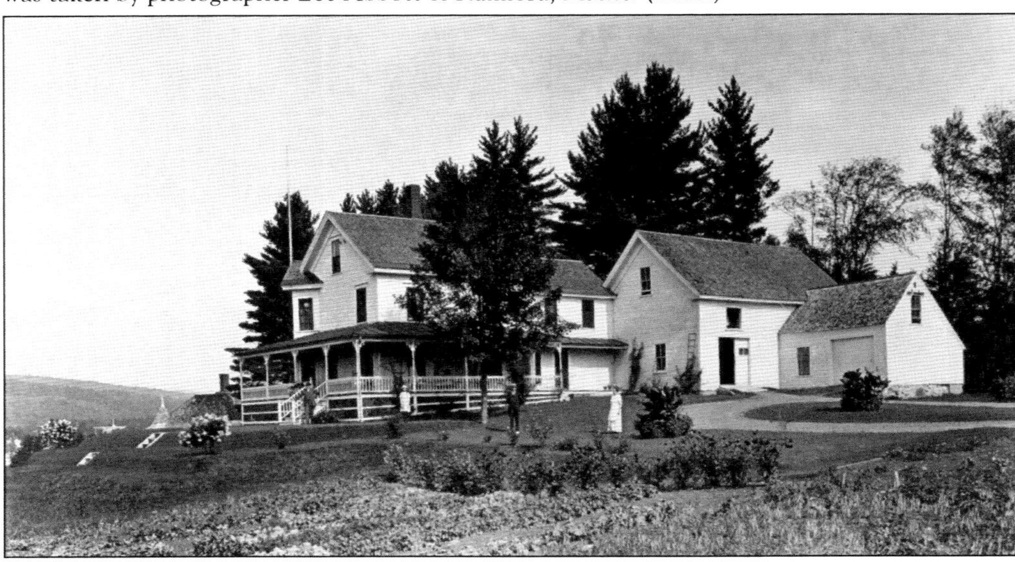

William W. Abbott created a very attractive estate for himself overlooking Dixfield Village from Abbott Hill. Like a lot of successful men of the day, he dabbled in racehorses, at one time owning and breeding Mercury Boone, listed in *Horse Breeders' Monthly* in 1887 by its publisher J.W. Thompson of nearby Canton, Maine. (DHS.)

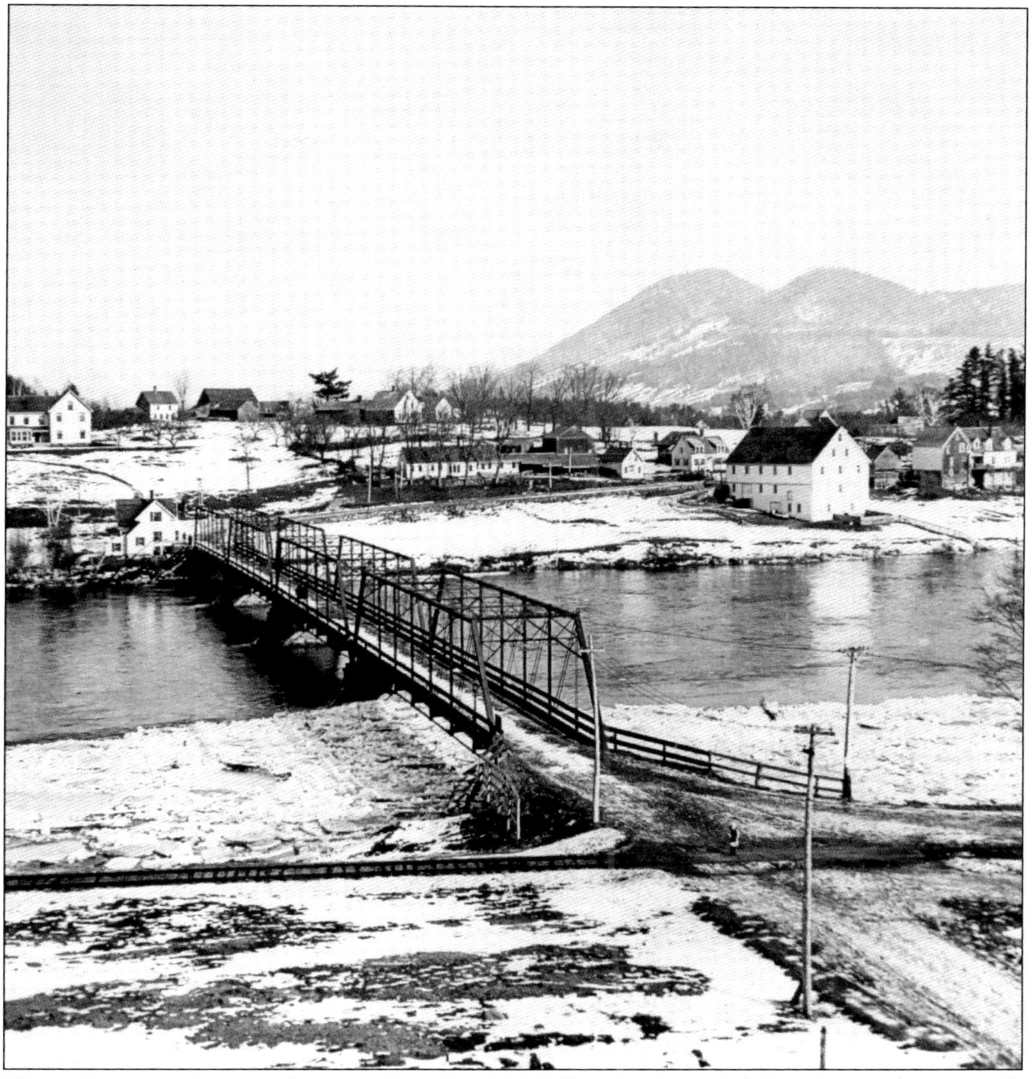

Winter has settled in over the area where Dixfield Village (to the right), Peru (in the foreground), and Mexico (across the bridge) come together. In this 1890s view, the viewer is afforded a clear glimpse of the buildings that used to dot the landscape. The large structure to the right center is the warehouse used by the Charles W. Forster toothpick mill to store products pending delivery to market. The box girder bridge was completed in 1895 and was replaced in 1931. The railroad tracks in the foreground were opened in 1893 and belong to the Maine Central Railroad. The large white house at the extreme left of the picture was once known as the Tucker house. The set of buildings to the right of the pine tree (center background) belonged to John Griffith Jr., who was in Dixfield by 1827, sawing shingles for James M. Williams near the site of the present opera house next to Webb River. Williams also operated a general store in partnership with Davis Washburn until Washburn's death 1832. (MHPC.)

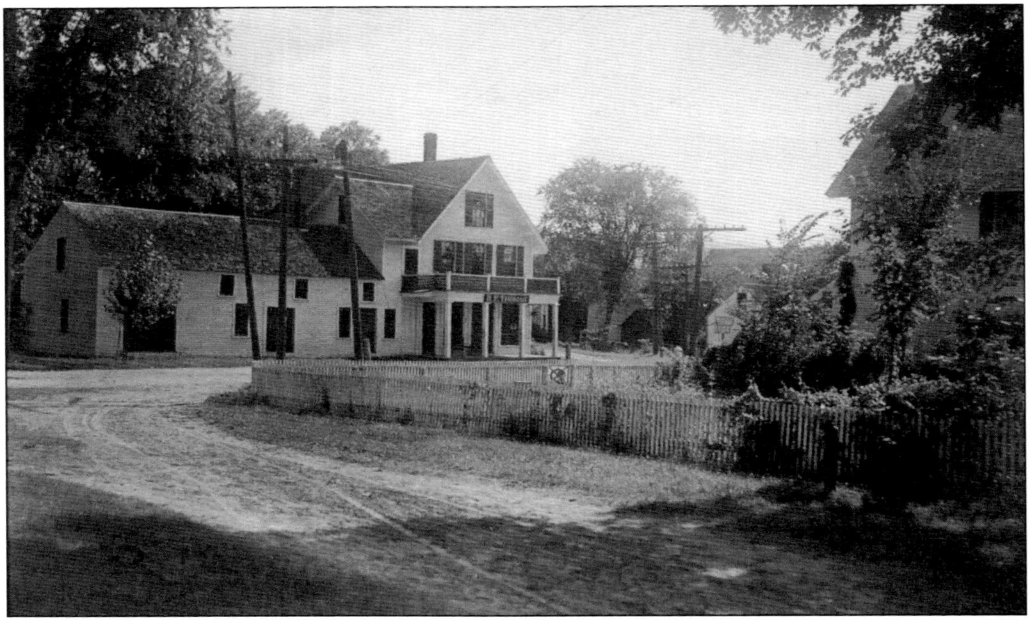

Bert F. Thomas was the successor to the Butterfield sisters at this East Dixfield general store. It became a favorite gathering place for townspeople as they sat by the stove and swapped their gossip and traded views. Besides his store duties, Thomas was also president of the East Dixfield Cemetery Association. (PRS.)

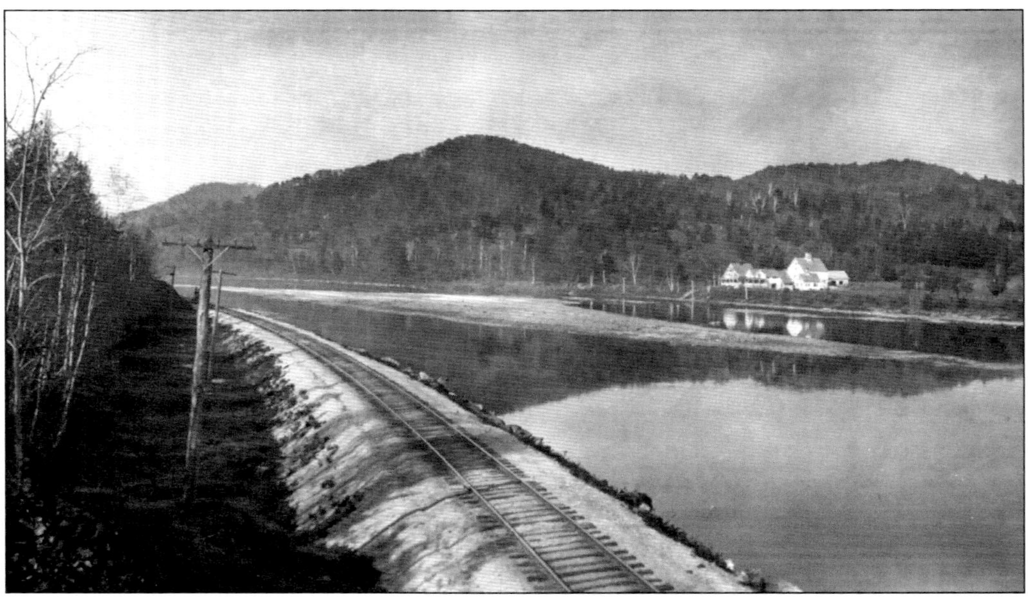

The tracks of the Maine Central Railroad parallel the Androscoggin River in this 1930s photograph. The neighboring town of Canton had long been served by the Maine Central before tracks were extended to Dixfield in 1893, then on to Rumford, a boomtown, which grew rapidly when Hugh Chisholm developed the Rumford Falls to provide electric power for papermaking. Shown across the river is the Gregory Inn in Mexico, Maine. (PRS.)

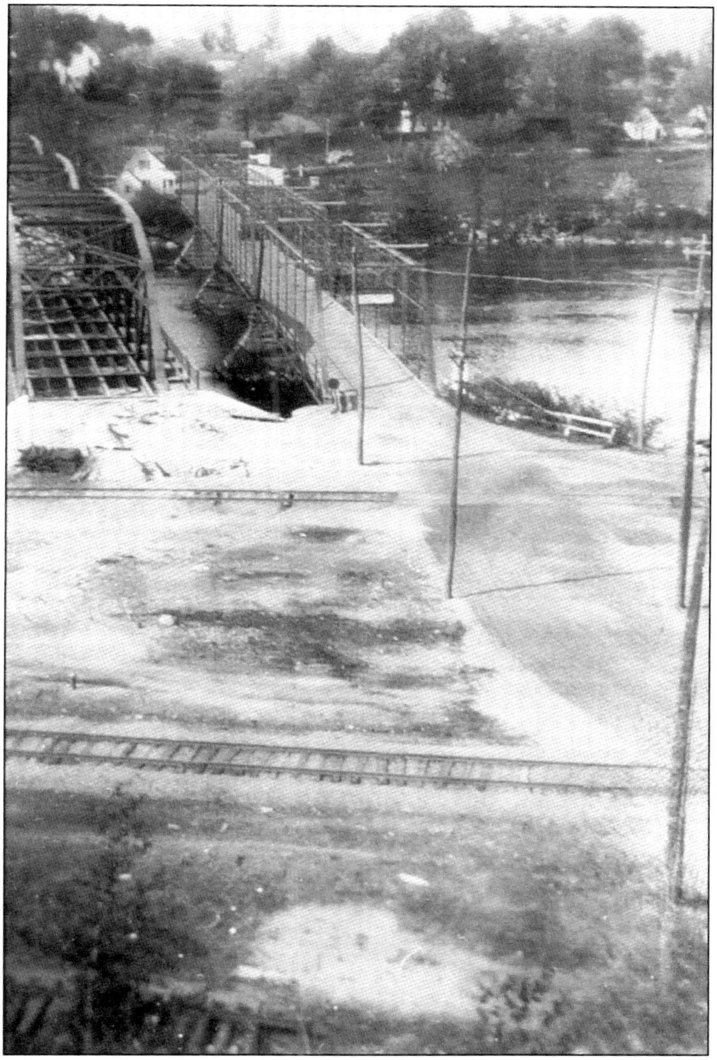

This is a rare view of two bridges spanning the Androscoggin River from Peru to Mexico, Maine. The original box girder bridge was built in 1895 and lasted only 36 years before being replaced. This picture, taken about 1930, shows the location of the new bridge to be several dozen feet upriver from the old bridge. Today, this bridge has reached the end of its useful life. (DHS.)

A growing population fueled by a booming economy in Dixfield and nearby Rumford led to new streets being developed in town. This is an early view of High Street several years after it was opened to development in the 1890s. Homes on Weld Street are shown to the right with the ever-present peaks of the Sugar Loaves in the background. Mill Street and Third Street were also laid out in the 1880s to accommodate economic expansion. (PRS.)

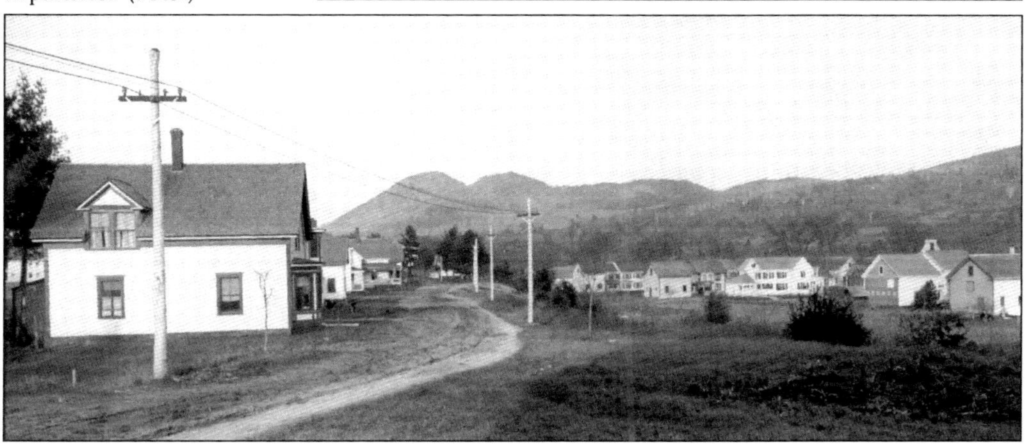

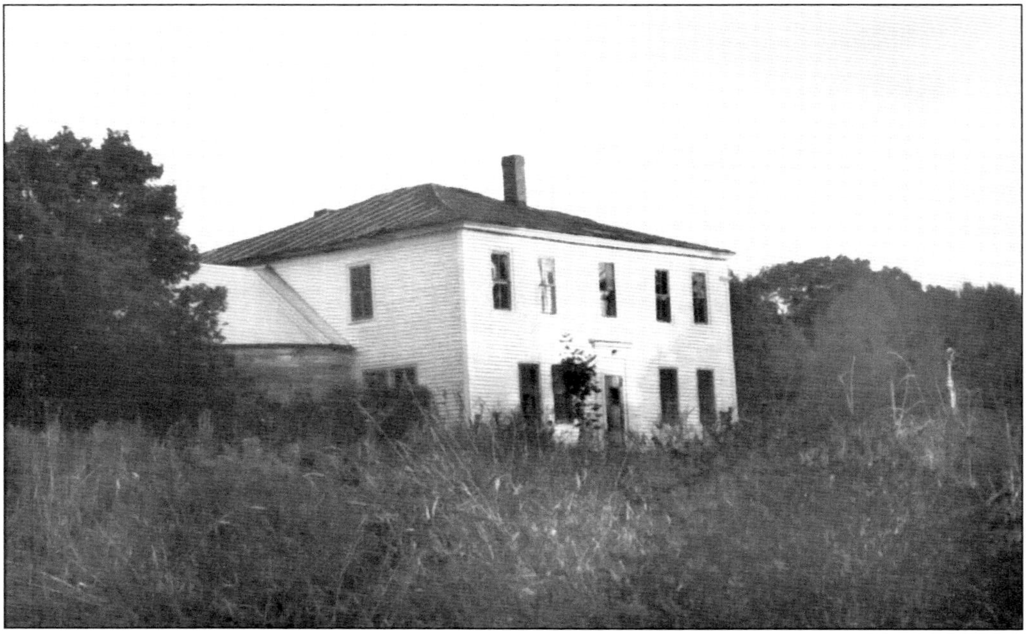

The Peter Holman house at Dixfield Common typified the homes built by Col. Jonathan Holman's three sons—Jonathan, Peter, and Ebenezer. Two of the houses were built of brick, but Peter's was constructed of wood, and, ironically, was the only one not destroyed by fire. (PDH.)

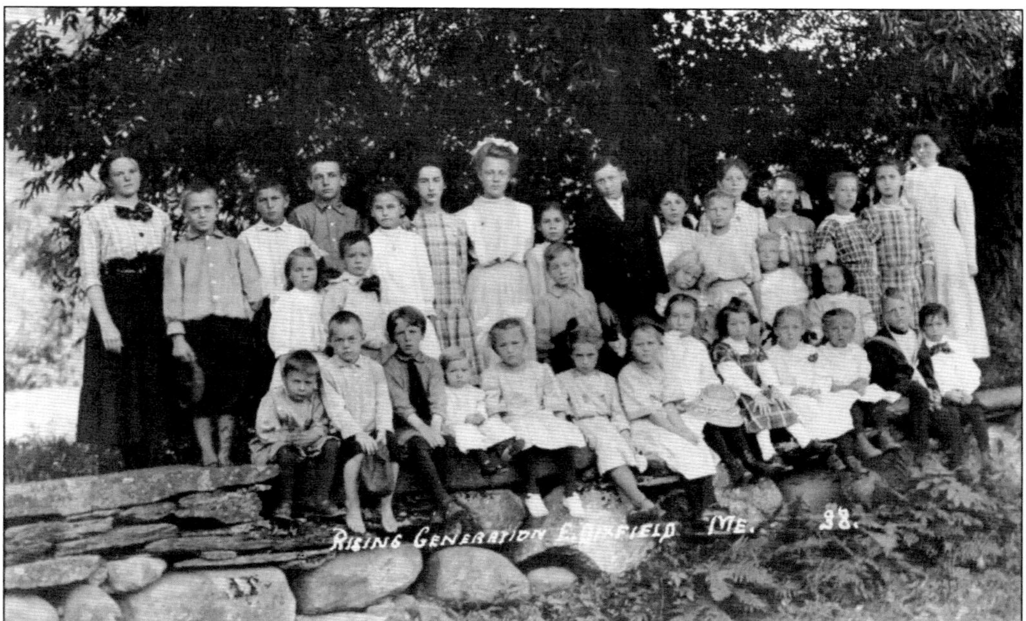

For many years, the tradition of posing for a group picture was practiced among the students and teachers of East Dixfield. Most of these photographs were released as postcards, each of them titled the "Rising Generation." This image was taken around 1911. (PRS.)

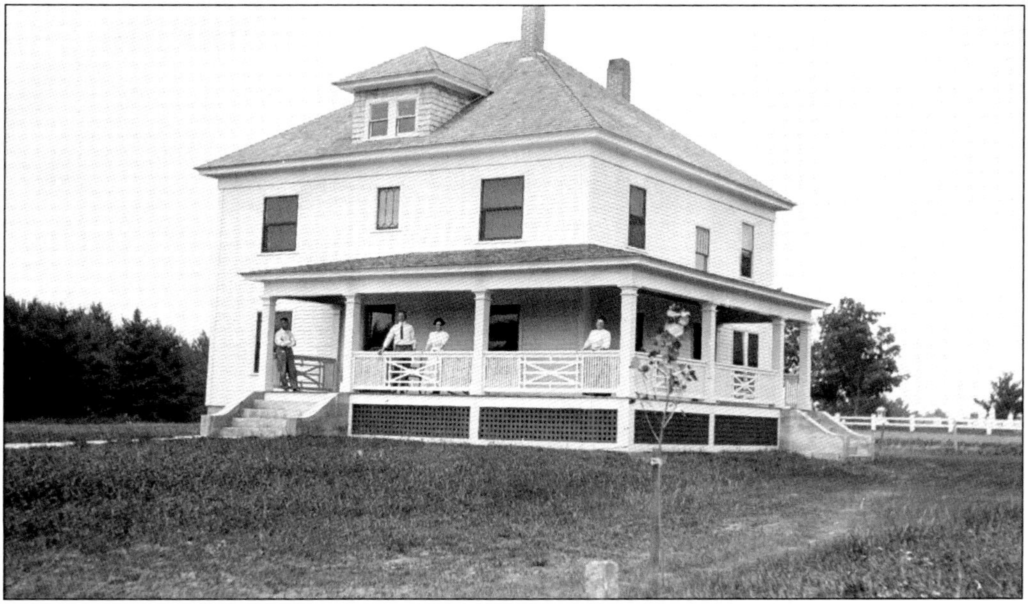

George P. Stanley, named for his cousin George Shepard Page, built this house for his wife, Netta Stanley on North Street, then known as Cliff Street, offering it as a Christmas present in 1911, roughly the date the photograph was taken. Stanley managed the Dixfield Toothpick Company mill on Pine Street. Also known as the Stanley Mill, it was built by John S. Harlow. (NDM.)

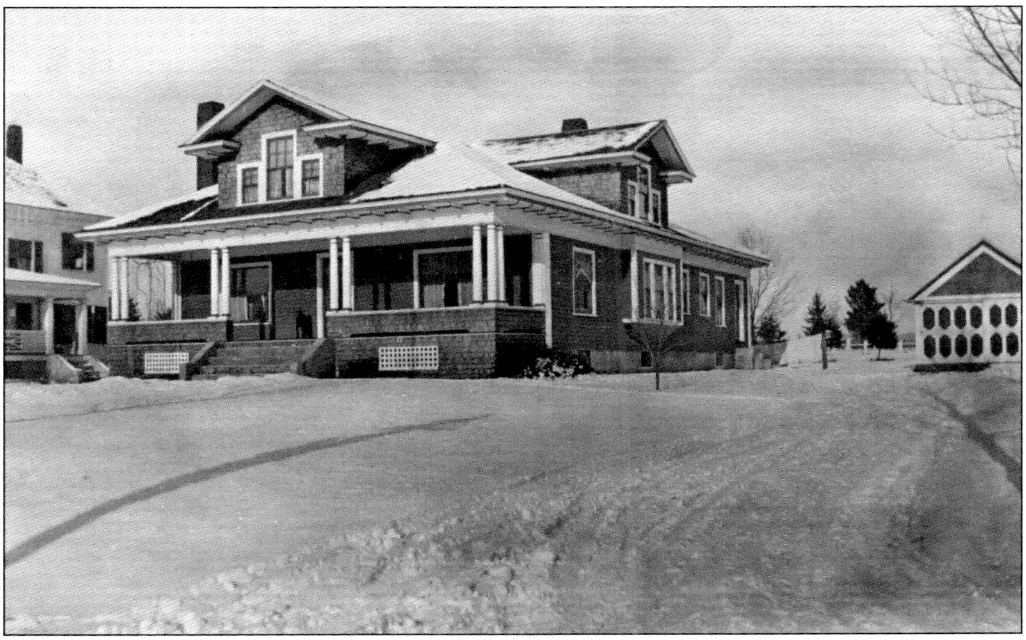

Fred Keene was a Dixfield merchant who operated a grocery store variously known as Cox and Keene or Kidder and Keene, depending on who his current partner was. In the spring of 1905, a fire leveled both the G.S. Holman store and the neighboring F.H. Keene store and damaged the post office. Fred and Ethel (Gates) Keene lived in this house on North Street, once called Cliff Street and Bungalow Street. (PRS.)

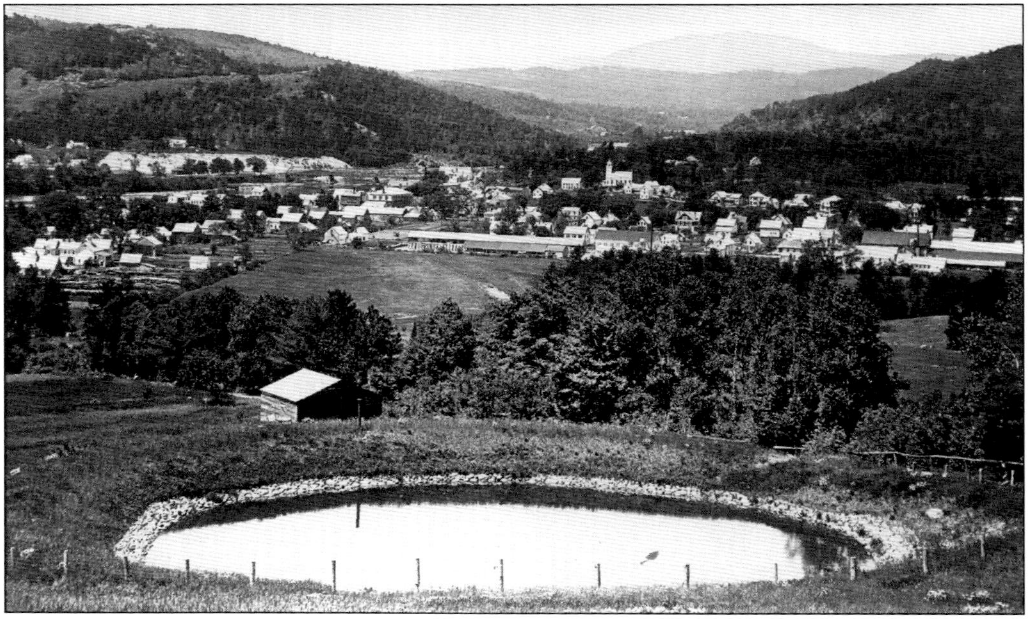

This view of Dixfield Village looks west from Abbott Hill. The long building in the center of the photograph is a drying shed used to store white birch "spool bars" for later use in turning spools for cotton thread. Dixfield was home to the largest spool-making operation in the world for many years. The Church on the Hill is seen in the distance. To the left is Peru, and in the background lies Mexico, once part of Dixfield. (DHS.)

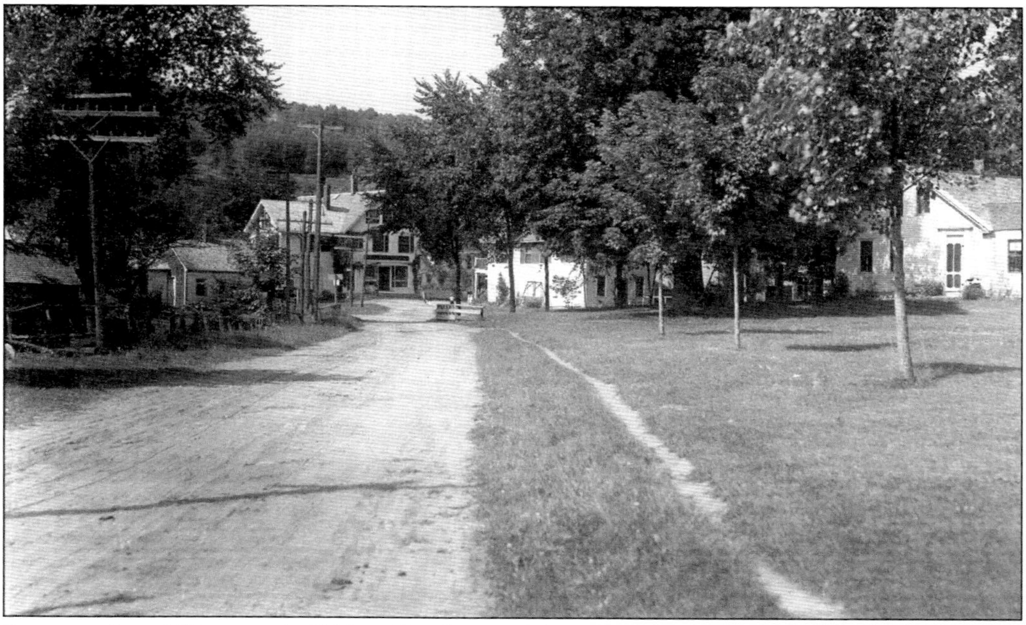

For more than 150 years, the Wilton Road turned sharply at the eastern edge of East Dixfield, as shown in this 1920s view. As automobiles gained speed and refinement and road building evolved to meet the increased demands of the motorist, this road was discontinued as a throughway, and traffic was routed straight through the village. (MHPC.)

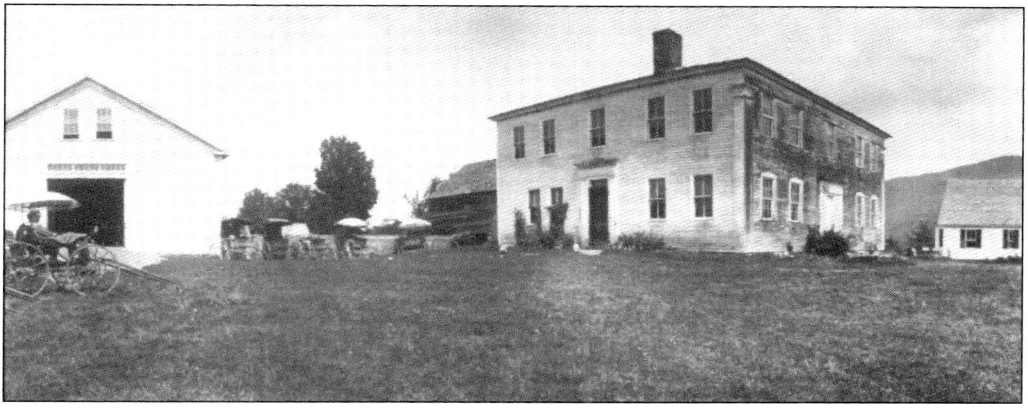

A gentleman of leisure seeks relief from the sun in this early-1900s photograph of the Peter Holman homestead. Peter was a son of Col. Jonathan Holman who brokered the purchase of Dixfield from the Committee for the Sale of Eastern Lands in Massachusetts in the 1790s. Even today this property remains in the Holman family. It is the same home pictured on the front cover of this book. (PDH.)

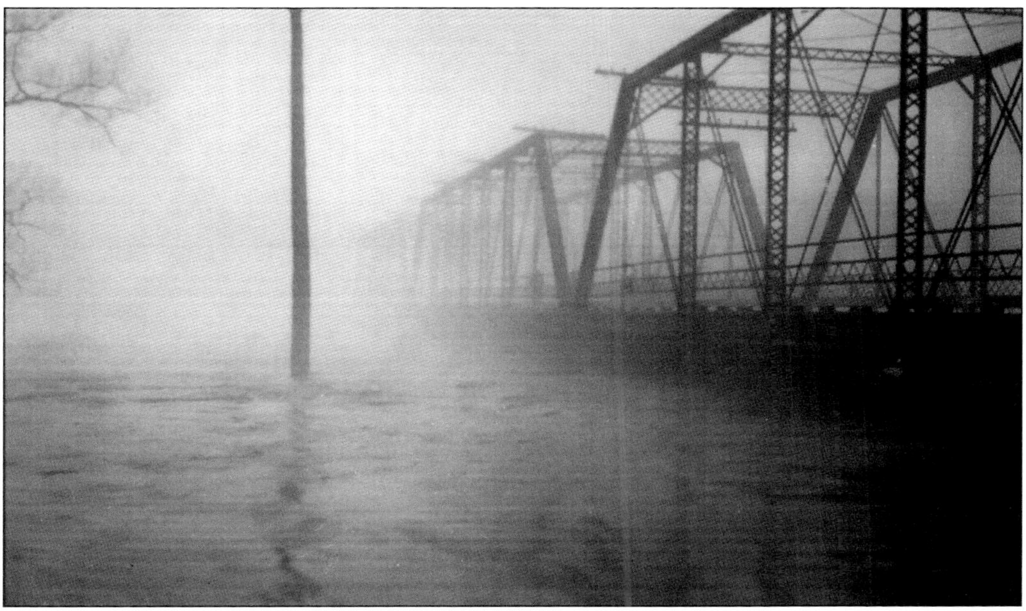

Built in 1895, the first Androscoggin River Bridge from Peru to Mexico was built to withstand the spring floods common to western Maine. At the time, wrought-iron box girder bridges were popular, and many of them were used. Their life spans on the Androscoggin were often less than 40 years. (PRS.)

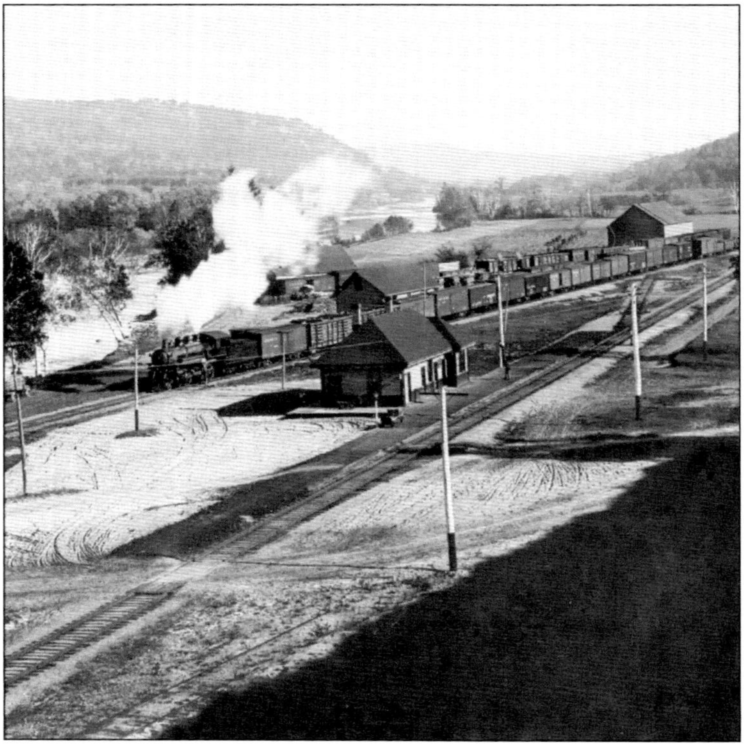

Much of western Maine had witnessed the development of local railroad stops decades before this Maine Central Railroad station opened in Peru, Maine, in 1893. Driven in part by the development of the Oxford Paper Company in Rumford, the railroad provided a nearby outlet for Dixfield Village mills that produced toothpicks, spools, and lumber. Previously, the nearest railway station was in Canton, Maine, 12 miles away. (MHPC.)

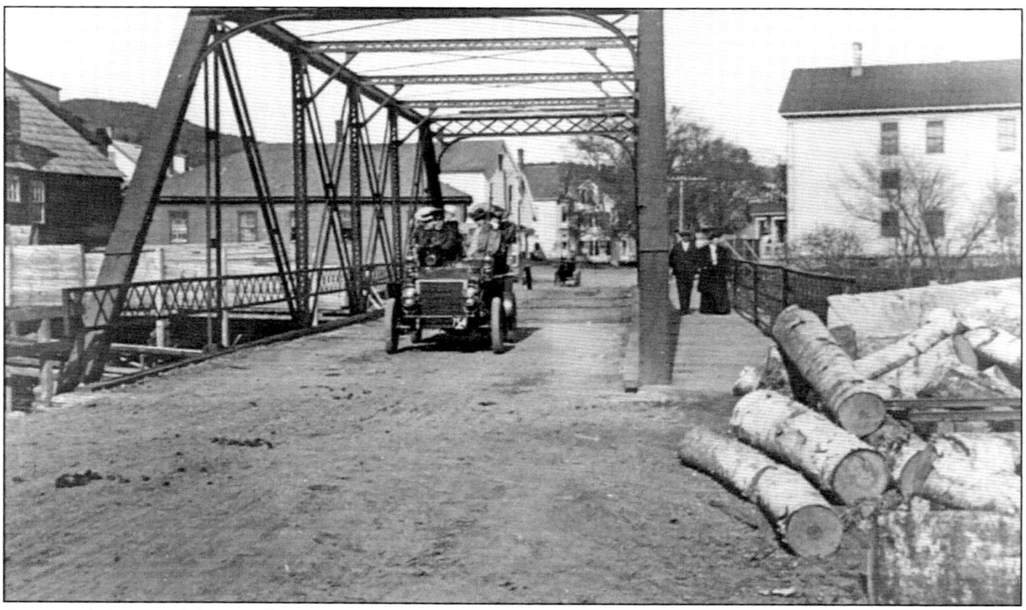

George Moy and his wife, Jennie, cross the Webb River Bridge from Dixfield into Mexico in this early-1900s photograph. The Moys resided on Main Street, and George was a carpenter and house painter. A charter member of the Dixfield Board of Trade, he later moved to Carthage. To the right are birch bolts to be turned into toothpicks at the Forster toothpick mill, which was managed by Charles Freeman. (DRH.)

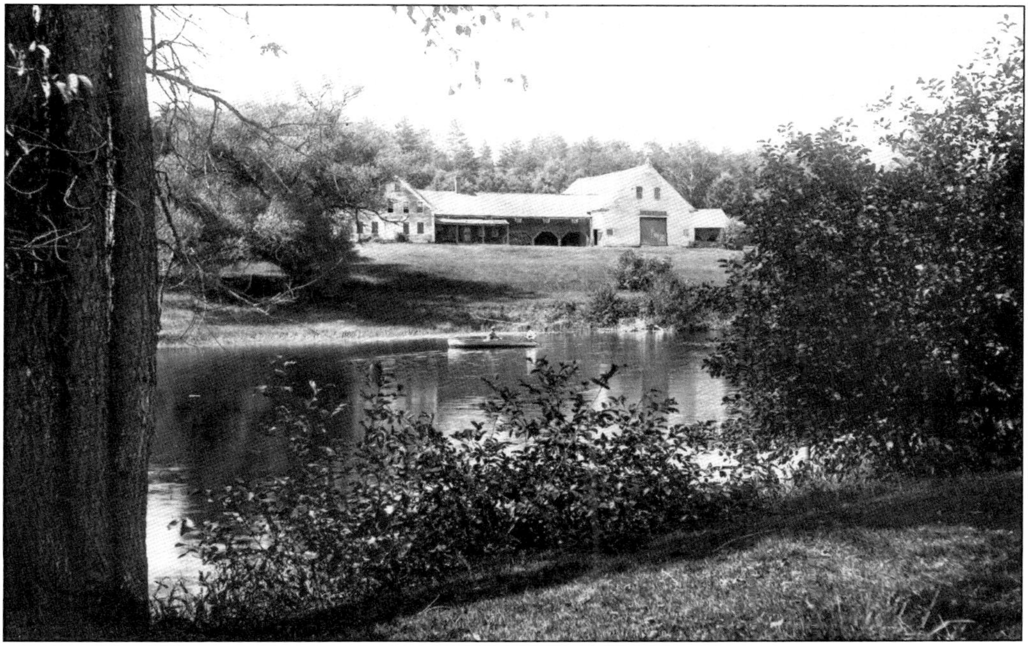

This is the home of Mexico resident Thomas Jefferson White and lies just across Webb River from Dixfield. Art experts believe that this farm was the house that Dixfield artisan Lucy Trask Barnard memorialized in her most famous hooked rug, sometimes called the "Rainbow Rug" for its stylized depiction of a broad rainbow over the farm. The Metropolitan Museum of Art in New York City now owns this masterpiece. (DRH.)

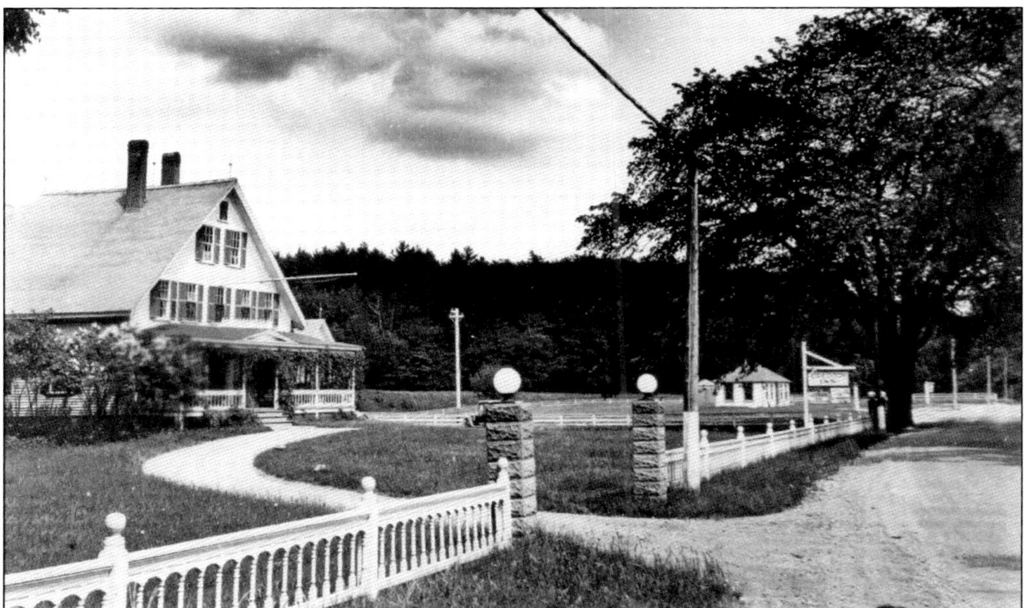

The Gregory Inn became an overnight stop for tourists back in the 1920 but, before that, it was the summer home of Gen. Charles A. Wilson, who was a summer resident of Dixfield Village and a member of the Dixfield Board of Trade. (PRS.)

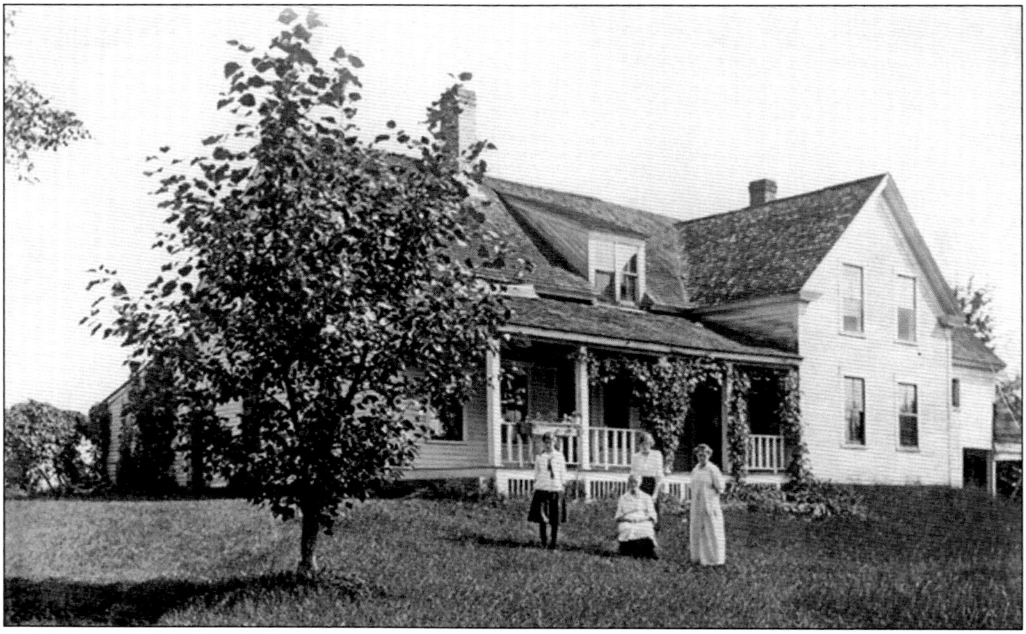

The Oscar Trask family home was on Leavitt Street in Mexico. Its porch served as the setting for family photographs for several decades. Pictured are, from left to right, Mary Fletcher; Oscar's widow, Jane Edmunds Trask (seated); Mary's sister Mathilde; and Ruth Rogers Trask, Jane's daughter-in-law and half-sister to the Fletchers. (DHS.)

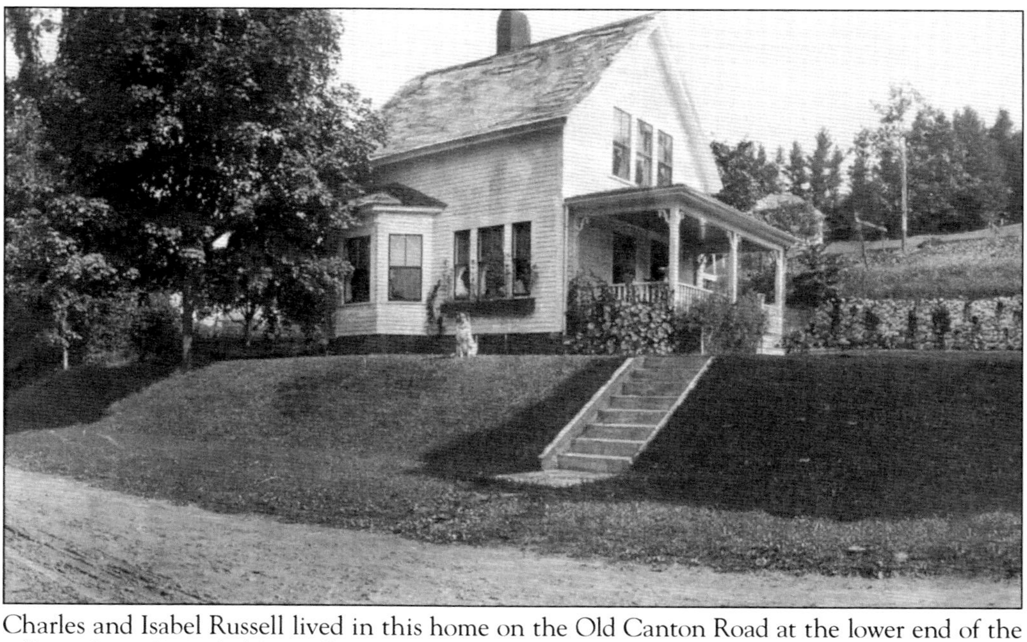

Charles and Isabel Russell lived in this home on the Old Canton Road at the lower end of the village. In 1959, Isabel Russell wrote a brief history of Dixfield for the Advance Club, a self-improvement social club for women focusing on issues of the day. Her account resonated with local citizens and remains popular today. The dog was called Laddy and belonged to a boy named George. (PPS.)

Five

THE MILLS

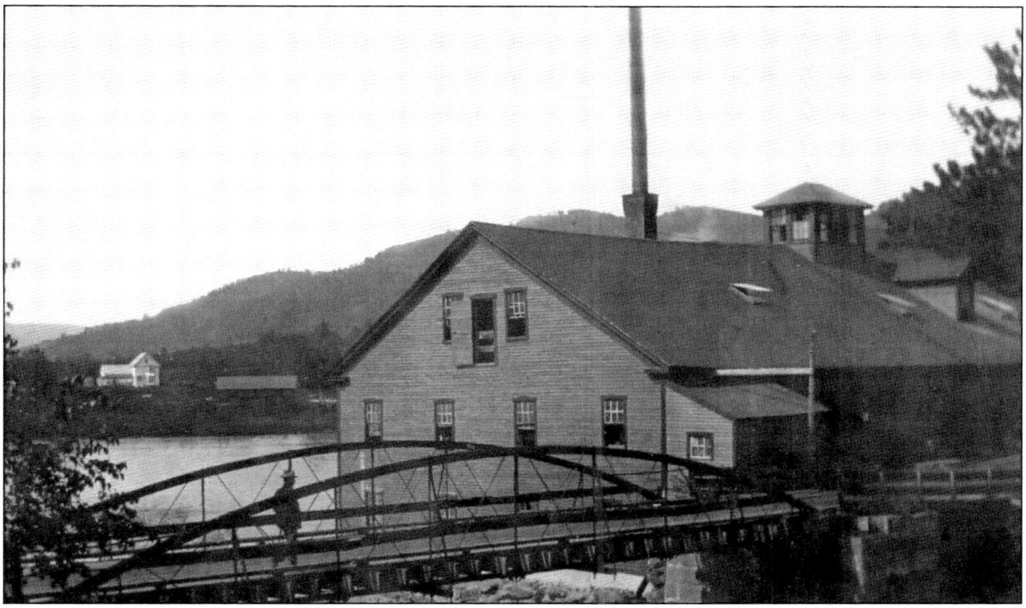

Soon after his toothpick mill in Sumner, Maine, burned, entrepreneur Charles W. Forster searched for a more suitable site to meet the increased demand for his product. After operating briefly in Canton, Maine, Forster moved his plant into the old Hosea Austin tannery in Mexico, Maine, where the Webb River empties into the Androscoggin River. This mill burned in 1904, but by this time, Forster had expanded into Strong, Maine, and (briefly) to Andover, Maine. Demand for toothpicks began slowly but grew rapidly once Forster hired stooges in Boston to ask for them at key restaurants. Dixfield happened to be situated amidst a generous supply of white birch, the preferred wood species for turning out toothpicks. Competition for birch was keen, with the three spool mills in town—birch was preferred by them as well for spools. (DHS.)

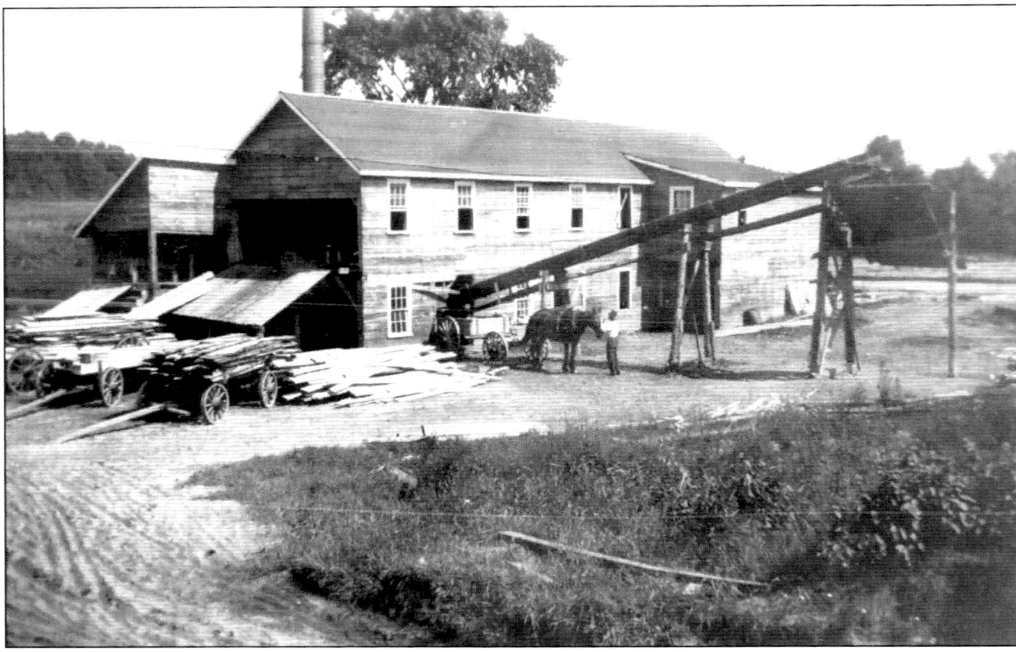

Once known as the Towle-Fairbanks Mill, this lumber mill was later owned by Arch L. Coburn of Carthage, Maine. It was here that C.L. Jackson was hospitalized after severely injuring his hand on an edging machine in April 1926. George Larsen was killed here in September 1926, and Floyd Chapman was killed at the mill in September 1928. Both men were just out of high school and both left families. (DHS.)

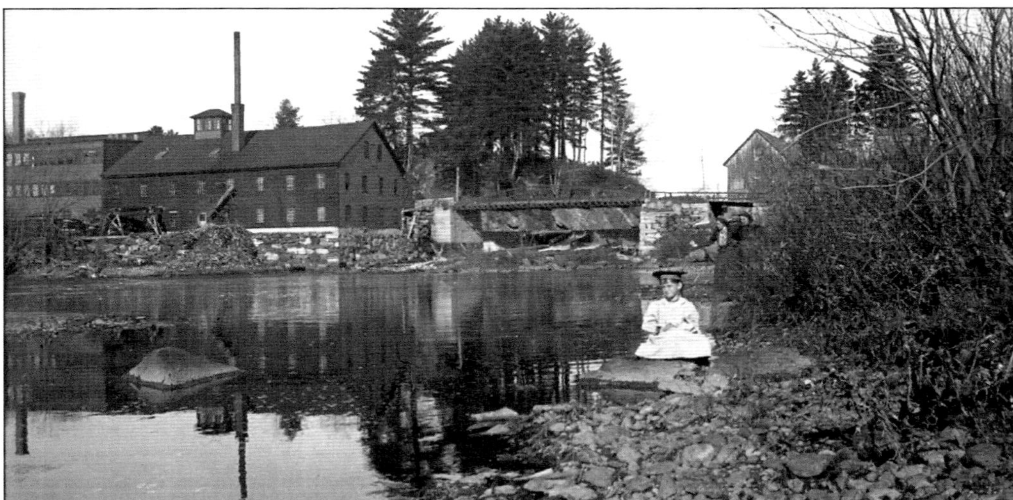

The Charles W. Forster toothpick mill is shown here at the height of its productivity in this c. 1900 photograph. The original Hosea Austin tannery is to the left of the bridge. An addition to the mill has been built as the demand for toothpicks appeared to be insatiable. Forster died in 1901, leaving his mills to his estate and forcing his son Maurice into the position of a salaried mill manager. Young Josephine Stanley is shown sitting on a rock where the Webb River joins the Androscoggin River. (NDM.)

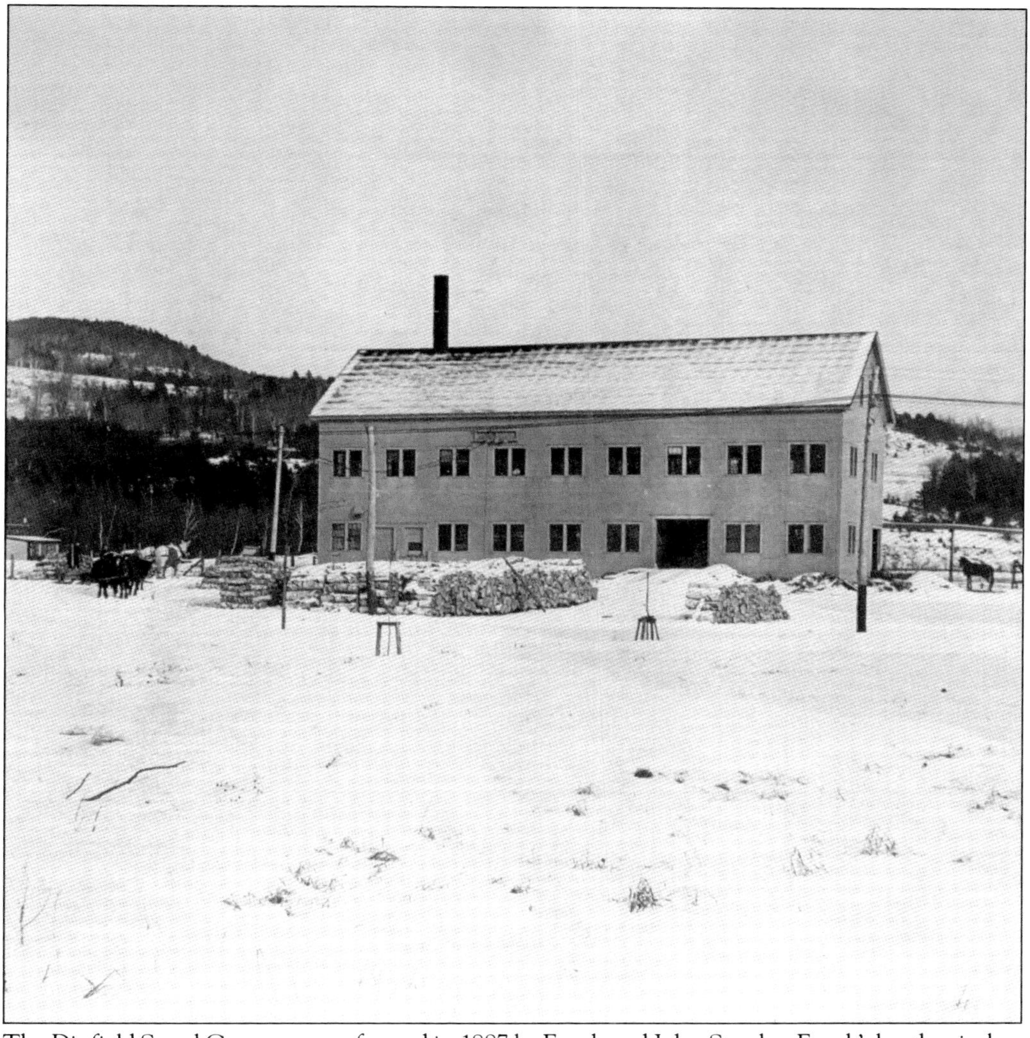

The Dixfield Spool Company was formed in 1887 by Frank and John Stanley, Frank's brother-in-law Ephraim Reynolds, and George L. Merrill of Searsport, Maine. When acquired by an out-of-state syndicate four years later, it soon went bankrupt. Purchased by Dixfield's John S. Harlow, the mill was resold to Merrill, who took Newton S. Stowell as a junior partner. Meanwhile, Frank Stanley built a second spool mill, and the first mill soon became known as Spool Mill No. 1. Pictured here in its earliest days of operation on Third Street about 1890, Spool Mill No. 1 depended on horses as well as men to operate. The initial labor supply for this mill came almost entirely from Searsport when 14 families moved to Dixfield with the machinery of the Searsport Spool and Block Manufacturing Company. (MHPC.)

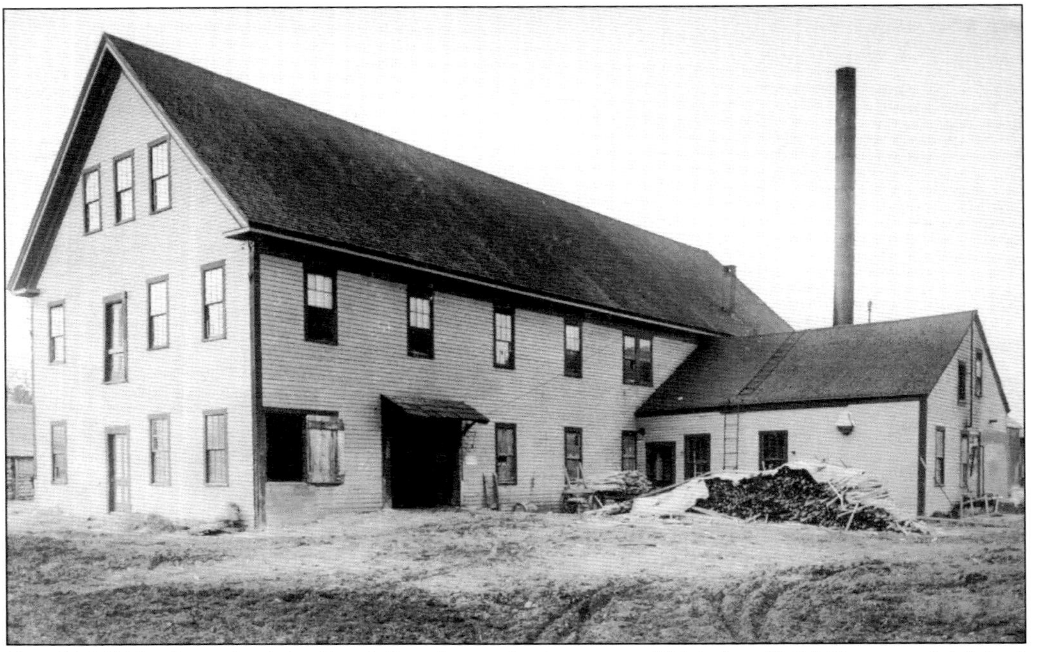

Spool Mill No. 2 was built by Frank Stanley at the juncture of Third and Mill Streets, which had been laid out to accommodate the spool mills. A short while later, John S. Harlow built another spool mill on Third Street. Known as the Stanley Mill and the Harlow Mill respectively, both of them became part of the G.L. Merrill and Company organization. (PRS.)

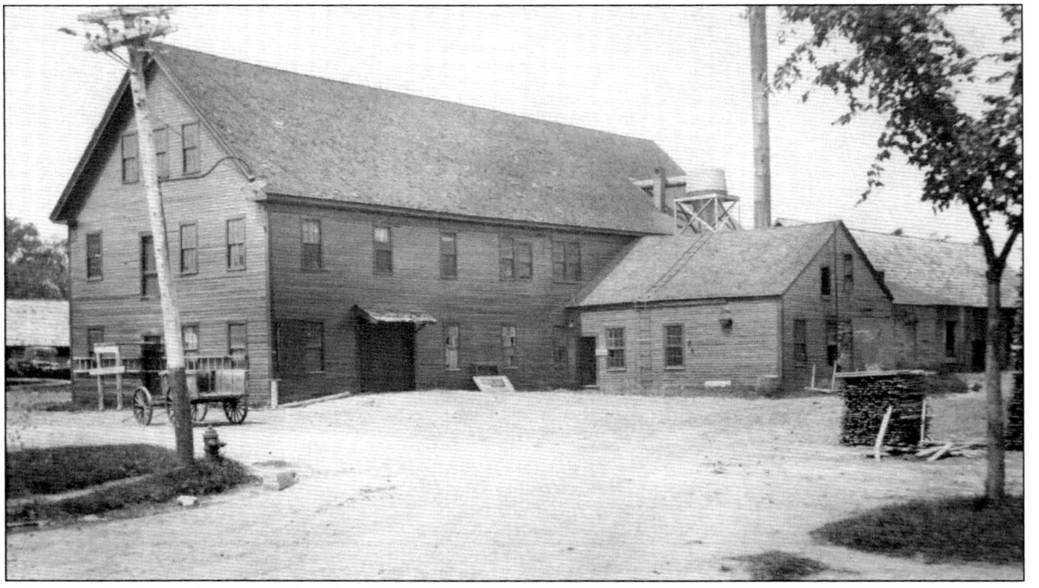

This is another photograph of Spool Mill No. 2 on Mill Street. Many changes were made to the spool mills over the years. More spool machines were added, and novelty manufacturing machines were installed or removed according to market conditions. More than once, worldwide competition was so fierce that US spool manufacturers were forced to ask Congress for protective tariffs. (PRS.)

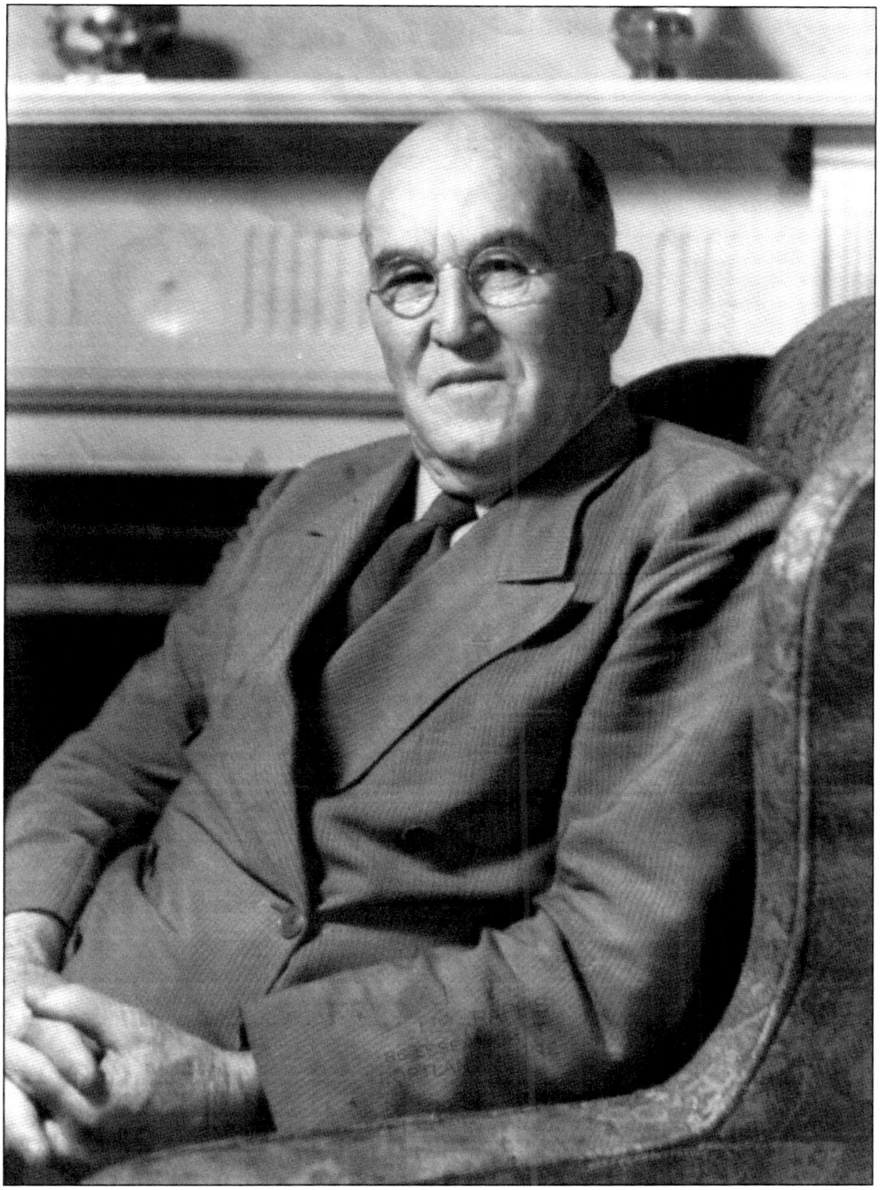

Newton Stanley Stowell was born in Dixfield in 1856 and moved to Canton, Maine, with his family in 1859. In his twenties, he returned to Dixfield, living with his uncle Henry O. Stanley in 1880. Among other jobs, he painted houses for $2 a day and taught in the local schools, quickly becoming superintendent. He operated a wool carding mill, which was owned by Stanley, and then went to work in the Dixfield Spool Mill for 90¢ a day. He soon took part in the management of the mills and became increasingly involved once his cousin John S. Stanley bought the mills from bankruptcy in the mid-1890s then sold them to George L. Merrill. Stowell was installed as vice president of Merrill's mills and gained control of them in 1903, forming the N.S. Stowell & Co., a corporation consisting entirely of his wife, Edith, and himself. By the time he retired 30 years later, he had owned 9 spool mills, 20 sawmills, and 90,000 acres of woodlots in nine Maine counties. (HSB.)

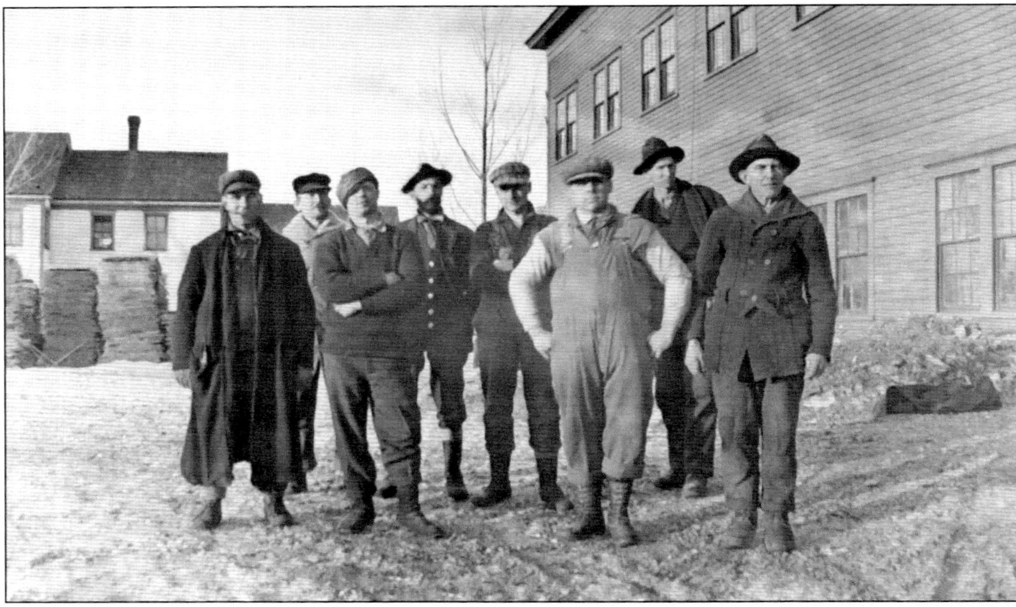

Spool mill employees of the N.S. Stowell & Co. Mill No.1 on Third Street are shown in this 1920s picture. Behind them are stacks of "squares" or "spool bars," to be processed into spools of various sizes for cotton thread. Much of Stowell's product was used by the J&P Coats Cotton Thread Company in Rhode Island. (PRS.)

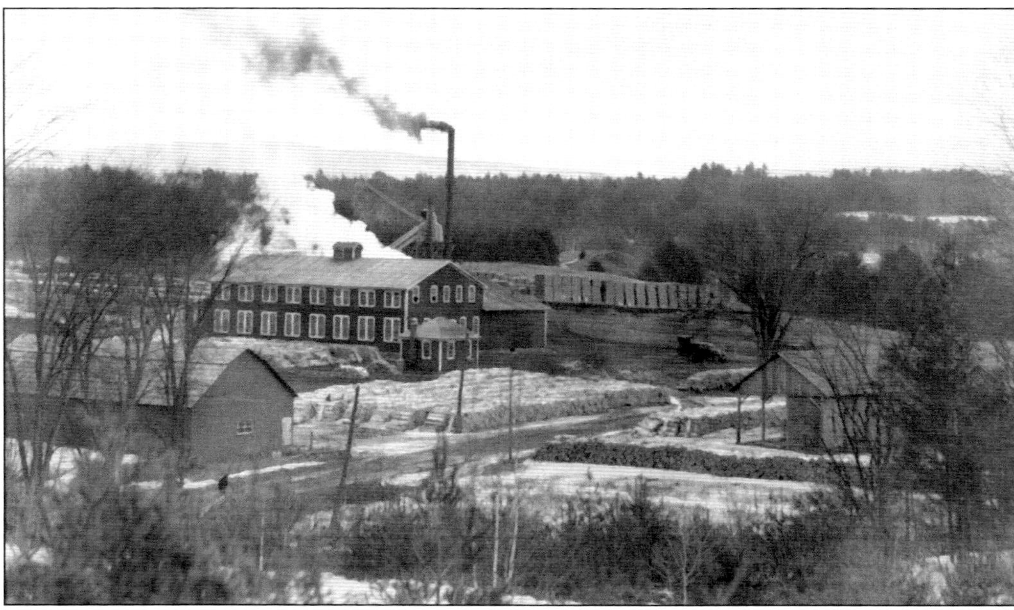

N.S. Stowell had acquired the Elliott and Bartlett spool mill, pictured above, in Andover, Maine, by the 1920s. Previously, he had taken over the Sanborn Mill in Weld, the Eli Oliver Mill in Farmington Falls, and the Dearborn Mill in Bryant Pond, Maine. This view of what would become Stowell Manufacturing Company was taken in the late 1920s. (PRS.)

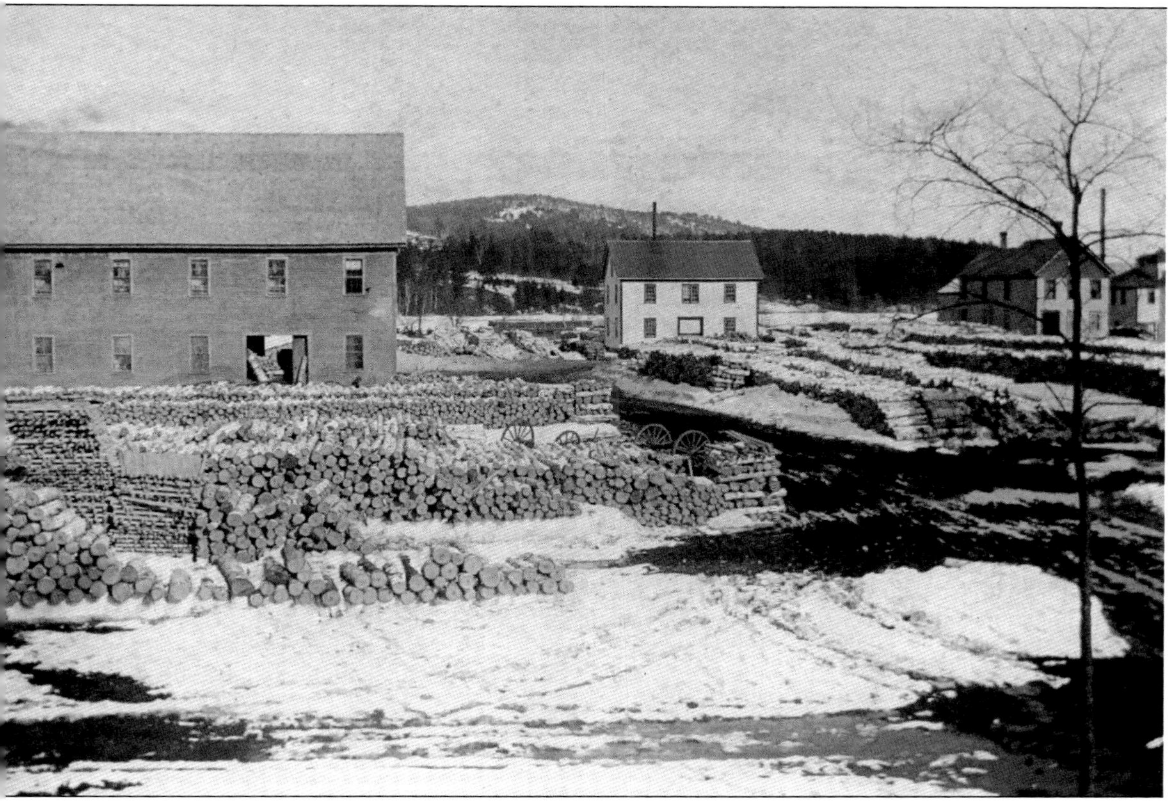

This c. 1900 view of Spool Mill No. 2 is the earliest known. The hundreds of cords of four-foot white birch bolts reflect both healthy economic conditions for the spool industry and the productivity of area farmers who cut wood in the winter months when there were no crops to tend. The wood was transported to the mill on "scoots," horse-drawn wooden runners capped with steel to slide with light effort over the snow-covered streets. Hidden behind the spool mill is the Burnham and Morrill corn-canning plant. The building in the center of the picture is the George Marsh box factory and sits at the intersection of Mill and Third Streets. Like many buildings of the day, it was heated by kerosene. Marsh managed Burnham and Morrill's Dixfield plant. (MHPC.)

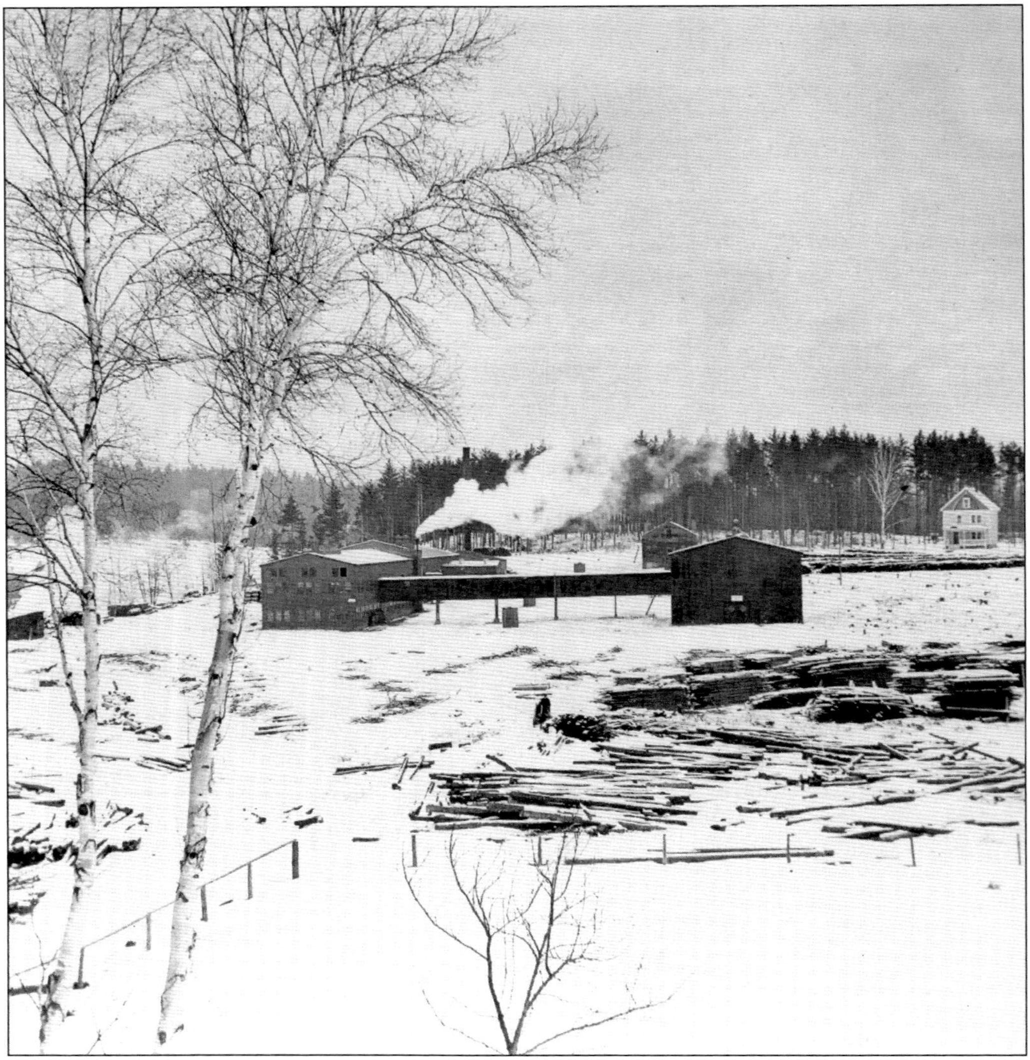

The Henry G. Thayer long lumber mill was located on the Webb River just above Dixfield Village on the site that had been home to sawmills since the early days of Dixfield's history. Hosea Austin sawed lumber here for many years, then was succeeded by Chase & Willoughby, and still later by Almena Austin (Mrs. Lamont C.) Willoughby who sold out to Thayer in 1899. Thayer provided employment for 25 men and hired French workers emigrating from Canada's Atlantic provinces. Thayer is credited with manufacturing fish hatchery troughs for Commissioner Henry O. Stanley and, at one time, stored more than 5,000 cords of wood in his mill yard. William F. Putnam was another lumber manufacturer and builder. When the Odd Fellows hall burned in 1901, it was Putnam who built its replacement, the Tuscan Opera House. (MHPC.)

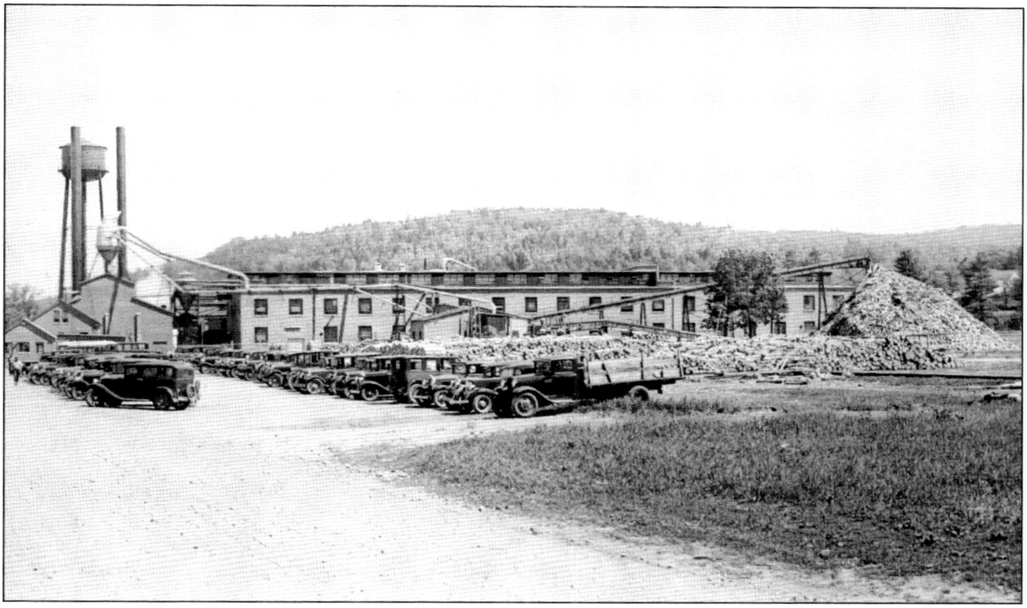

Worldwide competition forced many mergers in the toothpick industry in the early 1900s. The Berst Corporation of Minnesota merged with John S. Harlow's Dixfield Toothpick Company and Forster Manufacturing Company to form Berst-Forster-Dixfield, or B-F-D, as it was called. This plant, shown soon after is construction in 1931, was located in Peru, Maine, a half mile from Dixfield Village. (PRS.)

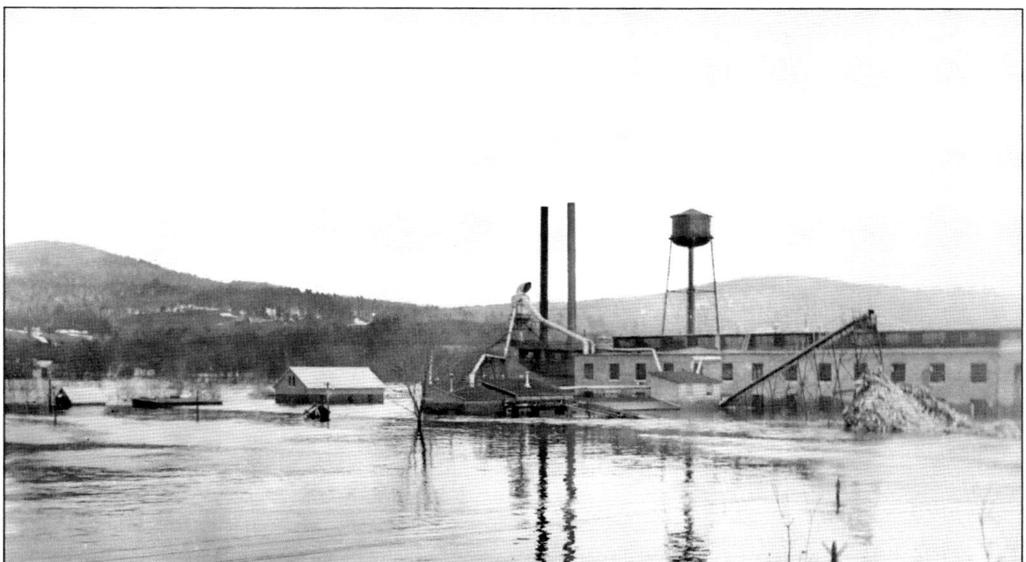

Just a few years after its opening, the B-F-D Mill suffered the flood of the 20th century when the Androscoggin River rose to damaging heights in March 1936. Much of the birch wood supply for this plant was swept away forever, and its machinery was heavily damaged. Items made here included toothpicks, matches, tongue depressors, Popsicle sticks, and similar items. (NDM.)

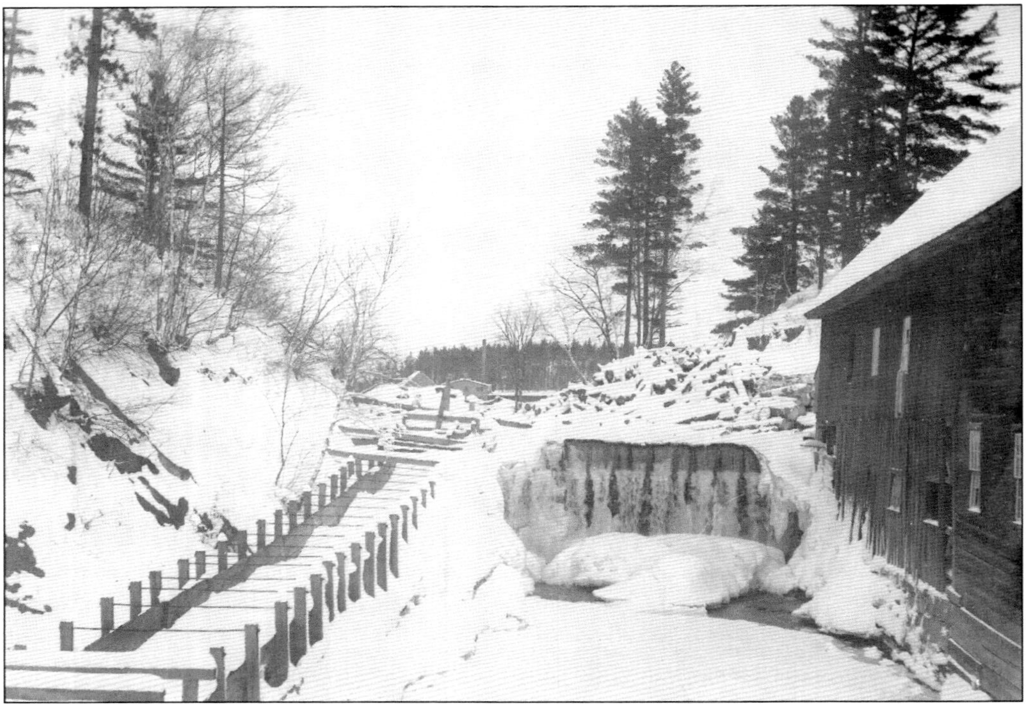

The importance of the dams of the Webb River to Dixfield's economy continued until electricity displaced the waterpower of small streams to work the mills. The flour mills of the midwestern United States sealed the fate of the local gristmills when they made flour conveniently available on the grocer's shelf. This dam has a fishway built into it, most likely initiated by Commissioner Henry O. Stanley. (DHS.)

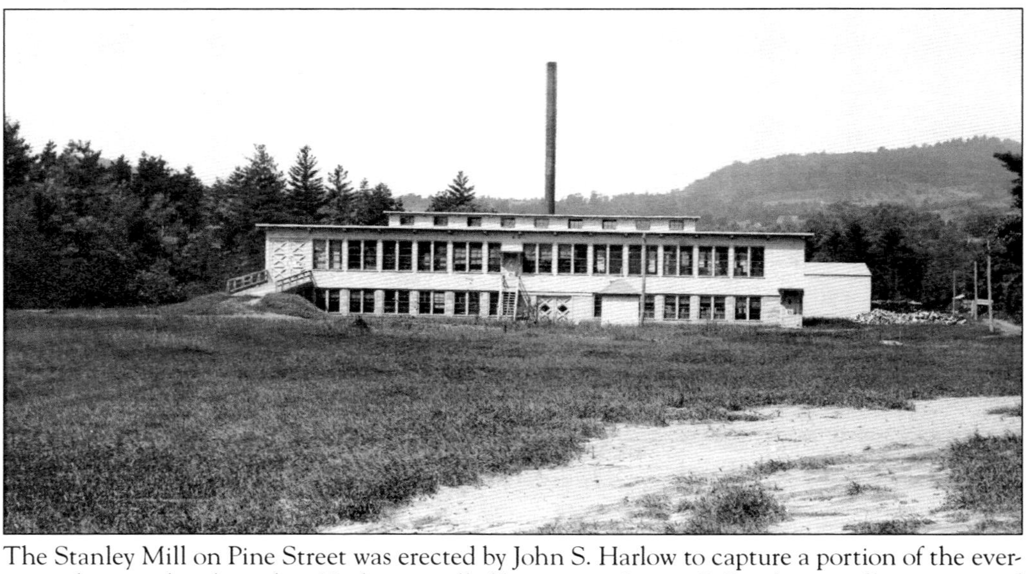

The Stanley Mill on Pine Street was erected by John S. Harlow to capture a portion of the ever-expanding toothpick market. Harlow installed his cousin George P. Stanley as mill manager and Charles P. Ricker as operations manager. Stanley invented many improvements in toothpick machinery, receiving patents for some of them. (PRS.)

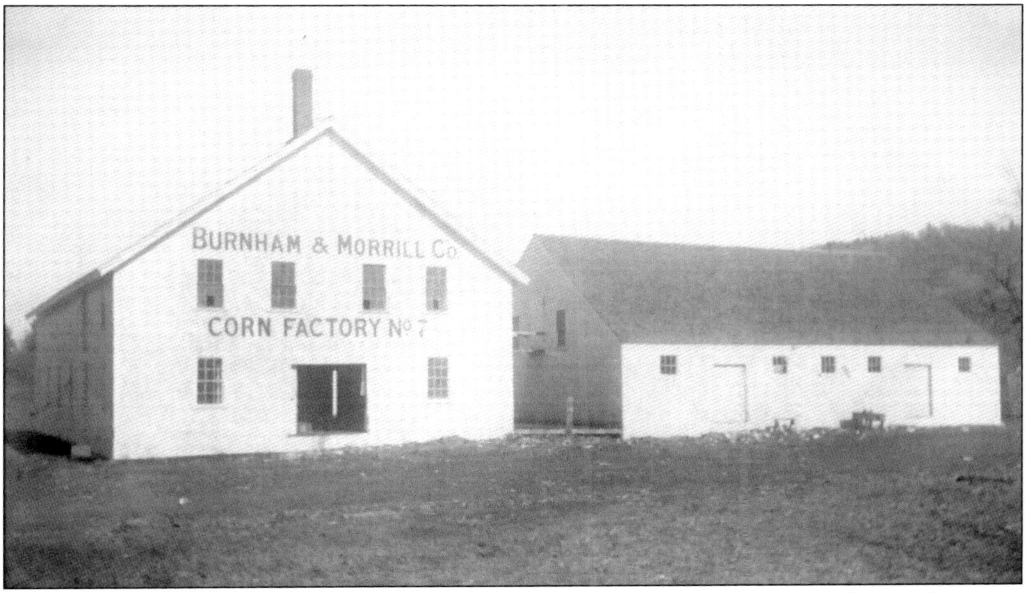

The Burnham and Morrill corn-canning plant was situated on Mill Street near the Stanley spool mill (also called Spool Mill No. 2). George A. Marsh came to Dixfield to run the operation after performing similar duties at their South Paris plant. He erected a can-making plant and owned the box factory as well. The canning plant later became the paint shop of the N.S. Stowell & Co. spool mills. (MHPC.)

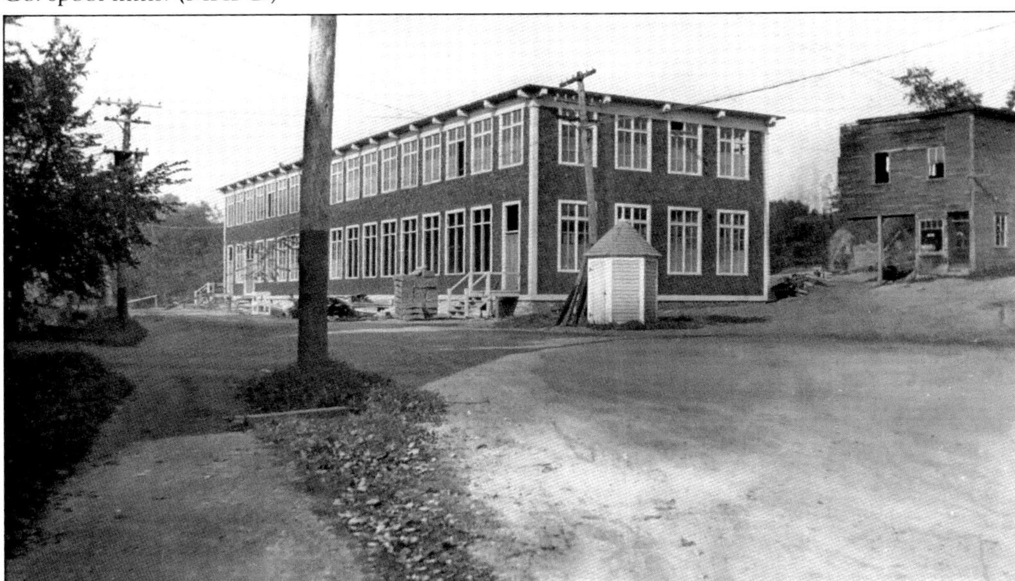

The Joseph P. Allen braid mill was incorporated in Rhode Island by Dixfield's John S. Harlow in the early 1920s. Harlow served as president and treasurer, his son John Jr. was secretary, and Joseph P. Allen joined them on the board of directors. $80,000 in capital was raised in a single evening at the opera house. When the mill failed to thrive because of changing tastes in fashions, toothpick machines were moved in briefly, but later the mill was turned into a bowling alley and billiard parlor. (PRS.)

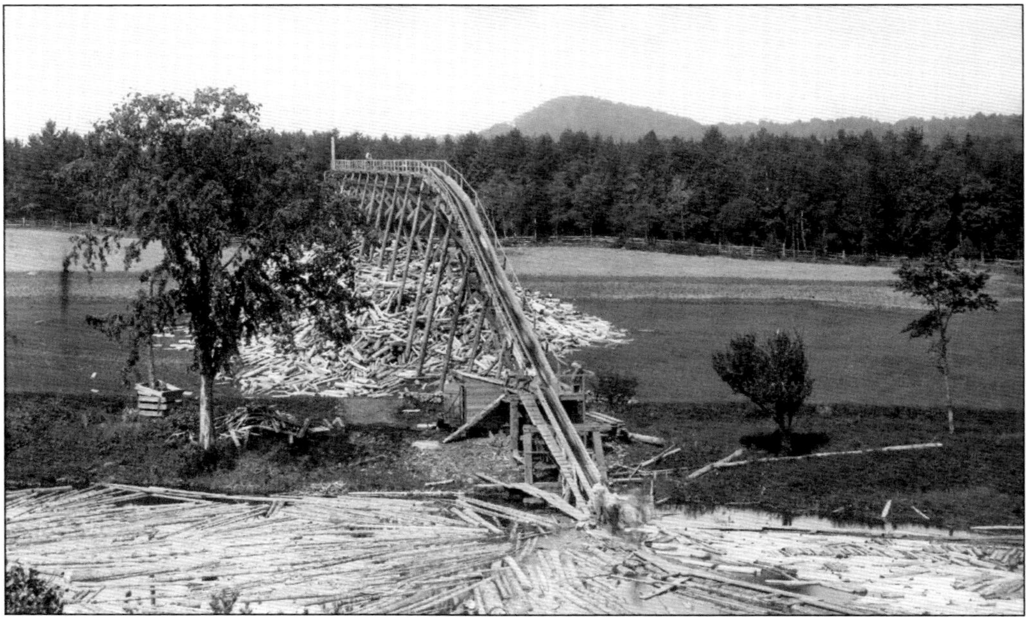

This wood conveyor was built by John S. Harlow on the Mexico side of Webb River on land owned by his cousin Oscar Trask. It lifted pulpwood and other forest products from the river prior to shipping them to paper mills and lumber mills. By 1914, Harlow and partner Don Gates had contracts to deliver thousands of cords of wood cut from lands near Dixfield, much of it in the so-called Siberia area near the Sugar Loaves. An estimated 300 cords of wood per day could be removed from the river. (PRS.)

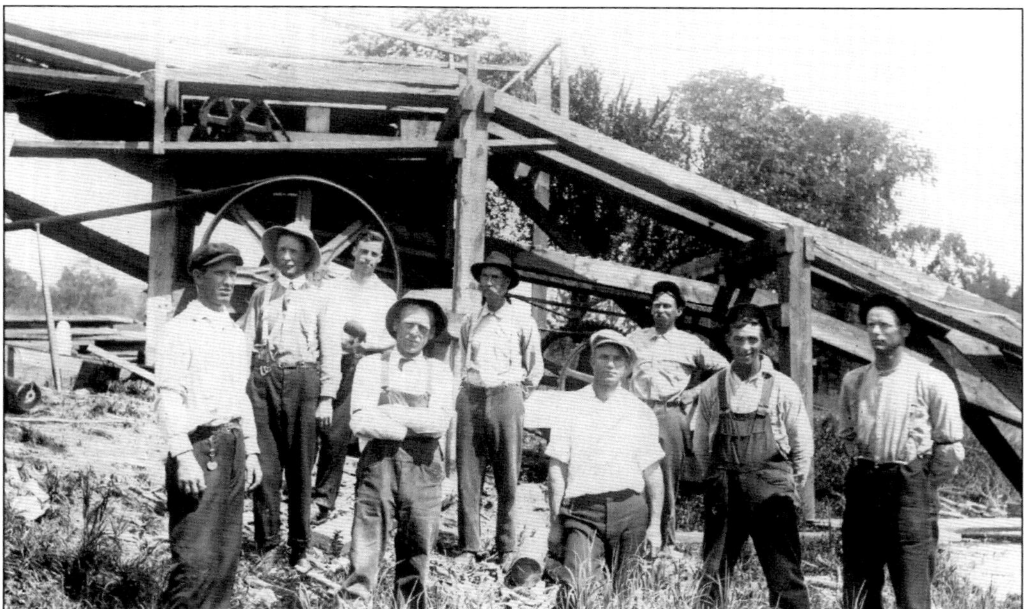

The wood conveyor was 40 feet high and 440 feet long. The men pictured who operated the machine are, from left to right, Maurice Horne, Austin Willoughby, Johnnie Harlow, Matt Morse, William Beedy, Ralph Williams, Vivian Horne, Neal Harlow, and Farnham Bishop. (DHS.)

Six

How Dixfield Lived

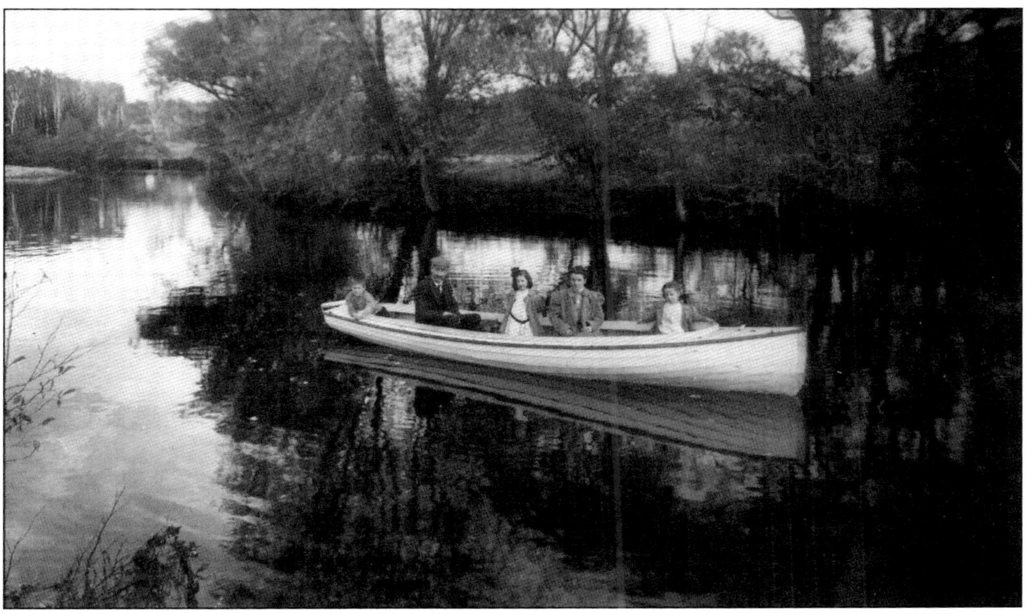

At one time, there were three dams on the Webb River in Dixfield Village to power its sawmills, gristmills, fulling mills, and shingle mills. Today, there are none. The river was much higher then, allowing for family recreation activities, such as boating and ice-skating. Horse racing on ice was popular, too, with events planned long in advance and widely advertised to entice Dixfield families to sweeten the purses of the winners and the profits of the promoters. (PRS.)

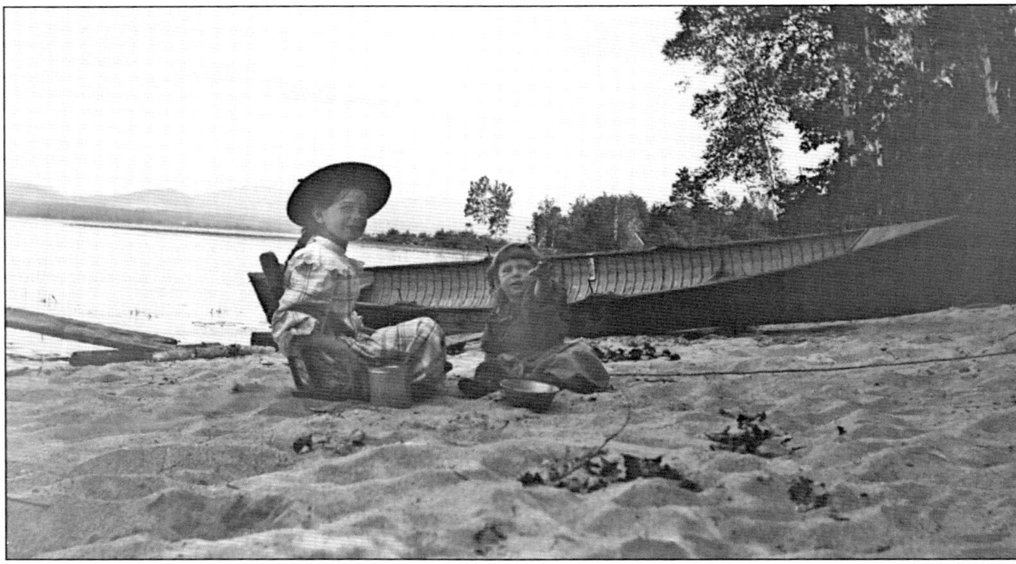

Lake Webb was once called Weld Pond and Webb's Pond, too. Whatever the name, this body of water located in Weld, Maine, has long provided summer recreation for many residents of Dixfield. In this c. 1900 picture, Josie Stanley and her cousin Mary Kimball enjoy the sandy beach of the Stanley cottage on the lake's west side. (NDM.)

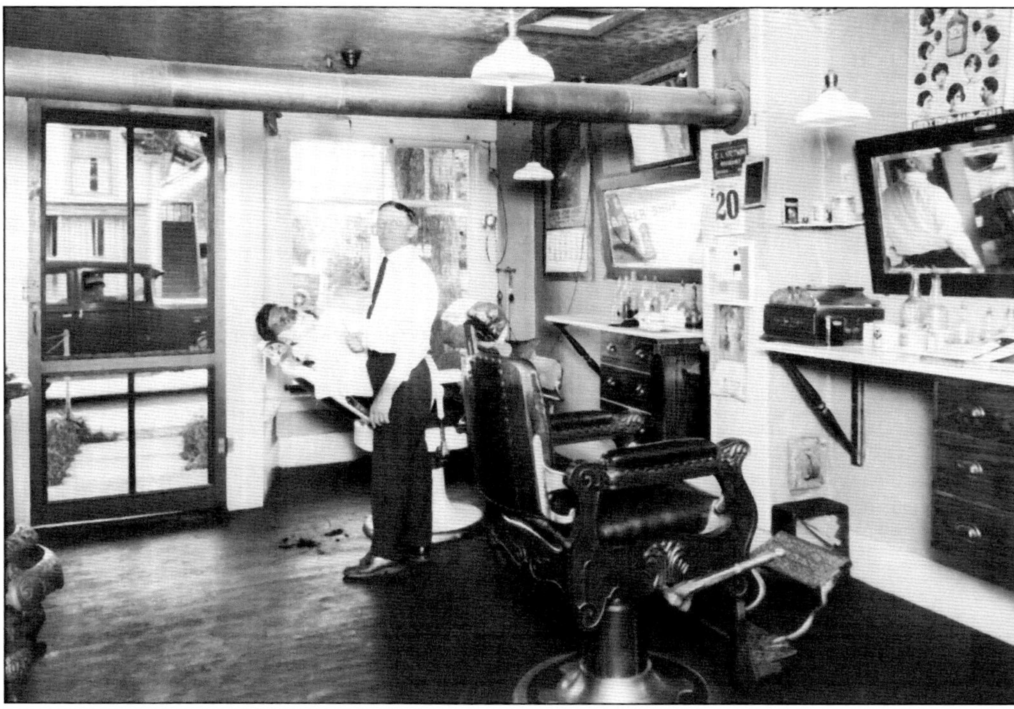

This is an inside view of Otto Holt's barbershop on Main Street in Dixfield in the Ludden home, later the site of the Ludden Library. Lewis "Snowball" Martin is the man in the chair. The Zenas Taylor home can be seen through the window. Taylor worked at the Charles W. Forster toothpick mill. His home was later occupied by Leona Taylor, a teacher. (DHS.)

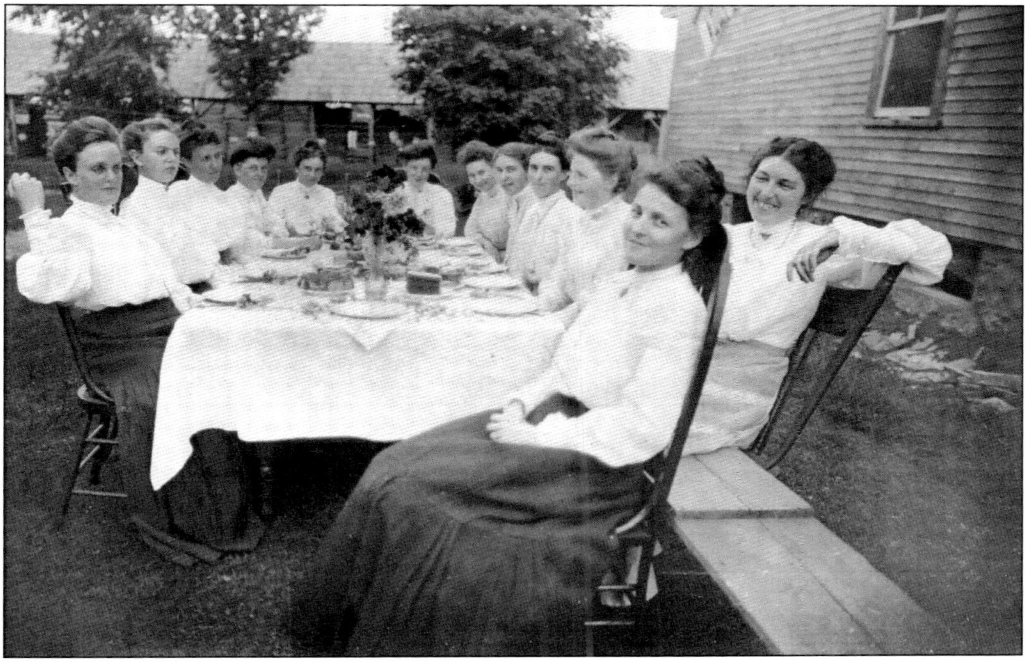

Several young ladies of Dixfield Village gather at a Third Street home. Pictured around the table are, from left to right, Edna Edmunds, her sister Ina Edmunds, five unidentified women, Mary Stowell, Edith Younkin, two unidentified women, and Isabel Stowell. (DHS.)

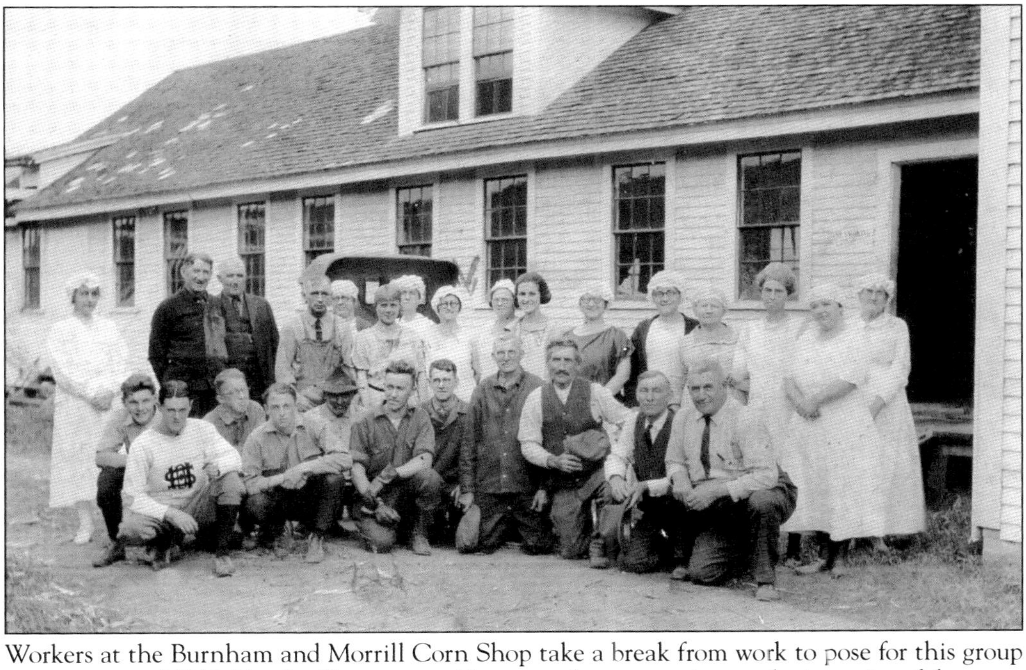

Workers at the Burnham and Morrill Corn Shop take a break from work to pose for this group portrait around 1910. Nearly all are covered by proper bonnets to insure the integrity of the corn, which was cooked and packed in cans made in Dixfield. George A. Marsh made the boxes the cans were shipped in. (DHS.)

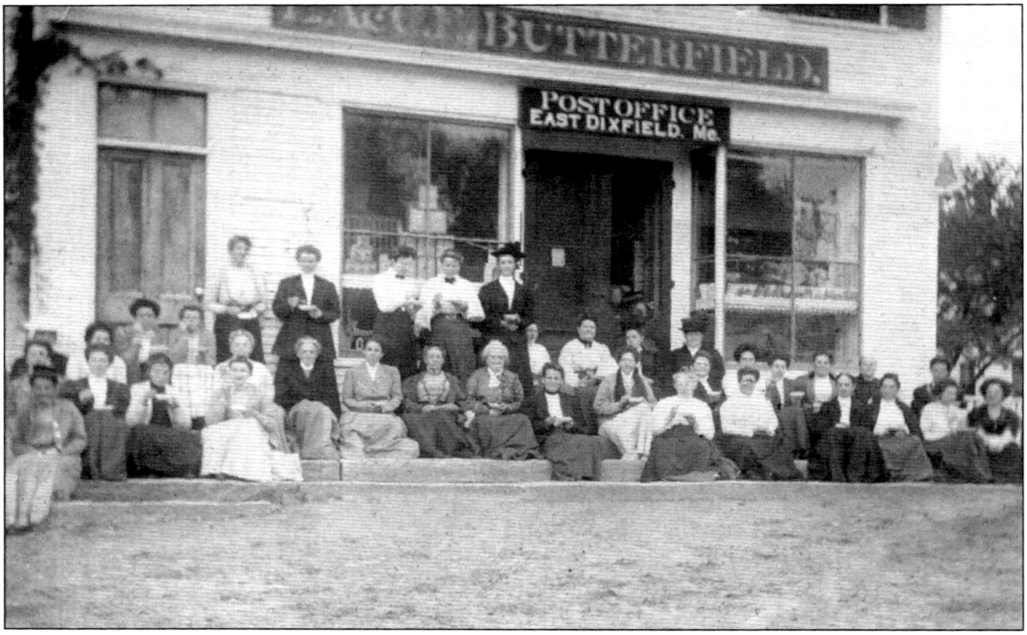

East Dixfield ladies assemble in on the steps of the Edith A. and Clara E. Butterfield store. They seem to be enjoying a celebration of some sort—perhaps strawberries were in season as many of them are holding a small dish of something undoubtedly quite delectable. The Butterfield sisters were locally famed for the fabric remnants they sold for many years at their store. (DHS.)

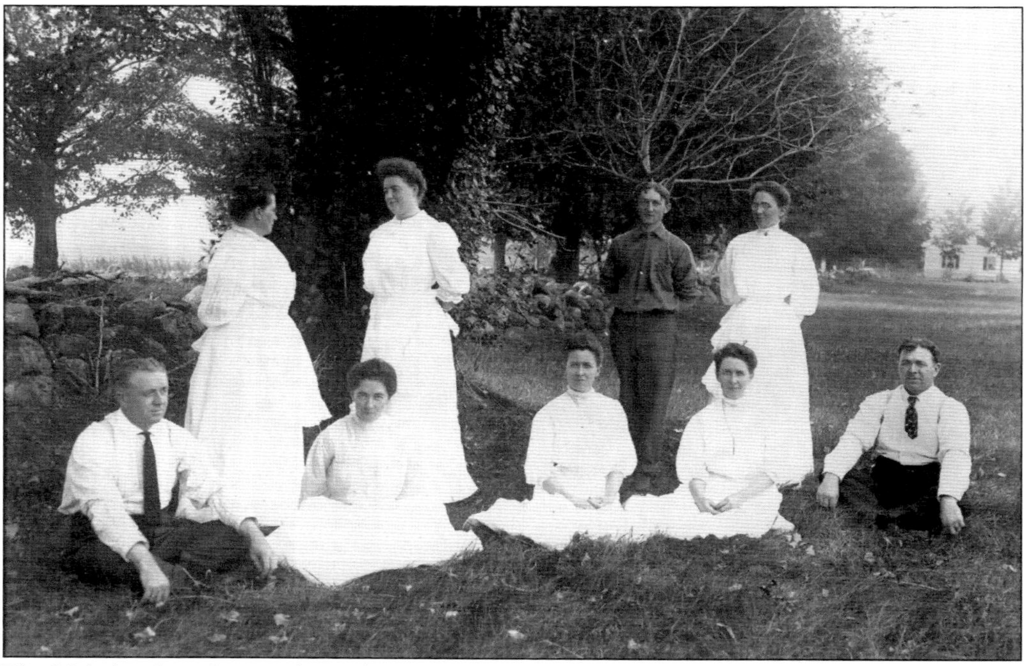

The Holt family gathers at the Coburn Farm on Center Hill in Weld. Pictured, from left to right, are Abel Holt, Ada Baker, Lelia Welch, Minnie Coburn, Mary Newman, Otto Holt, Martha Draper, Lura Nutter, and Henry Holt. Newman and Draper were friends of the family. (DHS.)

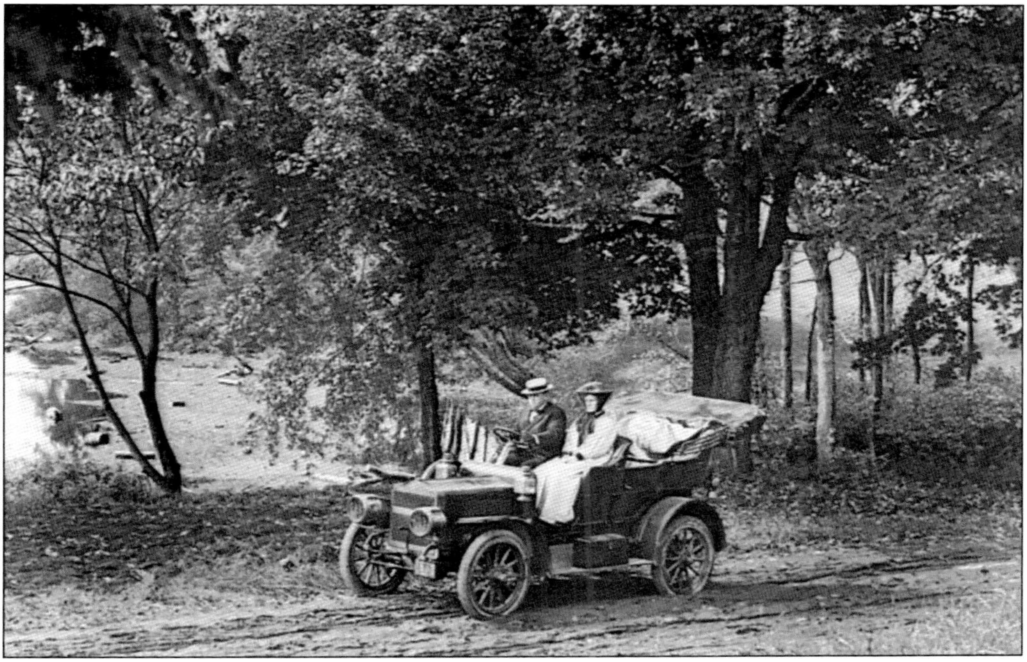

An early motorcar makes it way along a primitive roadway in Dixfield. At one time, Dixfield claimed the highest ownership of automobiles in the state, a claim hotly contested by the nearby town of Farmington. George Stanley owned the first car in town, a 1903 Stanley Steamer. (DHS.)

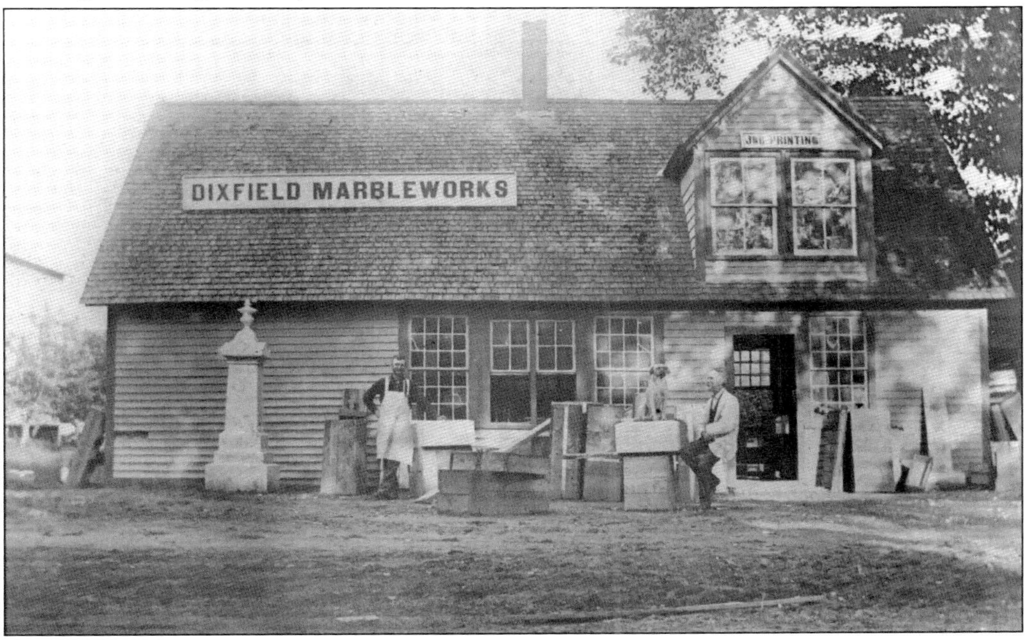

George Holt, seated, not only greatly expanded the Dixfield Marble Works, purchased from the widow of Henry Trask, but also added job printing and carpentry before he enlarged his shop on Weld Street. His three sons—Herschel, Dana, and Thomas—joined him in his efforts, even selling Cameron automobiles at one point. (DHS.)

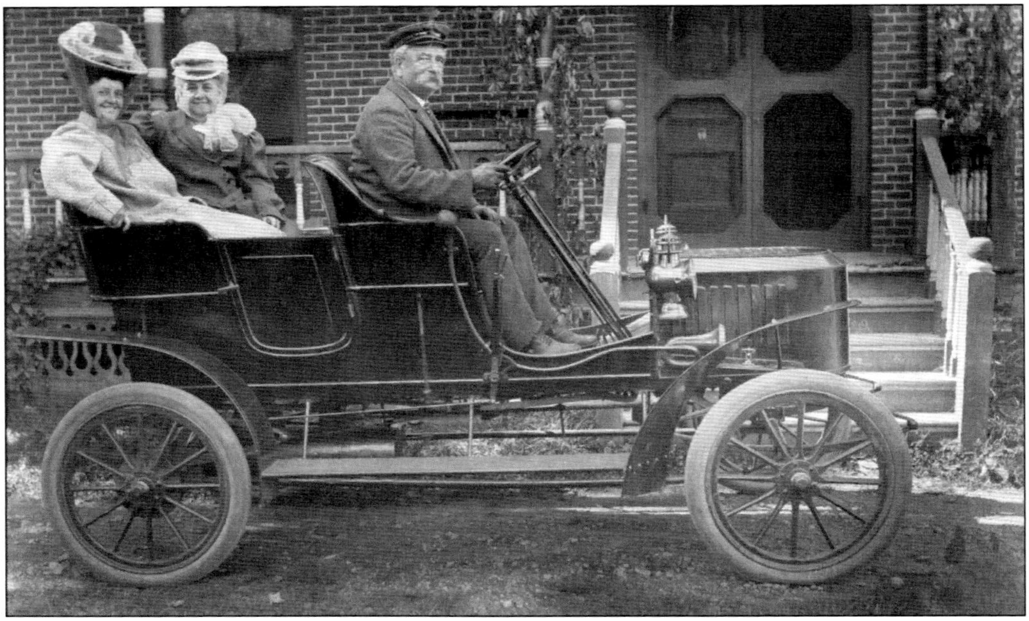

George Marsh, retired as manager of the Burnham and Morrill Corn Shop, chauffeurs his wife, Josephine, and his daughter Josie Walters in a Stanley Steamer in this c. 1910 photograph, taken in front of the Marsh home on lower Main Street in Dixfield. (NDM.)

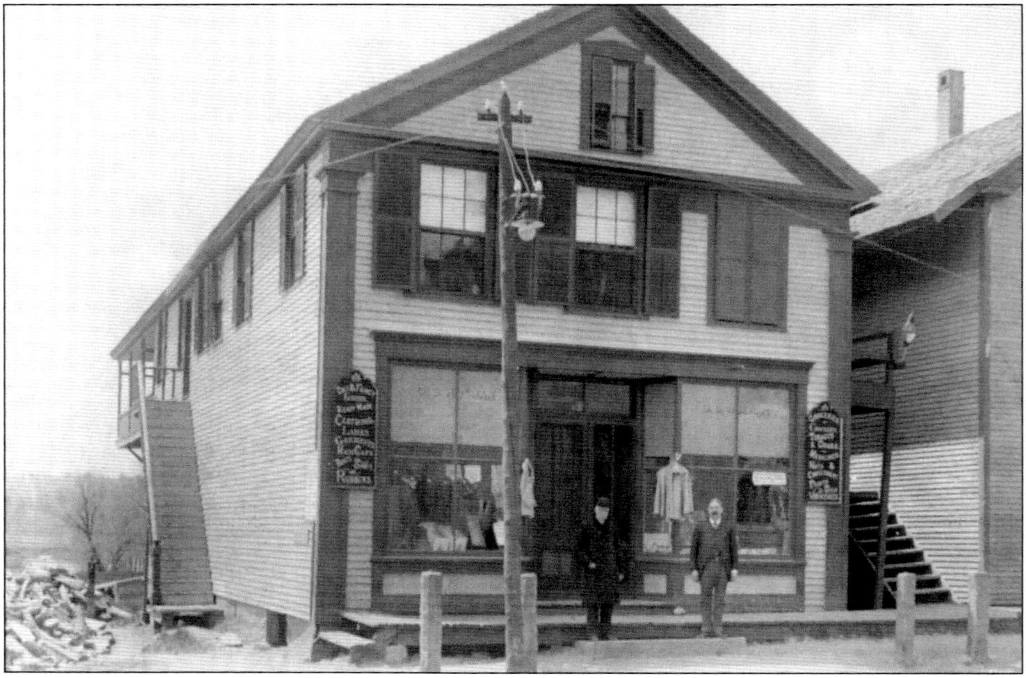

A Dixfield shopper could buy almost anything at George S. Holman's general store—from dry and fancy goods to ready-made clothing, from tobacco and cigars to paints, oils, and varnishes. The Holman Store burned flat in a 1905 fire, which also leveled the Fred H. Keene store to its right. (DHS.)

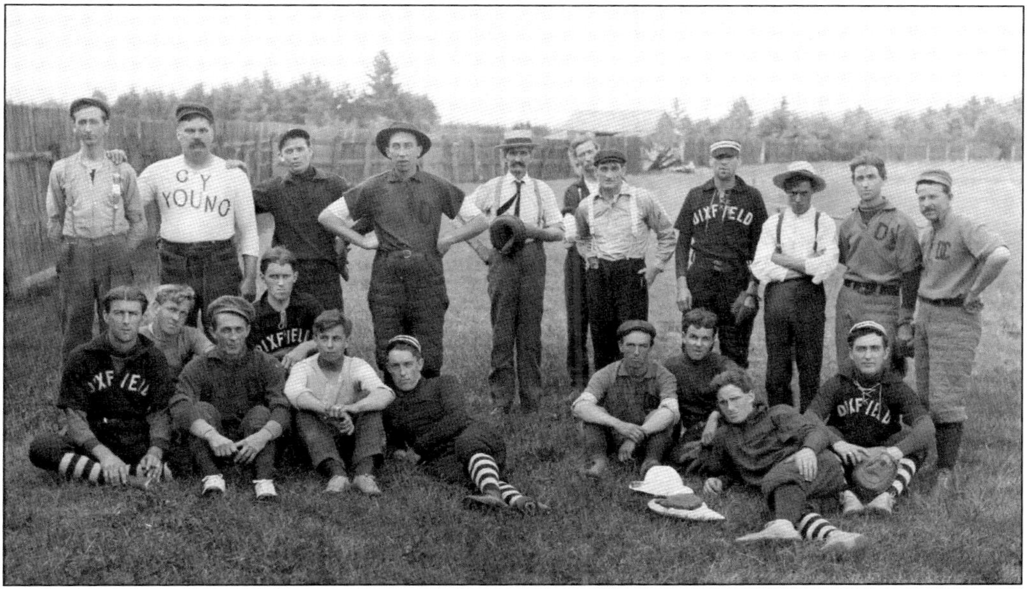

Boston Red Sox pitcher Cy Young was held in high regard by one member of this Dixfield baseball team assembled for a group portrait about 1910. Simon Tainter, sitting at the far left, is the only person who can be identified. Baseball was played in Dixfield for many decades, often in organized leagues consisting of local teams from nearby towns. (DHS.)

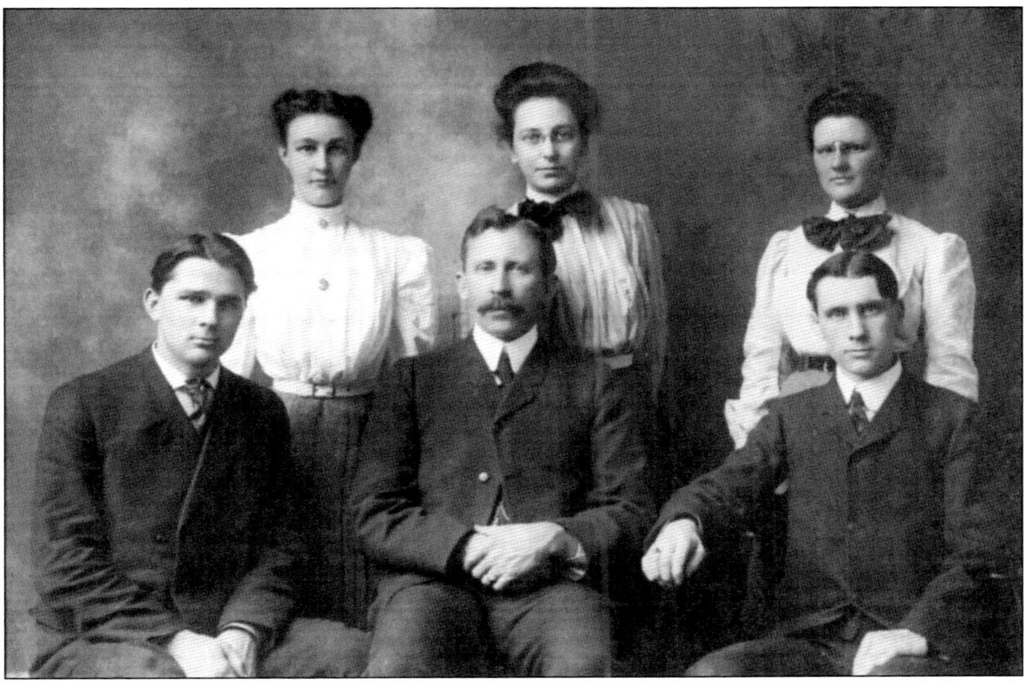

Dixfield could feel justifiably proud when the Rumford Bank and Trust Company opened a branch in the Hotel Stanley. Pictured are, from left to right, (first row) Elisha Stetson, branch manager; Elisha Pratt, cashier; and Lewis Irish; (second row) Louise Kidder, Alice Towle, and Julia Irish, wife of Lewis. Stetson was also an insurance agent who served Dixfield residents. (DHS.)

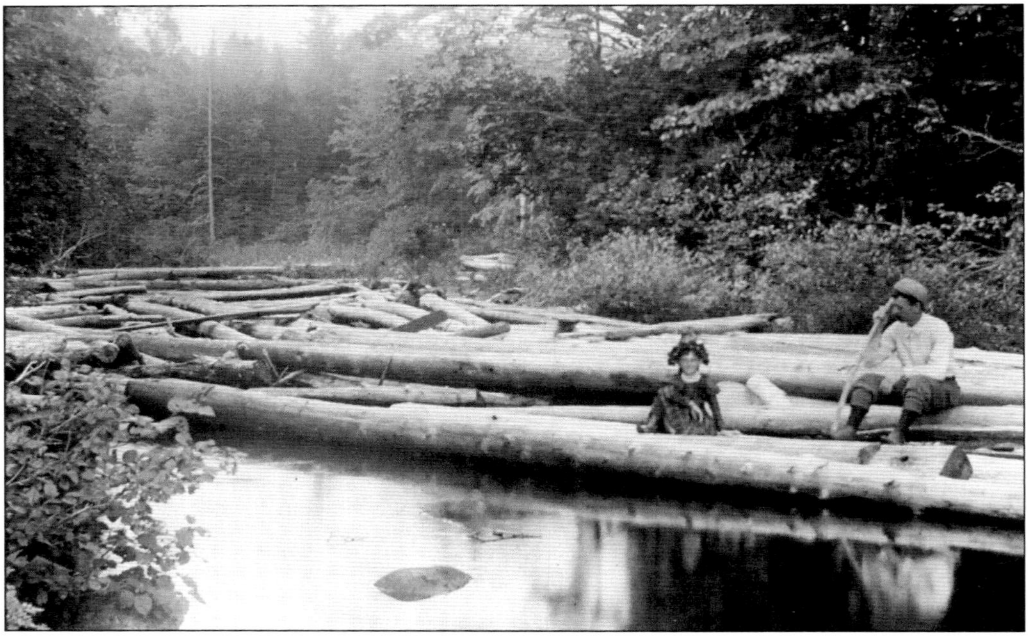

Low water strands many logs in the Webb River following the annual spring log drive. Here, George Stanley and his daughter Josie sit and ponder the situation. Millions of board feet of trees were transported by high water from Dixfield's woodlands to the waiting sawmills in the village. (NDM.)

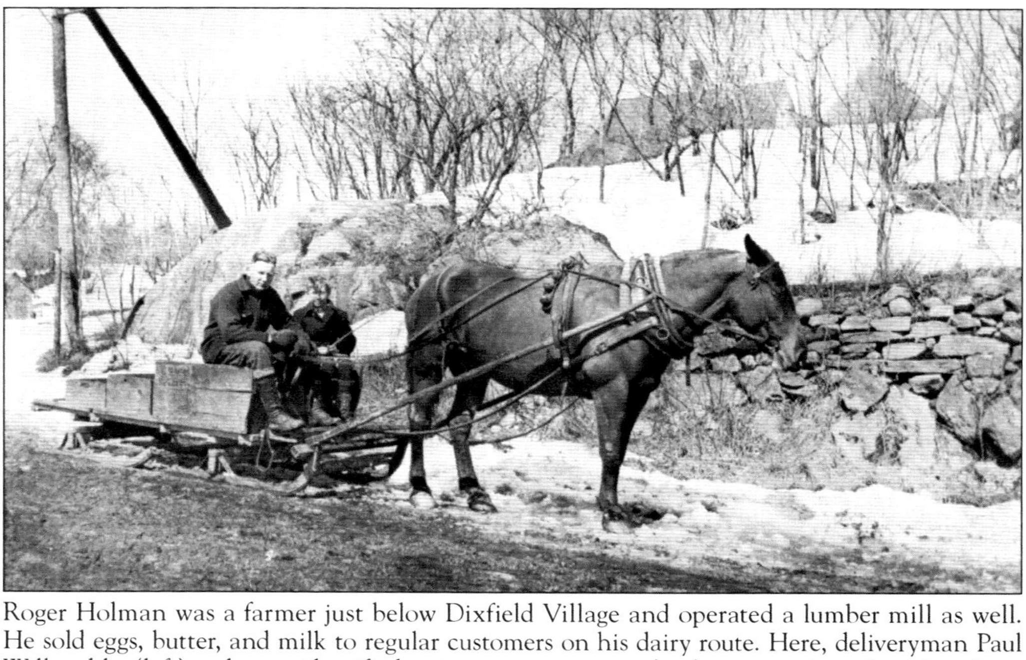

Roger Holman was a farmer just below Dixfield Village and operated a lumber mill as well. He sold eggs, butter, and milk to regular customers on his dairy route. Here, deliveryman Paul Willoughby (left) and an unidentified assistant pause to pose for the camera in early spring about 1910. (PRS.)

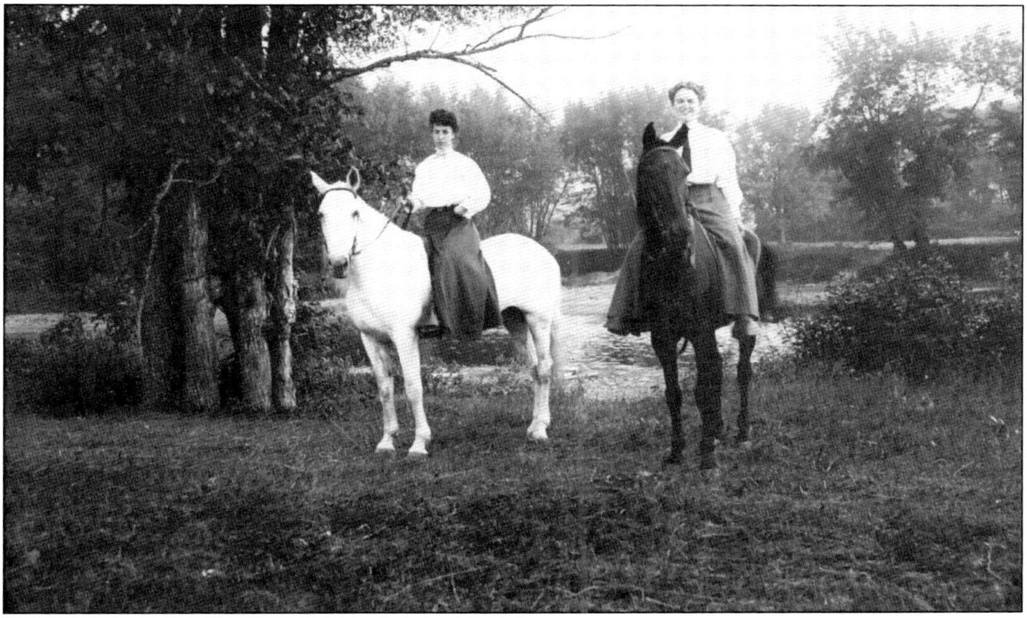

First cousins Lucie Reynolds (left) and Ina Reynolds enjoy riding horses in Dixfield near the Androscoggin or Webb River. Lucie was the daughter of Ephraim and Abbie Edmunds Reynolds, and Ina was the daughter of Joseph and Emma Edmunds. This photograph was taken about 1905. (DHS.)

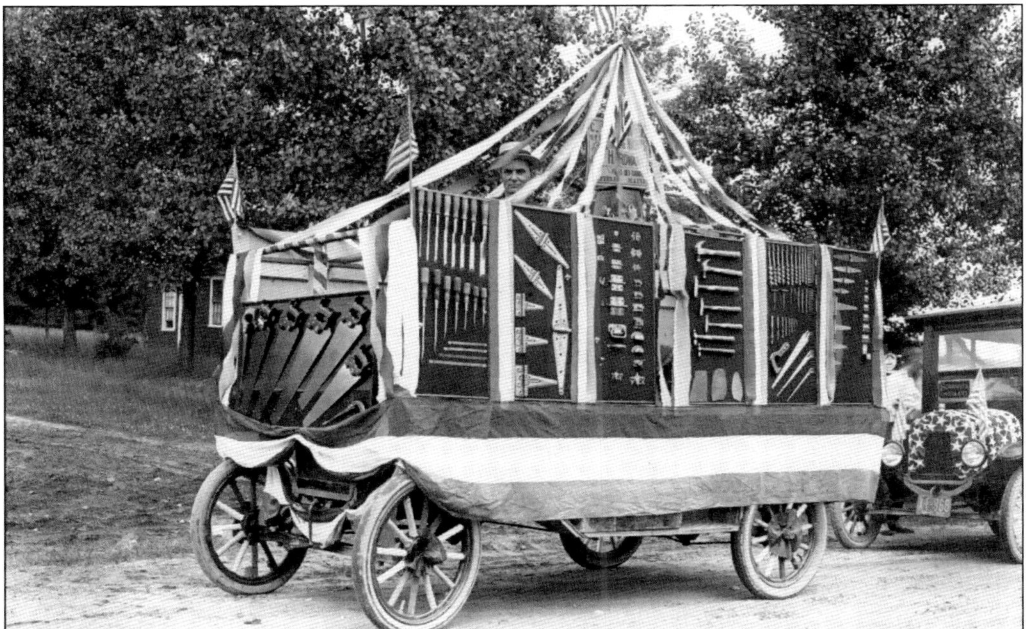

Ever the promoter, Charles H. Towle created this impressive float for the Fourth of July parade in Dixfield in 1924 to promote Towle's Hardware. Consisting of samples of handsaws, woodworking tools, outside door hinges, cabinetry hardware, hammers, bits, and the like, Towle's float represents an impressive display of dedication and local spirit. (DCT.)

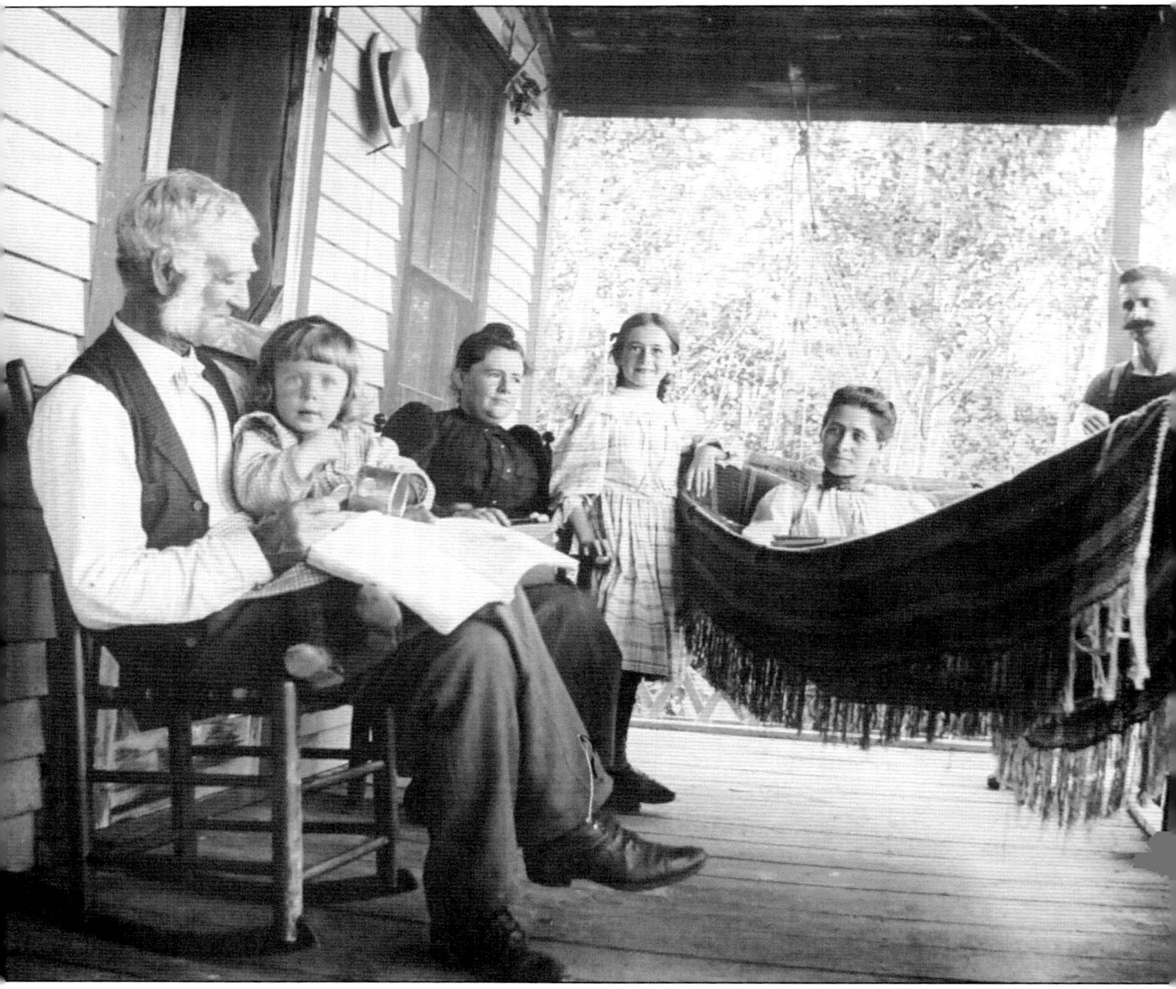

State of Maine fisheries and game commissioner Henry O. Stanley and his family are shown at the Stanley cottage at Weld Pond in this c. 1900 photograph. They are, from left to right, Stanley, his granddaughter Mary Kimball, Netta Stanley and her daughter Josie, Henry's daughter Nellie Kimball and his son George. In 1852, Stanley went to California during the Gold Rush via the Isthmus of Panama but stayed only briefly. In 1872, he undertook a tour of fishways on principal Maine rivers, keeping notes on both their condition and an accounting of his daily expenses. While commissioner, he also began a personal scrapbook, consisting of newspaper columns discussing conservation issues of the day. When he retired in 1904, his fellow commissioner Leroy T. Carleton presented Stanley with another scrapbook comprised on many articles Stanley penned for Carleton's *Sportsman Journal* over several years. His cottage was built in 1885. (NDM.)

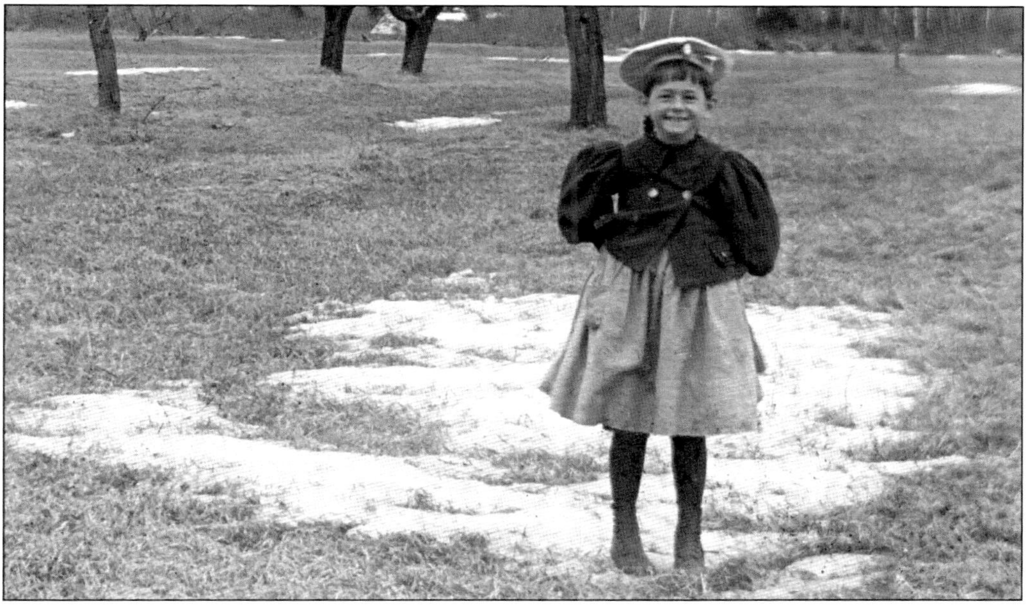

Young Josephine "Josie" Stanley smiles for the camera in this c. 1902 picture taken in the late attorney Isaac Randall's field. This is where future president of the Confederate States of America Jefferson Davis delivered a speech more than 50 years earlier. Josie lived on nearby Mill Street, just a few dozen feet from the field, but soon would move into a new house on Cliff Street (now North Street). (NDM.)

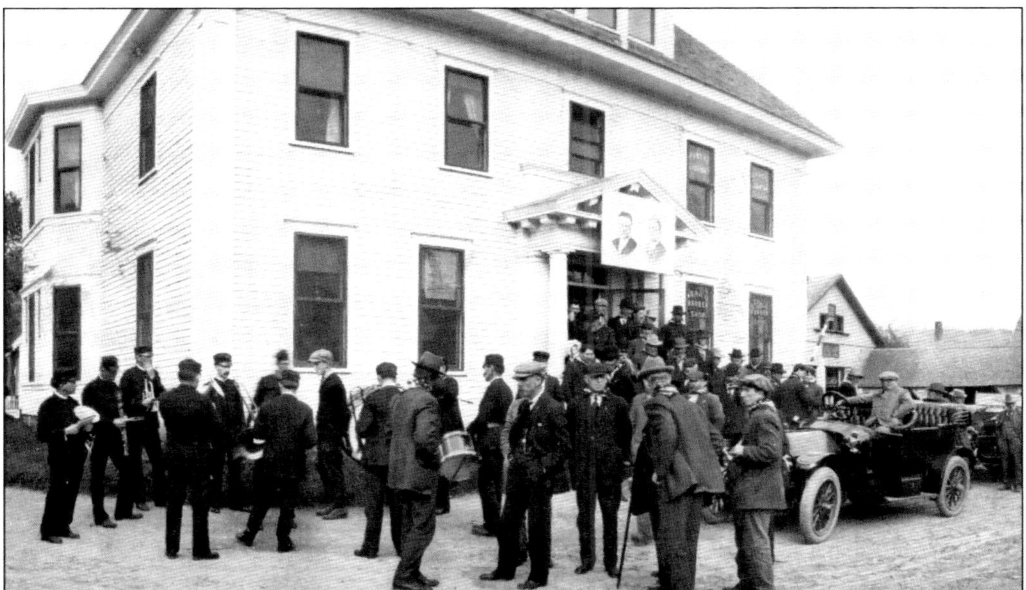

A crowd awaits the arrival of Theodore Roosevelt, the "Bull Moose" candidate for president in 1912. The Harlow Building has been decorated, and a band assembled to strike up a welcoming tune. A poster featuring Roosevelt and running mate Hiram Johnson are in place. Harlow family tradition holds that Roosevelt was fishing with John S. Harlow, just across the Webb River in the Back Kingdom section of Mexico. (DHS.)

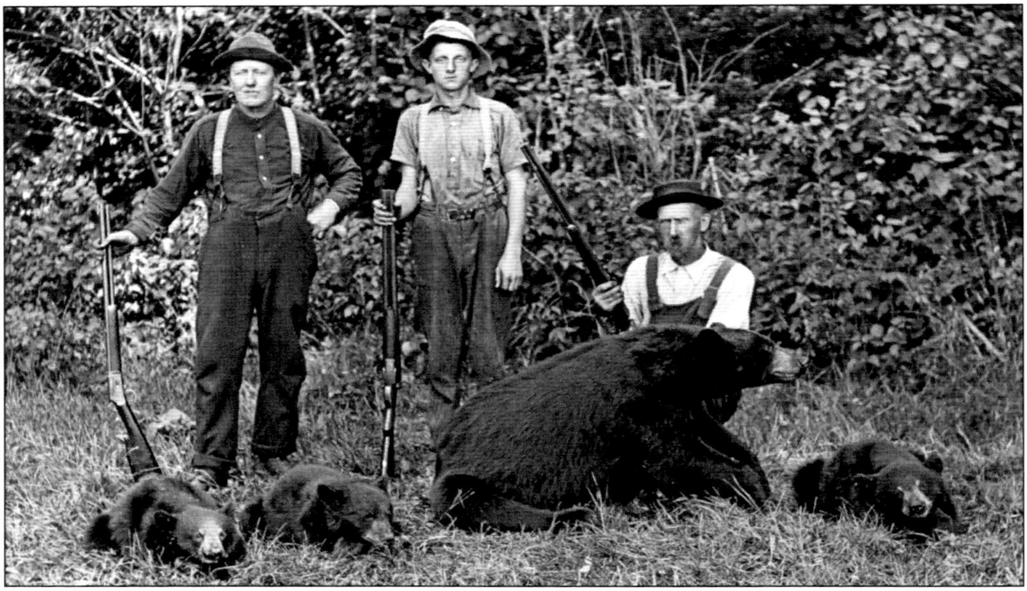

Hunting of all kinds was popular with Dixfield area residents, much more so than today. N.S. Stowell was a noted foxhunter, Henry O. Stanley hunted passenger pigeons, Lee Dillingham was fond of deer hunting, and the Hutchinsons of Carthage, Maine, were among those who sought out bears. Pictured, from left to right, are Frank Hutchinson, his son Lee Hutchinson, and their friend Elmer Holt. Tavern keeper Samuel Morrill killed a bear in the village in 1836, displaying the carcass beneath the tavern's sign. (DHS.)

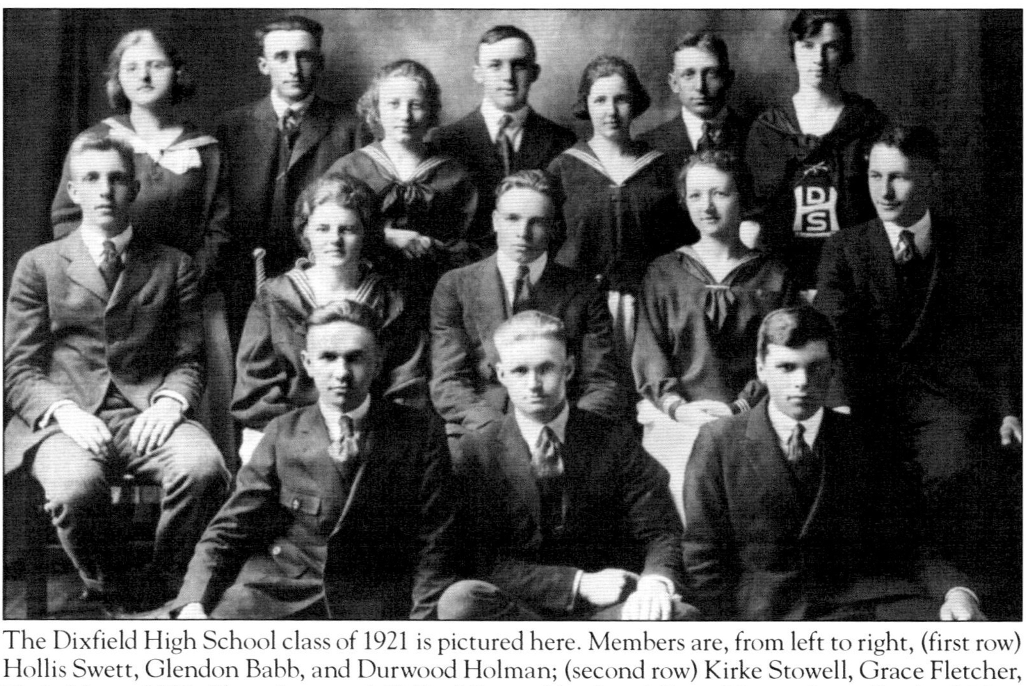

The Dixfield High School class of 1921 is pictured here. Members are, from left to right, (first row) Hollis Swett, Glendon Babb, and Durwood Holman; (second row) Kirke Stowell, Grace Fletcher, Elwin Noyes, Hilda Humphrey, and Clifford Swett; (third row) Doris Harvey, Isaac Searles, Velma White, Archie Holman, Isabel Welch, Cleon Adams, and Cora Bisbee. (DHS.)

Seven

The People of Dixfield

Col. Jonathan Holman (1732–1814) is credited with founding Dixfield. A valiant soldier and veteran of the French and Indian Wars, the Revolutionary War, and Shays's Rebellion, Holman molded his fellow townspeople from Sutton, Massachusetts, into the core of Dixfield's first settlers. Three of his sons built fine homes at Dixfield Center, which was sometimes called "the Common" as civic functions were held there for many years. Following the Revolution, he was so disillusioned with the falling value of the country's paper money that he deliberately lined the interior walls of his foulest outhouse with them. For the rest of his days, it is said, he could not stop talking about the war and his high hopes for his country's future. He would live through the presidencies of George Washington, John Adams, and Thomas Jefferson, before dying in 1814 midway through the first term of James Madison. (PDH.)

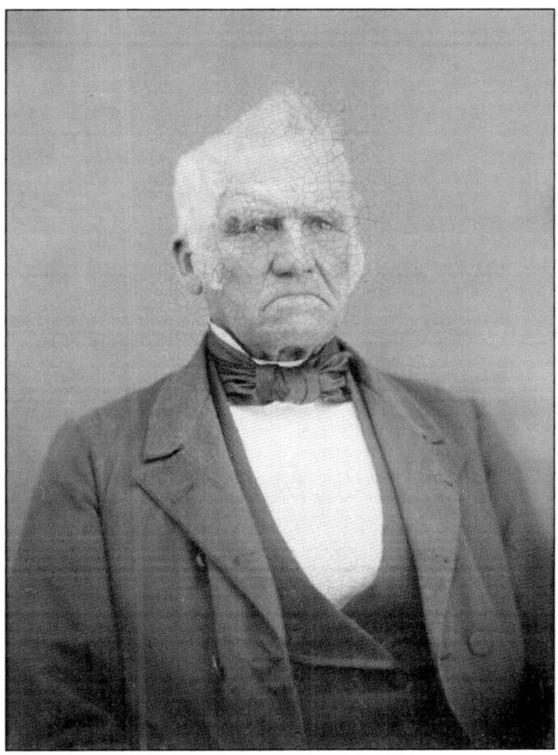

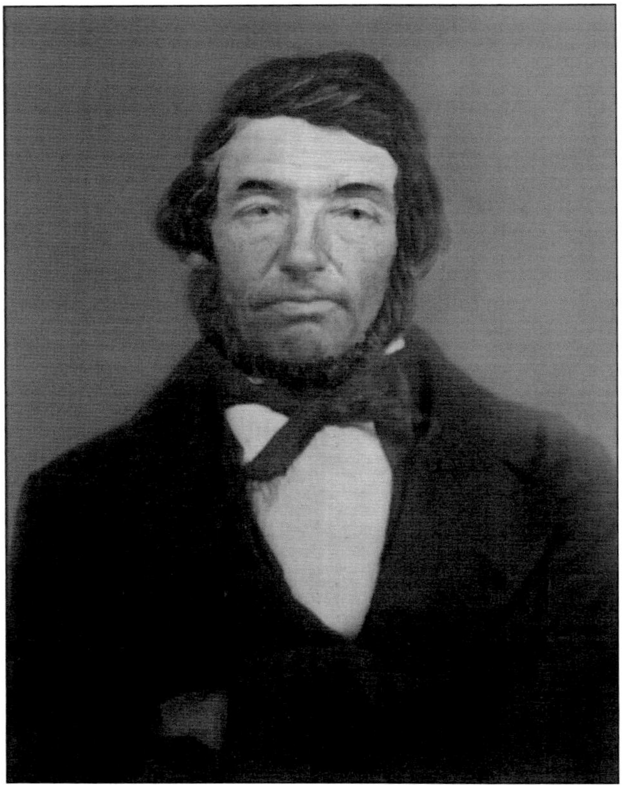

Peter Holman (1769–1829), son of Colonel Holman, along with his brothers Jonathan and Ebenezer, settled at Dixfield Common, each of them building large houses. They were influential in Dixfield's early history, holding several offices and serving as interpreters of their father's vision for the town. Dozens of present-day Dixfield families proudly trace their descent from Colonel Holman and his offspring. (PDH.)

Leila Holman, a great-great-granddaughter of Dixfield proprietor Col. Jonathan Holman, married Ralph Walton in 1915. She is shown in this 1920 photograph with two of her children, Althea and Earle "Bud." Althea became a librarian for the Ludden Library in Dixfield and amassed many photographs of early life in Dixfield, generously sharing them with the Dixfield Historical Society. (DHS.)

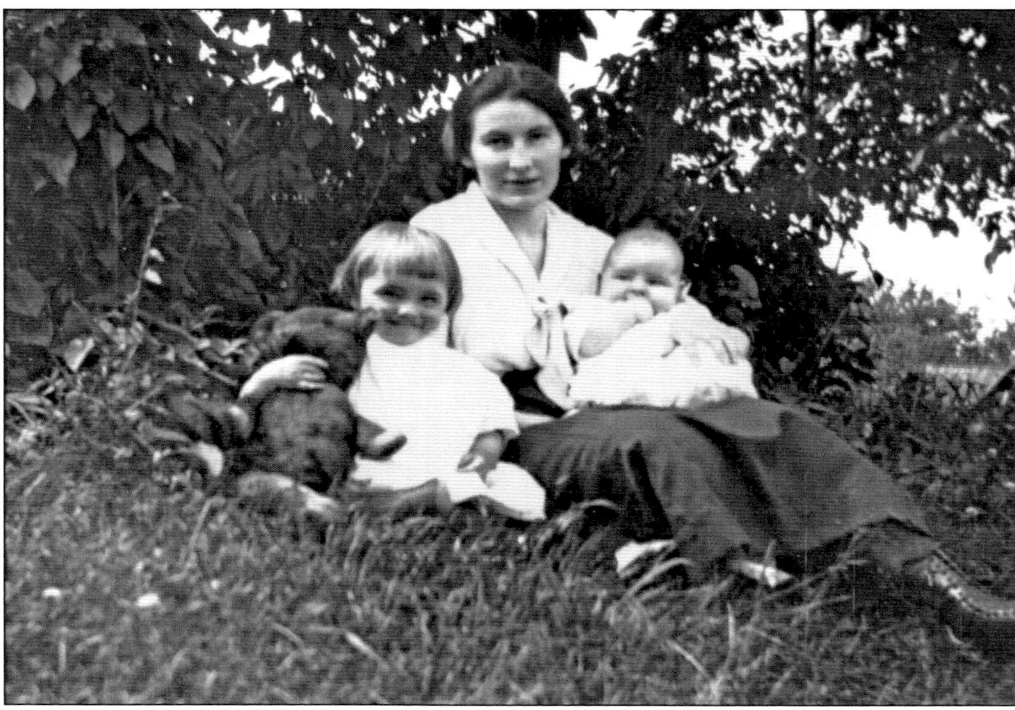

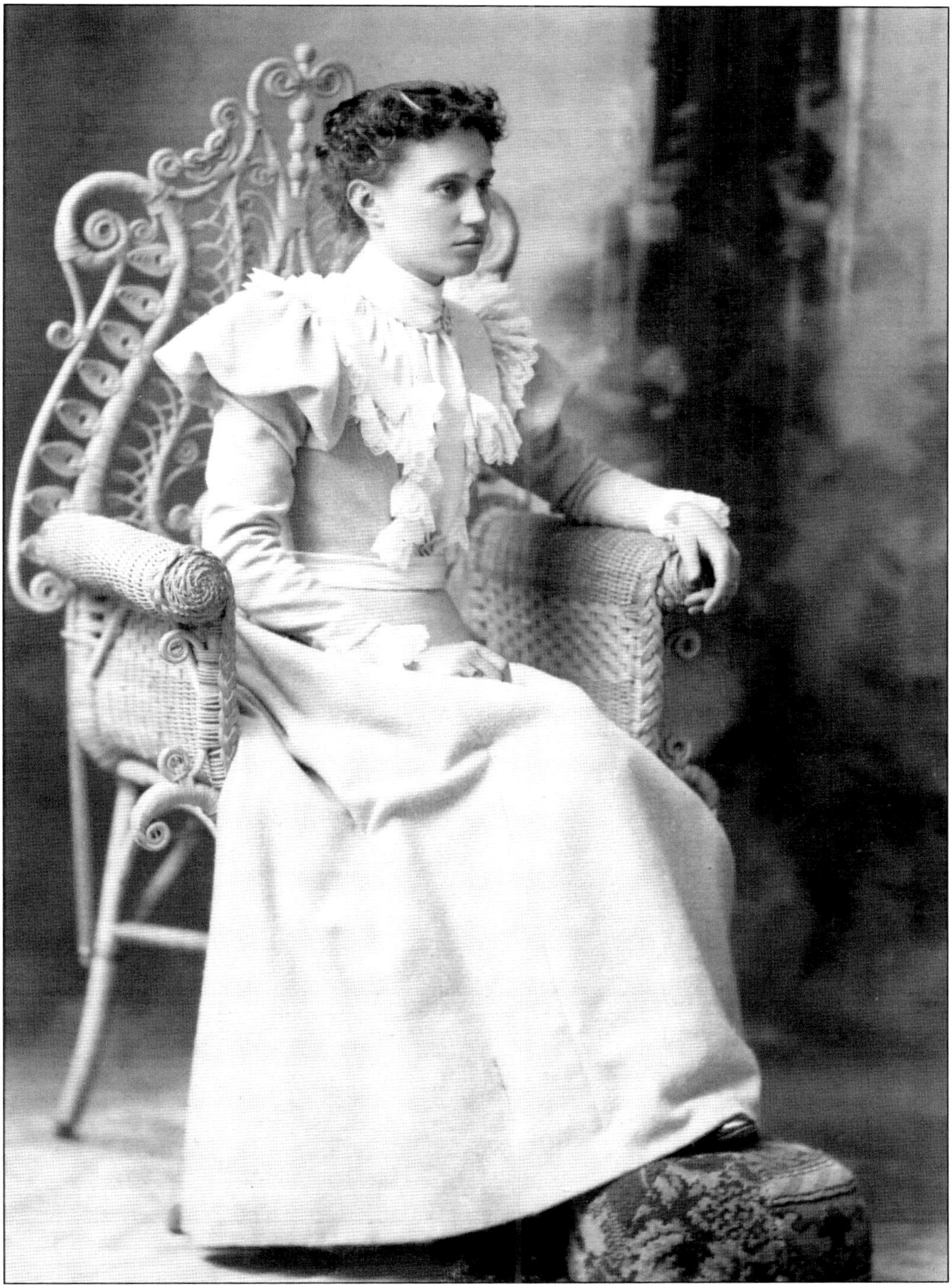

Myrtie Walker (1871–1962) was born at East Dixfield, the daughter of Samuel and Rose White Walker. She married Warren Look in 1899 and, in 1912, married Philetus Torrey, a Dixfield resident and longtime member of the Mount Sugarloaf Grange. She survived him by more than 40 years. (JMB.)

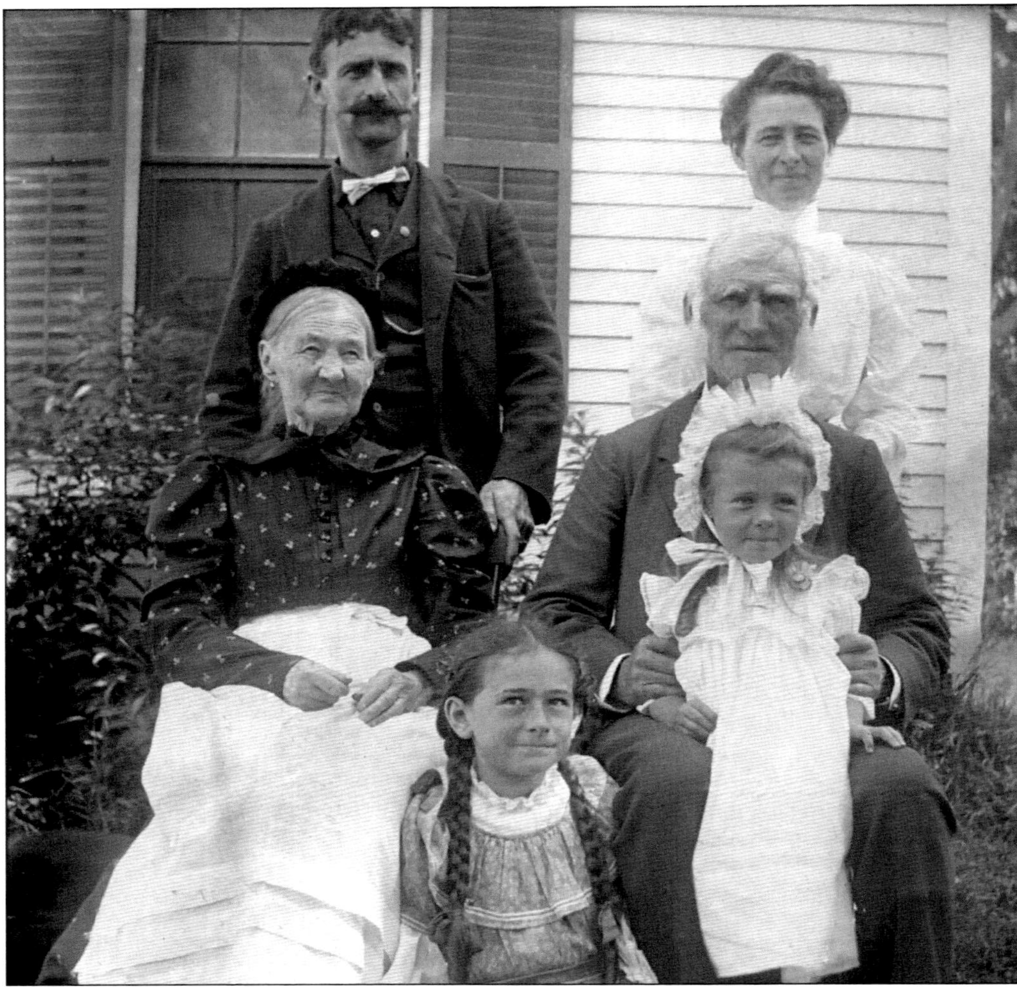

Amos Trask fathered one son and five daughters, who all made their marks on Dixfield Village history. His youngest daughter and family matriarch Susan Trask Stanley (1809–1901) is shown in this c. 1900 picture with her son Henry O. Stanley to her left. His son George and daughter Nellie Kimball are behind him. Henry O. is holding Nellie's daughter Mary, and George's daughter Josie is at the front. Descendants of Amos Trask were significant in the development of the town's industrial might, an influence that lasted nearly 200 years. Henry O. Stanley pioneered the development of the Maine Warden Service while serving as commissioner of the Maine Department of Fisheries and Game. Researchers are now cobbling together his contributions to early wildlife conservation efforts. His achievements were extraordinary, but he remained a humble man, lending his meager assets to support to local businessmen. When he died, his estate was owed money by some of Dixfield's most-noted industrial leaders, including John S. Harlow and Newton S. Stowell. (NDM.)

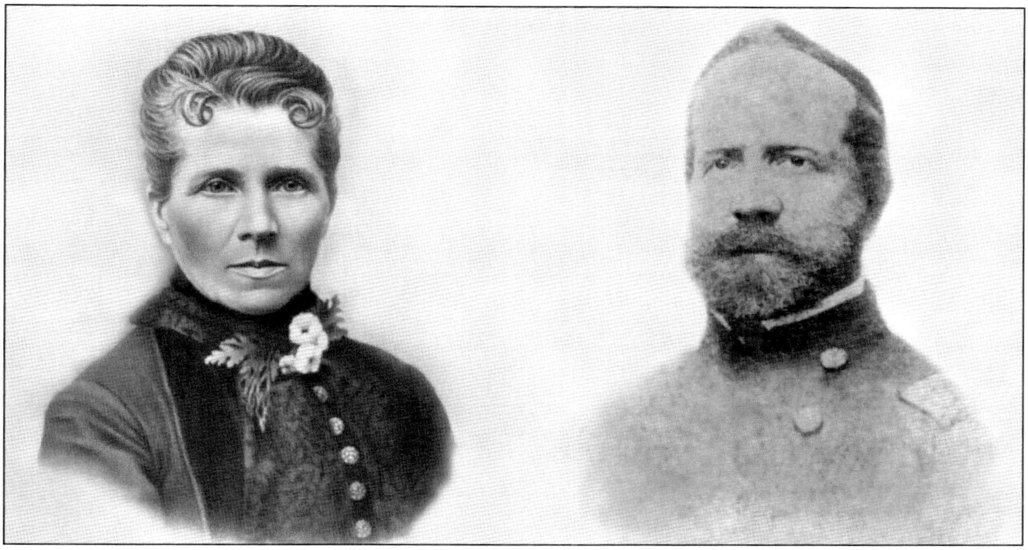

Sophronia Stanley (1832–1924) married attorney major David Porter Stowell (1816–1884) on New Year's Day 1854. They lived in the Ned Stockbridge farm on Mitchell (now Holt) Hill before moving in 1959 to Canton where they could raise and race their horses. Stowell served with the 1st Maine Cavalry and captured rebel soldiers near Aldie, Virginia. The image of Sophronia was done in charcoal and airbrushed by her cousin Francis Stanley, inventor of the Stanley Steamer, for her 50th birthday in 1882. It was a gift from her daughters—Mary, Elizabeth, and Susan. (DHS.)

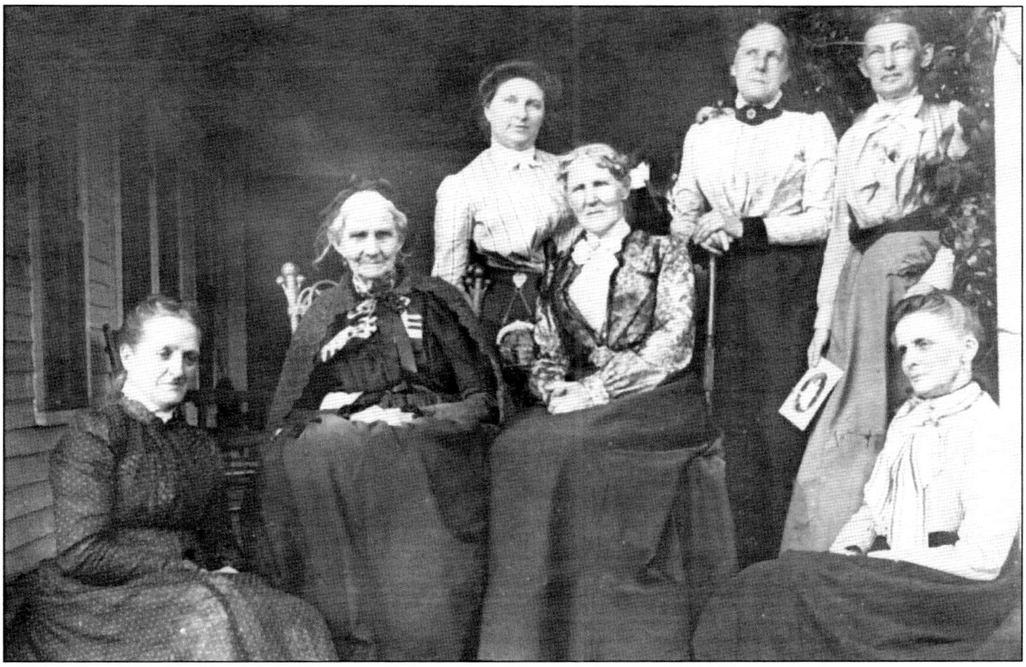

Several Dixfield Village ladies are gathered for a portrait at the Trask homestead on Leavitt Street in Mexico. They are, from left to right, Jane Edmunds Trask, Melissa White Randall, Elizabeth Eddy, Delpine Barnard Root, Emily Barnard Knight, Louise Trask, and Francella Marble Smith. (DHS.)

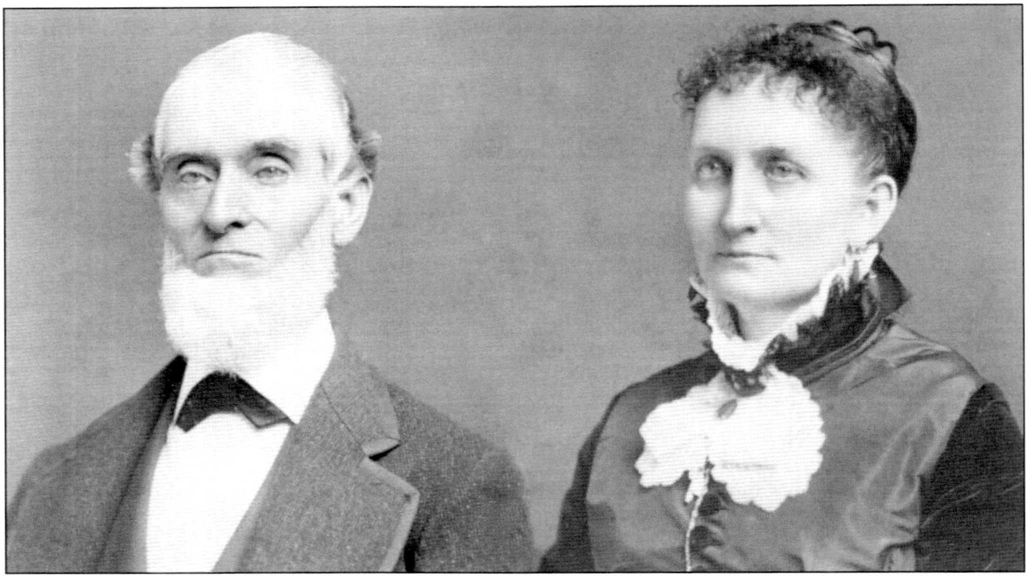

Two grand old Dixfield families were united when Amos Griffith married Azuba Stockbridge in the 1840s. The Griffiths were early settlers in Dixfield Village—Amos's ancestors sawed the first clapboard in Silas Barnard's mill on the Webb River in 1810. Amos was born in 1821 and, early on, waited tables, first in Boston then Dixfield, for Col. Samuel P. Morrill. Later, he became a carriage maker. Azuba was born in 1824, a granddaughter of Revolutionary War lieutenant John Stockbridge, who settled in Dixfield before moving to Stockbridge Hill in Byron, Maine. She was descended from the Warrens, Eustises, and Buckminsters of Massachusetts. (WWE.)

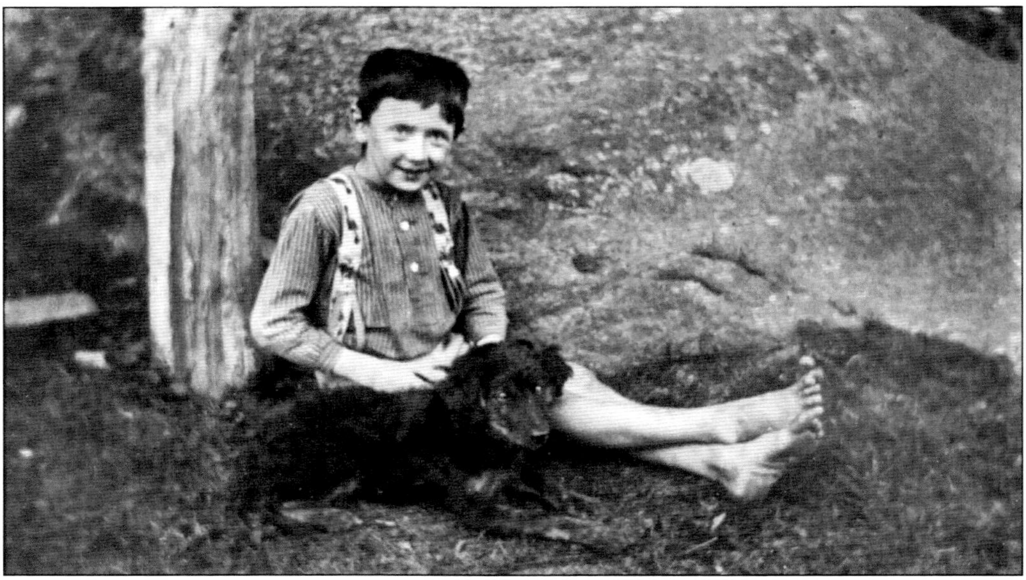

Vivian Morrison (1892–1984), the son of Fred and Ella Morrison, poses with his dog in East Dixfield. He married Mildred Look in 1921. As a young man, he became an airplane pilot and built his own airplane in the 1930s. He was the elder brother of Erlon Morrison, who operated Morrison Motors in Mexico, Maine, for many years. Vivian was a heavy-equipment operator and self-employed mechanic. (JMB.)

Mary Greenleaf was the youngest of John Mason and Anna Trask Eustis's 10 children. She married Charles Greenleaf and lived in the Wallace Greenleaf house on upper Main Street. Here, she is shown with her son Mace Greenleaf, a leading silent film star in Hollywood between 1910 and 1912. His film *Falling Leaves* was one of the top-grossing movies of 1912. (DHS.)

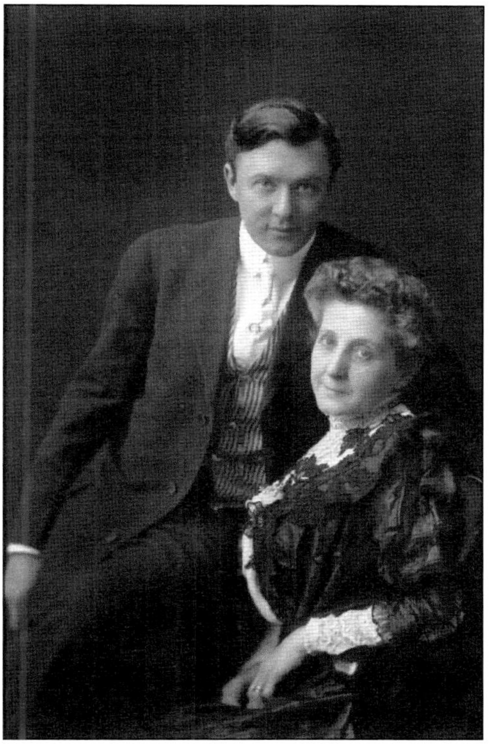

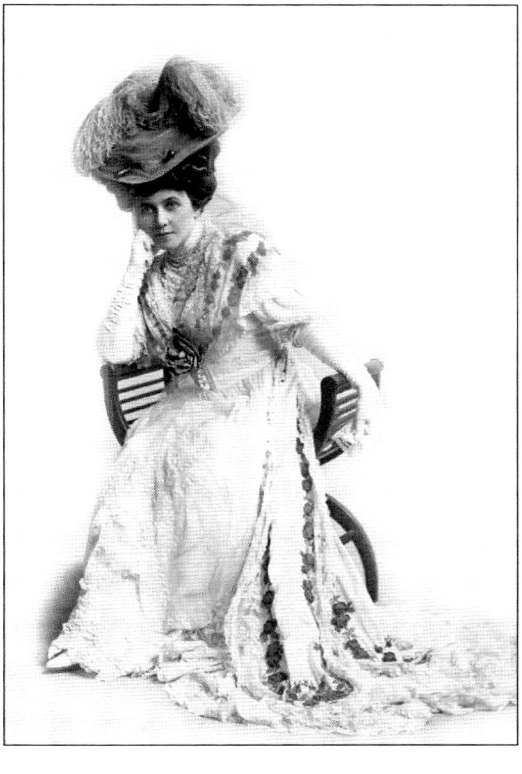

Actress Ida Adair was a friend and consort of Dixfield's Mace Greenleaf. As such, she played a minor role in Dixfield's history as she was also the mother of actor John "Jack" Gilbert, whose film career rivaled silent movie star Rudolph Valentino's in stature. Occasionally, Greenleaf and Adair brought young Jack to Dixfield where his hand-me-downs found their way into the Eustis family. Newspapers later reported his few visits to Dixfield. (WWE.)

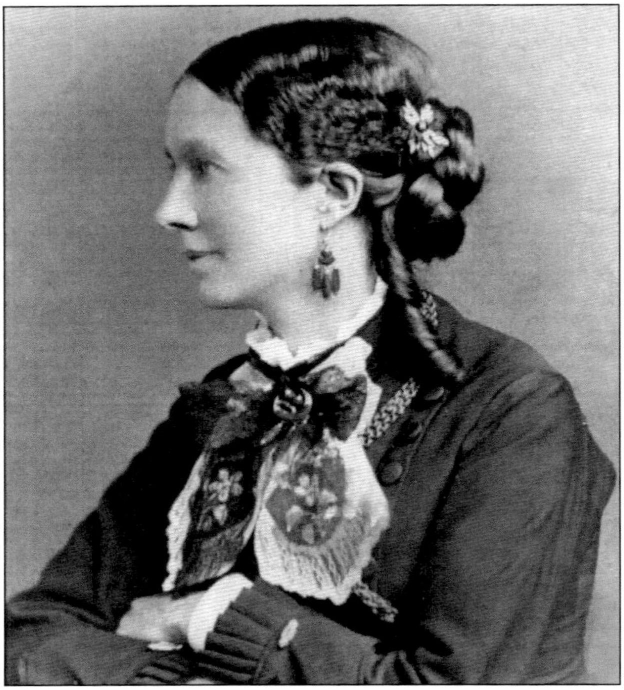

This is a picture of Sarah Edmunds Chase Lake dressed in the fashion of the day. The eldest of five daughters of Eli and Harriett Stockbridge Edmunds, she was born in 1838 and married first Wade Chase of Dixfield. Upon his death, she married Charles Lake of Roxbury, Massachusetts, where she went to live. She attended her brother Montello as he lay dying from tuberculosis in 1861. (DHS.)

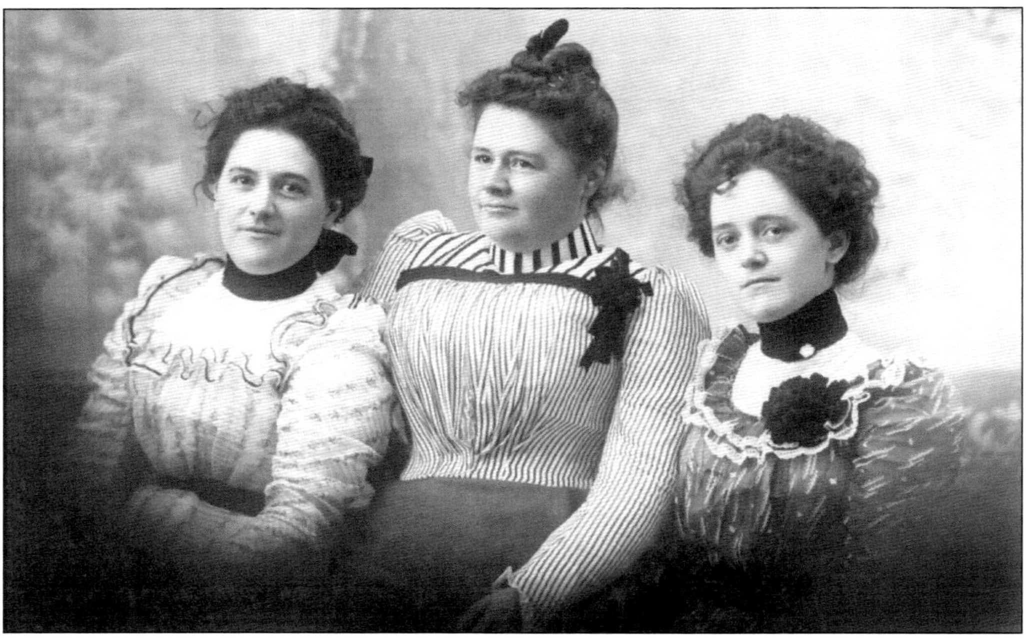

When George A. Marsh came to Dixfield in the mid-1880s, his three charming daughters changed its social life. They are, from left to right, Alice Marsh, who married Maurice Keith; Netta Marsh, who married George P. Stanley, superintendent of the Stanley toothpick mill; and Josephine Marsh, who married Adolph Walters, a bookkeeper for the Niles and Butler wood-turning plant in Jay, Maine. In the 1890s, George and Maurice formed Stanley, Keith & Co., manufacturing items from the leftover tin from George Marsh's can-making process. (NDM.)

Henry W. Park, born in Dixfield in 1834, the son of Isaac and Emeline Park, preserved much of Dixfield's history through his personal accounts and as correspondent for the short-lived newspaper the *Canton Telephone*. Although most of his writings were discarded upon his death, enough material survived to provide information on hundreds of Dixfield residents of the 19th century. Park spent much of the Civil War as a clerk in Washington, DC, where this photograph was likely taken. (DHS.)

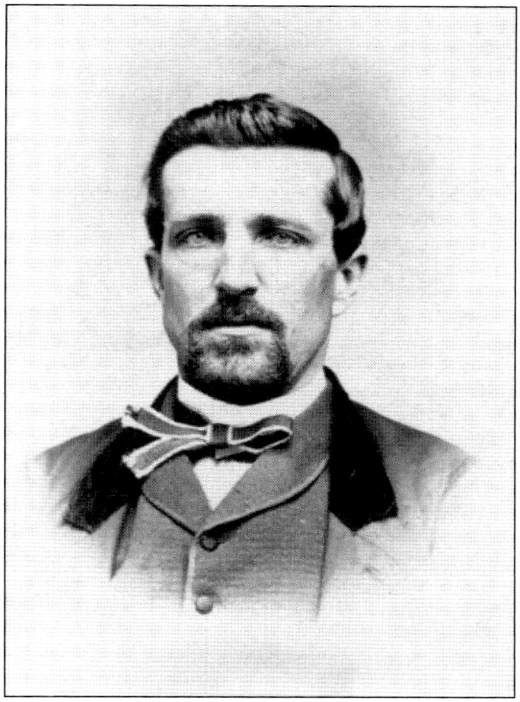

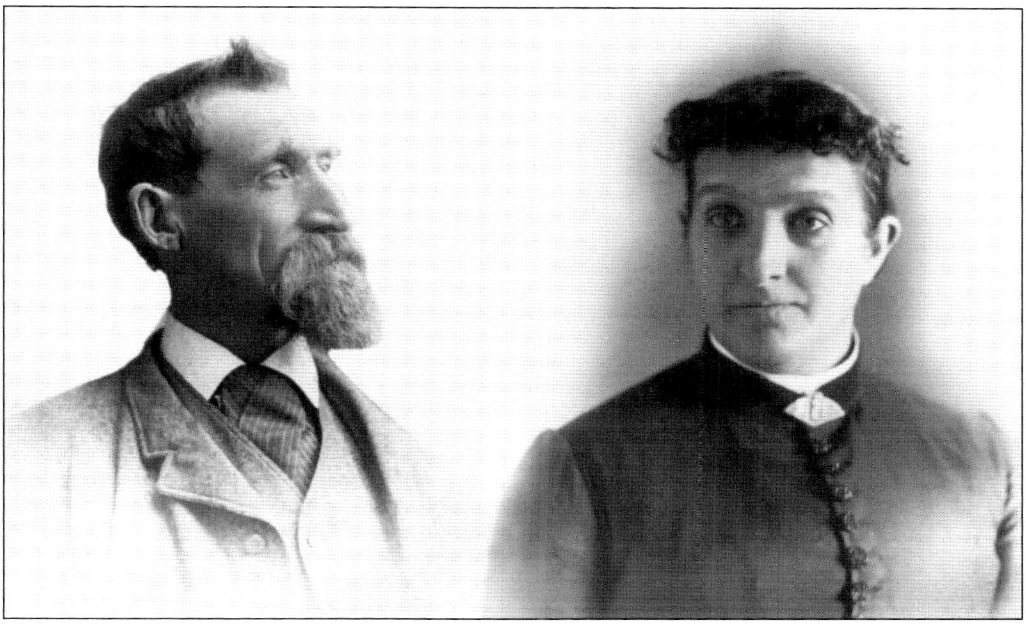

Oscar Trask married Jane Edmunds in 1868; they were neighbors in the Mexico section of Dixfield Village. Oscar was the grandson of Amos Trask through Peter Trask. He was a farmer, a logger, and a longtime deputy sheriff for Oxford County. Jane, the daughter of Eli and Harriett Stockbridge Edmunds, was born in Mexico, Maine, in 1839. Oscar cryptically noted his marriage in his diary by writing, "Got married today." They were the parents of four children—Albert, Wade, Bessie, and Harriett. (DHS.)

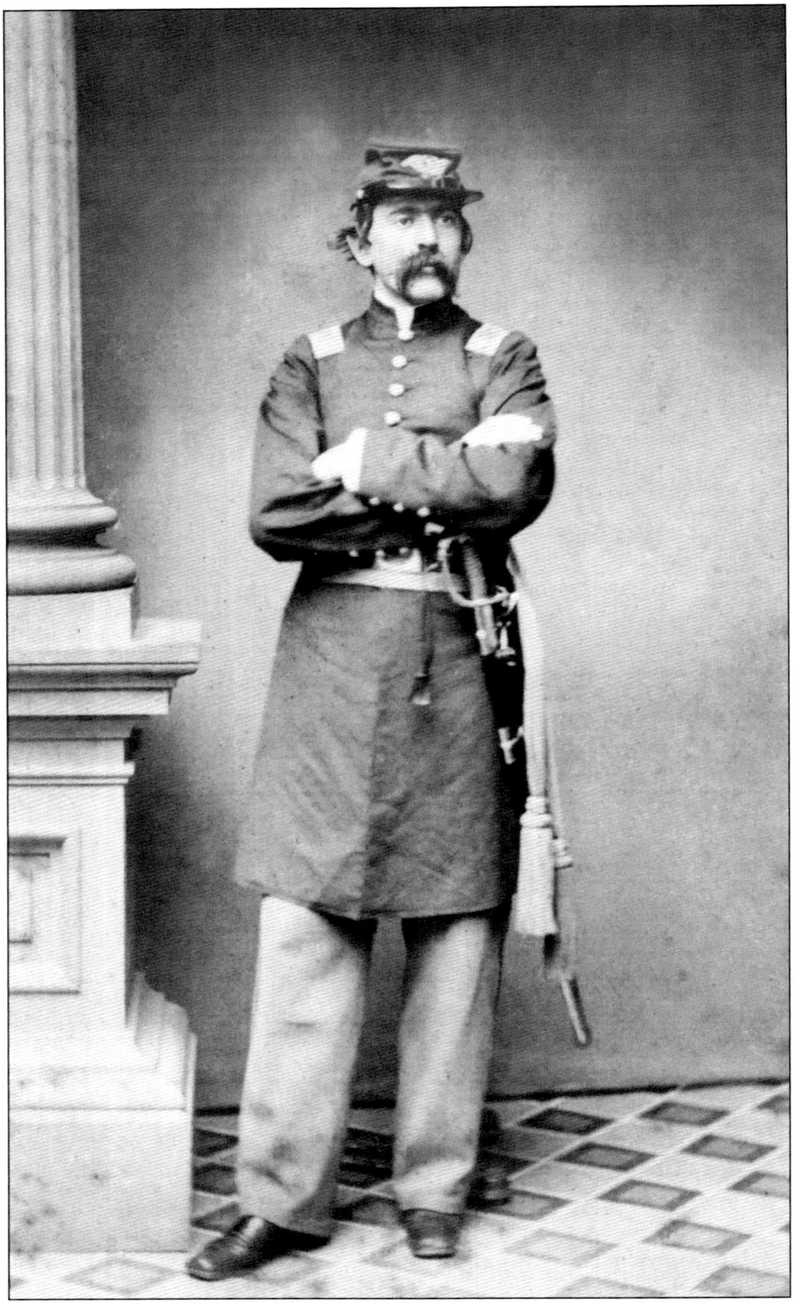

Col. William Tappan Eustis (1836–1925) enlisted in the 5th Massachusetts Regiment during the Civil War. The fifth of John M. and Anna T. Eustis's six sons, he was a natural-born leader. A strong prohibitionist, he ran for governor of Maine several times and for the US Congress as well, always on the Prohibition ticket. He was a historian for the 5th Massachusetts, a gifted and respected orator, and an accountant for the Maurice Forster toothpick mill. When his two daughters, Anne and Augusta, needed special services to address their deafness, the Eustis family moved to Portland, Maine, for several years to allow them to be educated. (MSA.)

Frank Carlos Griffith (1851–1939) was the son of Amos and Azuba Stockbridge Griffith of Dixfield. At 25 years old, he was starring on the stage in Boston. Later, he became the American road manager for the noted actress Lillie Langtry, the "Jersey Lily," during her three-year tour of America. He then managed Millie Maddern Fiske for more than 20 years. On one of his tours of England, he briefly sat on the throne of the king of England at Edinburgh Castle. (DHS.)

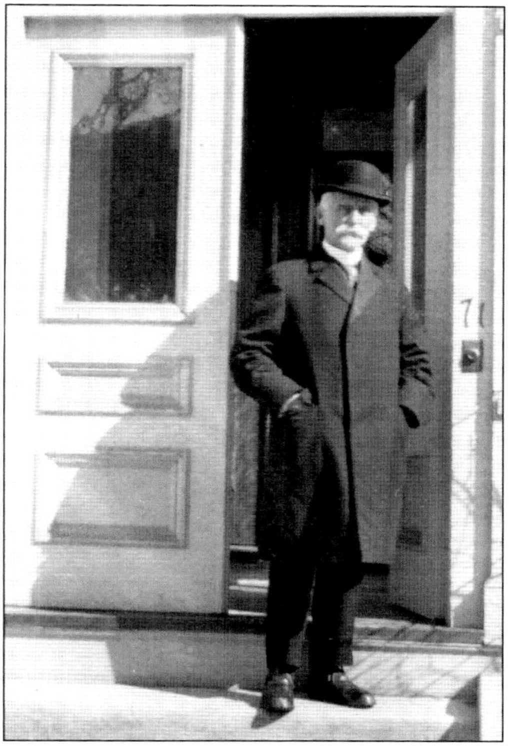

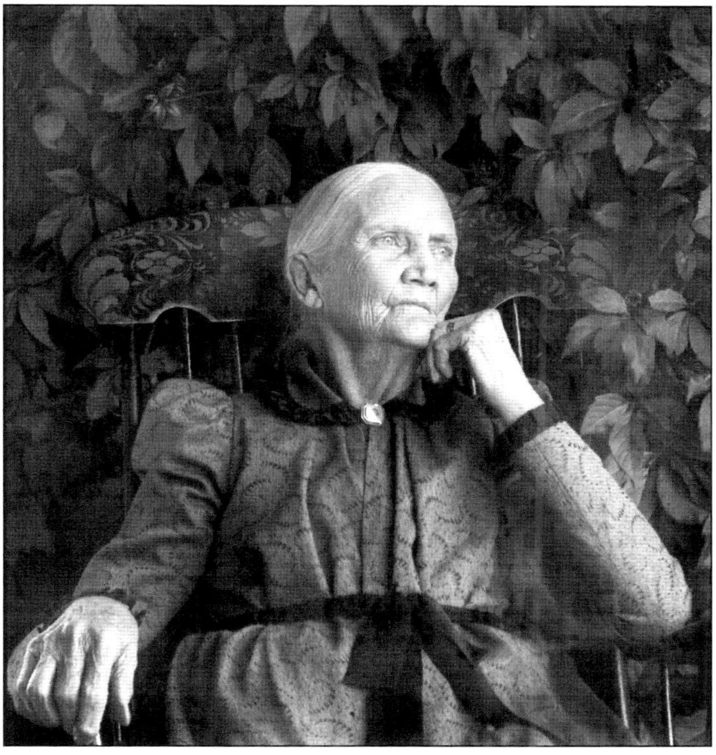

Harriett Stockbridge (1817–1916), the eldest daughter of William Stockbridge and granddaughter of Revolutionary War veteran John Stockbridge, married Eli Edmunds and had seven children with him, five surviving to adulthood and another, Monticello, dying of tuberculosis at age 19. When Eli died, a mourner said, "Mr. Edmunds always stood up for the absent and accused—and never spoke unkindly of others, no, nor listened to it." (DHS.)

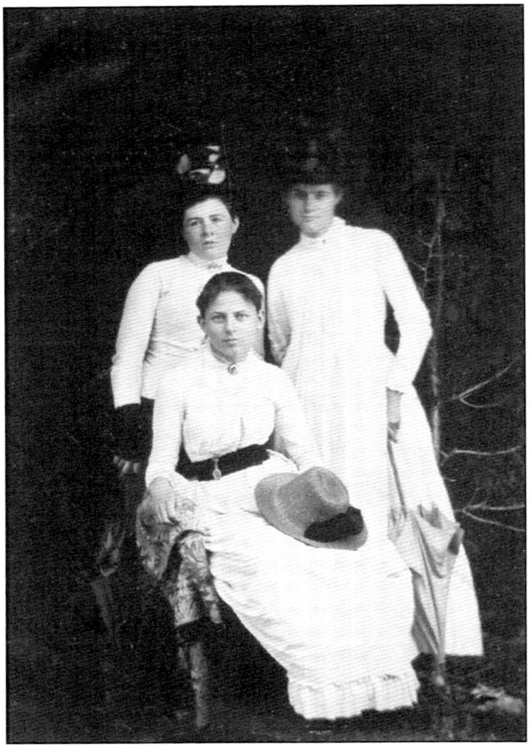

Three young Dixfield ladies pose for a picture around 1890 in Dixfield. Sitting is Susie Stanley (Bailey), daughter of Frank and Mary Stanley; standing are, from left to right, Netta Marsh (Stanley), daughter of George A. and Josephine Marsh, and Ione Harlow, daughter of Elbridge G. and Rosella S. Harlow. (NDM.)

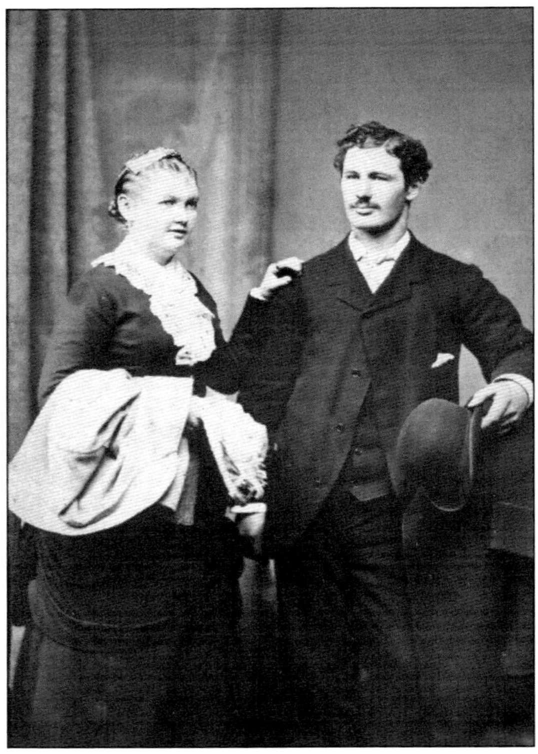

Nellie Leach (1862–1942) married Albert Barnard Root (1858–1937) in 1881. Born in Dixfield, Albert became a blacksmith in Boston, with his wife's father helping him to finance his business. The Roots later returned to Dixfield to care for his mother Delphine. Albert became a noted antiques dealer in the 1820 House on Weld Street, while Nellie carefully compiled and preserved volumes of Dixfield's vital records. Albert died in 1937, along with three octogenarian friends, when the automobile he was riding in landed upside down in a stream, trapping all inside. (KRG.)

Guy O. Gardner was a native of Buckfield, Maine, but was best known as the proprietor of the Guy O. Gardner drugstore on Main Street in Dixfield. For a time, he sold fishing flies and leaders when fellow Dixfield resident and former fish commissioner Henry O. Stanley sold his business in the early 1900s. (DHS.)

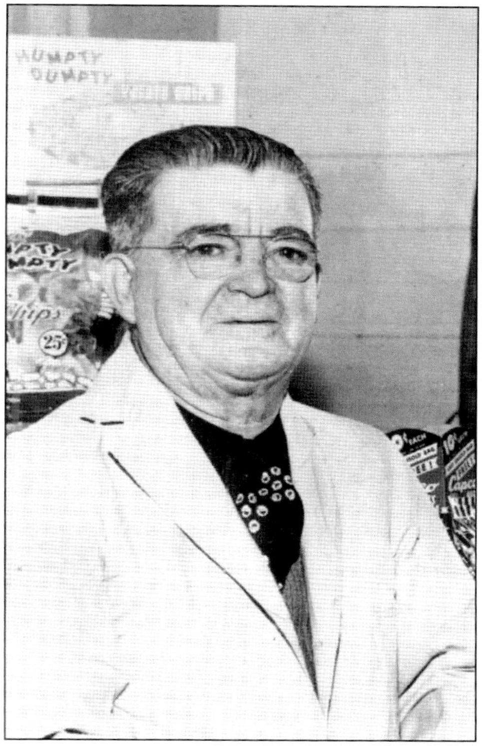

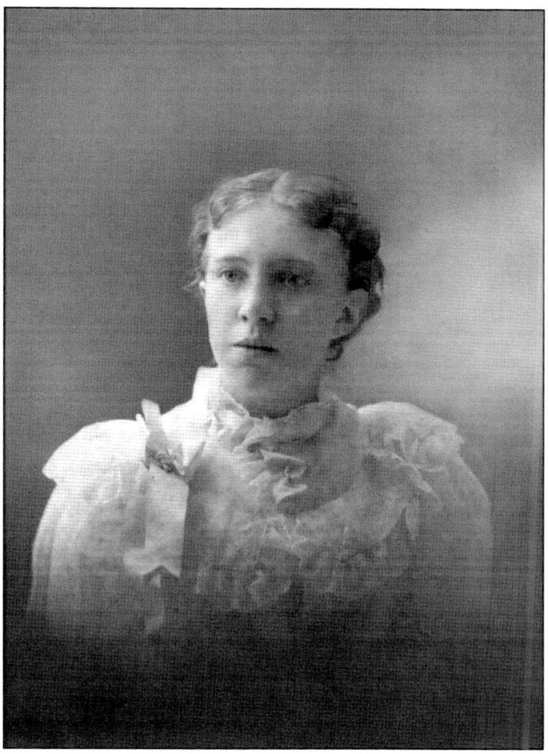

Zerua Walker was the great-granddaughter of one of East Dixfield's first settlers, Osgood Walker, whose presence was discerned by a neighbor, Asa Severy, when he heard the distant sound of an axe felling a tree. They became fast friends. Zerua married Henry Monroe Babb and they had four children. A sister to Myrtie Torrey, she died of breast cancer in 1928. (JMB.)

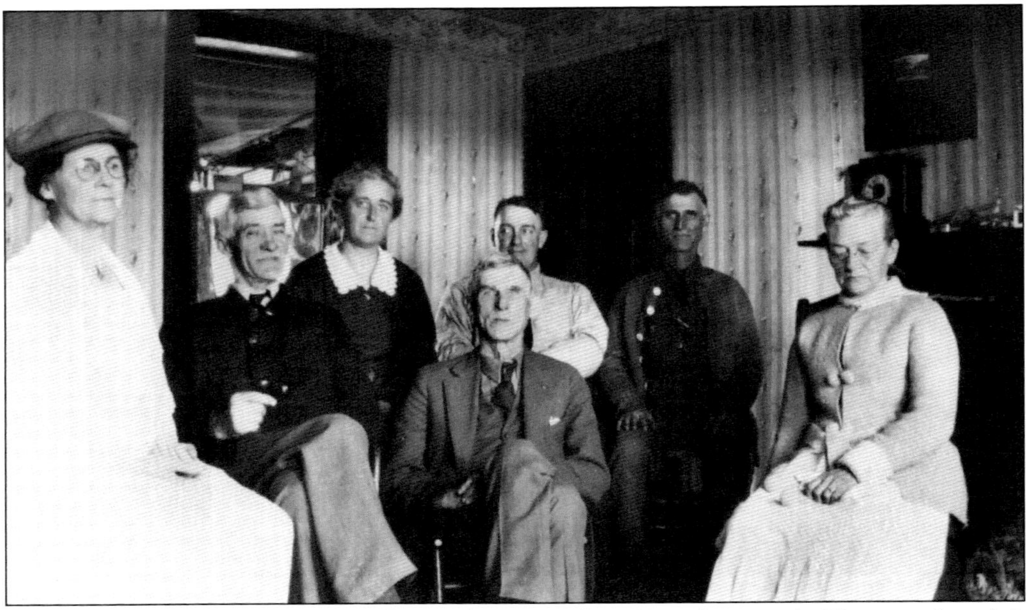

A group of Dixfield people gathers for good times in this 1920s photograph. They are, from left to right, Lottie Ricker; her husband, Charles Ricker, supervisor at the Stanley toothpick mill; Mae Payne; Frank Stanley; Mae's husband, Olie Payne; George Stanley; and Frank's wife, Mary Stanley. (NDM.)

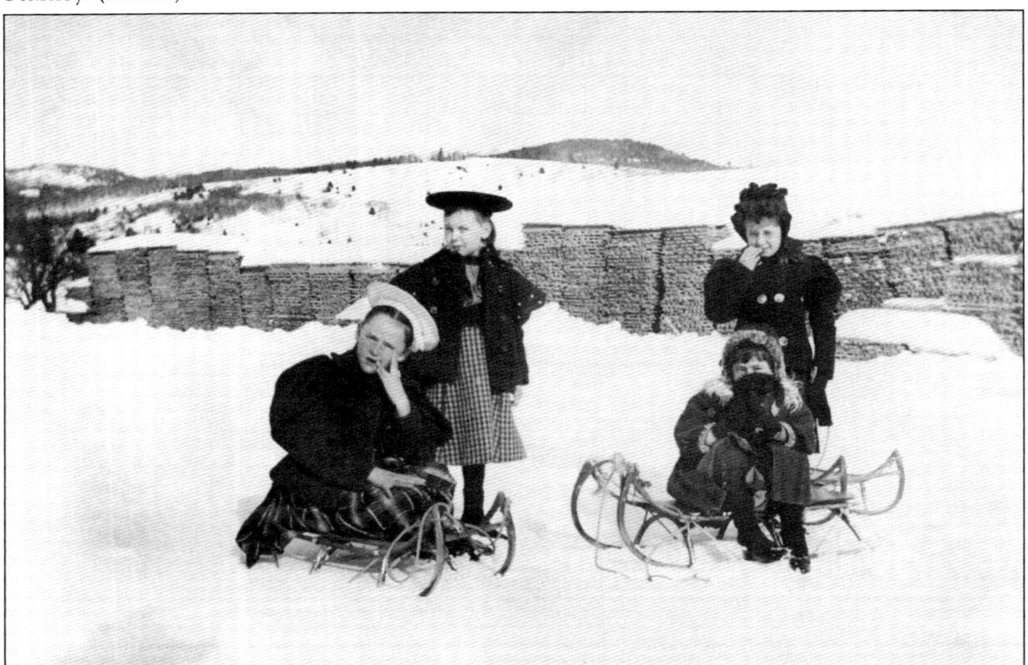

Four young Dixfield girls enjoy the snow on Mill Street in this c. 1900 photograph. Their names are Florence Thayer, Sadie Wait, Henrietta Thompson, and the only one to be clearly identified, Josie Stanley, holding the dog. (NDM.)

Spool magnate Newton Stanley Stowell poses with his five children in this late-1930s photograph taken at the family cottage in Weld, Maine. Pictured, from left to right, are Arthur Stowell, Anna Isabel Russell, Kirke Stowell, N.S. Stowell, and George Stowell. (HSB.)

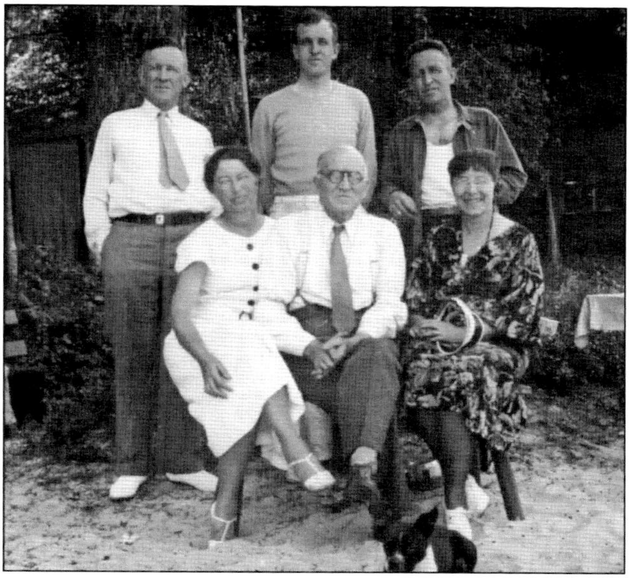

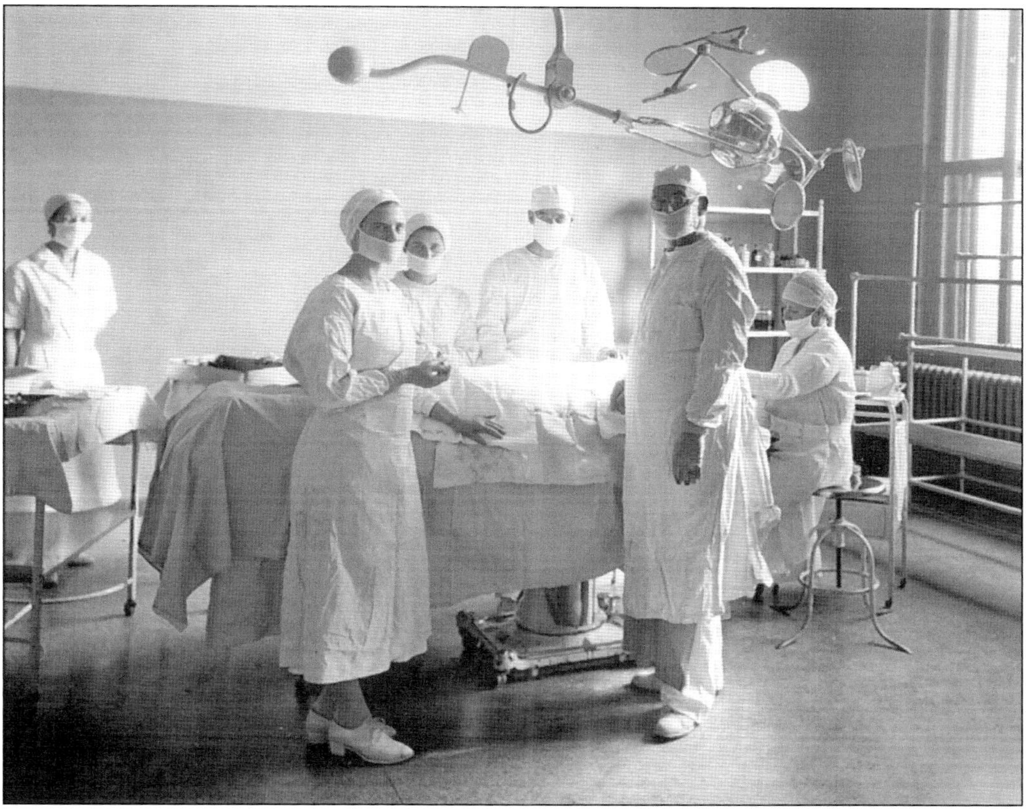

Dr. Dexter Elsemore, who practiced medicine in Dixfield for more than 20 years, is shown at the rear center of this picture at the Portland General Hospital in Portland, Maine, where he served his residency. The Elsemore family was treated to a weeklong retirement celebration by Dixfield area residents upon his retirement in 1977. (MES.)

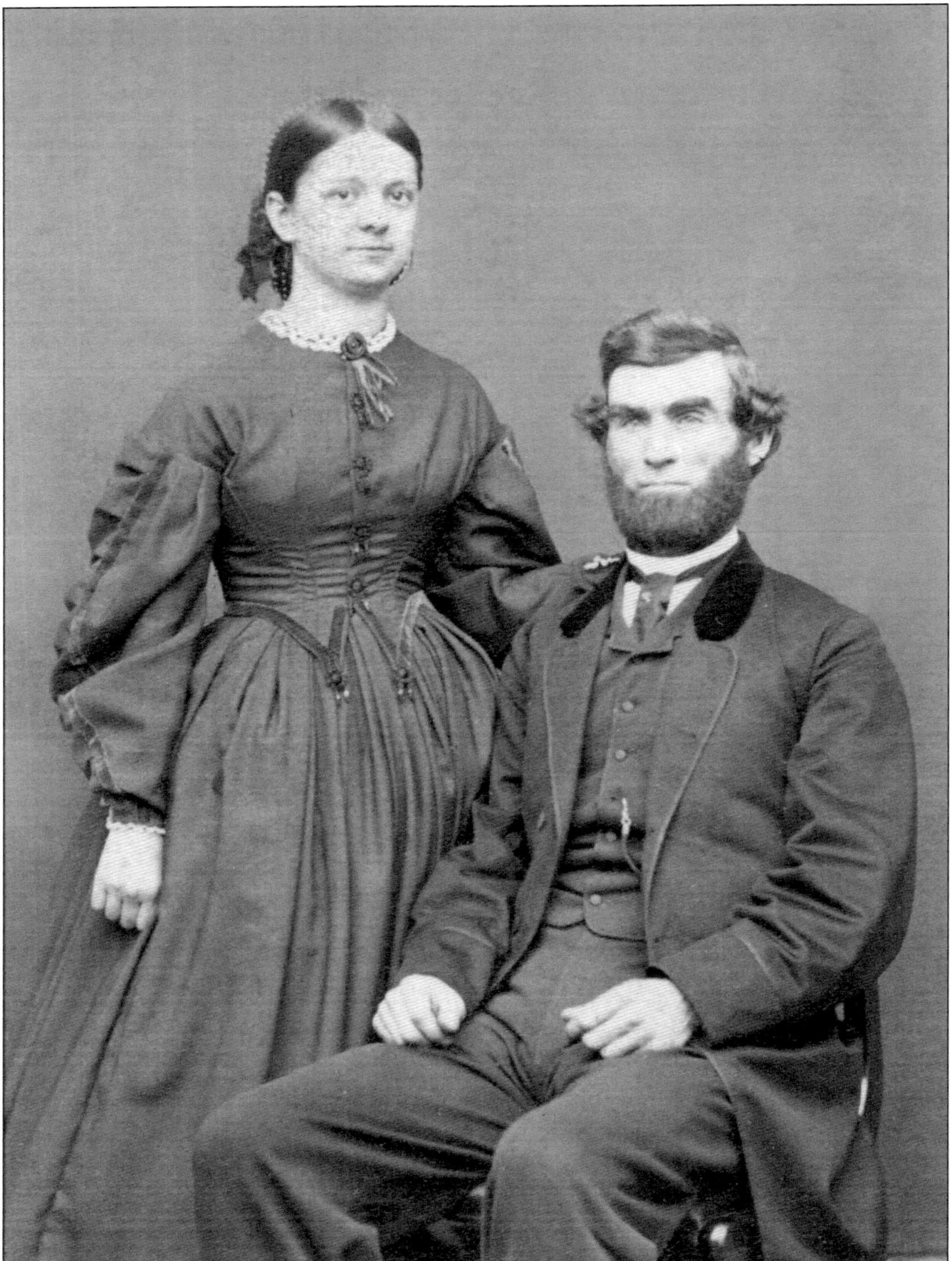

Henry O. Stanley's first wife, Helen Randall Sawtelle, died in 1861. Three years later, he married Mary E. Bennett of Gorham, New Hampshire. They had two children, Nellie (1865–1953) and George (1869–1955). Mary died in a Portland, Maine, hospital in 1881 while Henry was on a business trip in Wiscasset, Maine. He never again married. (NDM.)

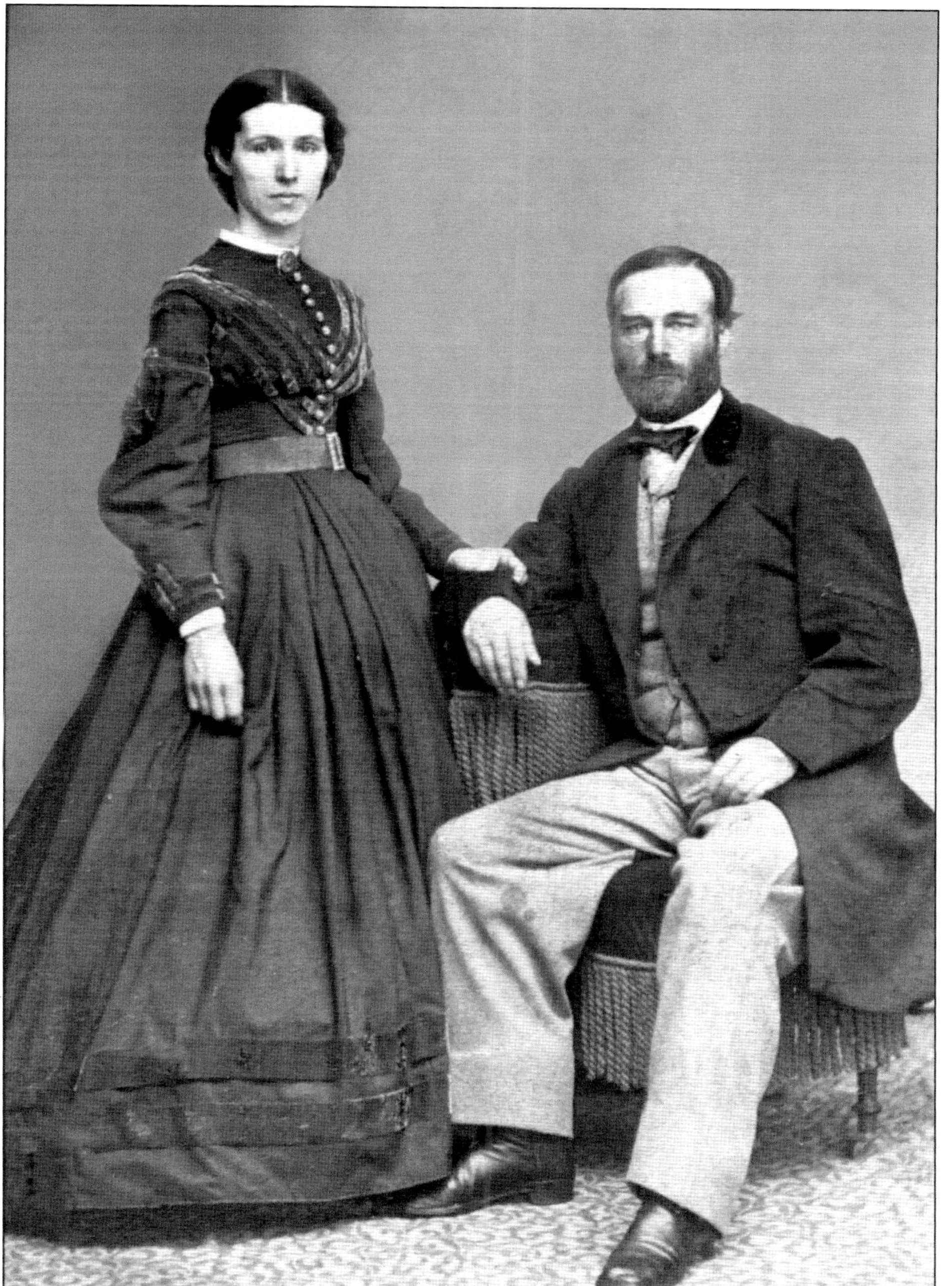

Rosella Stanley Harlow and her husband Elbridge Gerry Harlow are shown in this photograph taken in Boston about 1875. Harlow's first wife, Harriett Sanborn, had died. The Harlows had eight children, prompting Rosella's cousin Emily Knight to write prophetically in early 1865, "Rosella Harlow is going to have another baby and her health is very poor. She will not live but a short time if she continues to have children so fast as she has. I would get a divorce as soon as possible." Whether or not having children contributed to her early death at age 46 is not known. (WWE.)

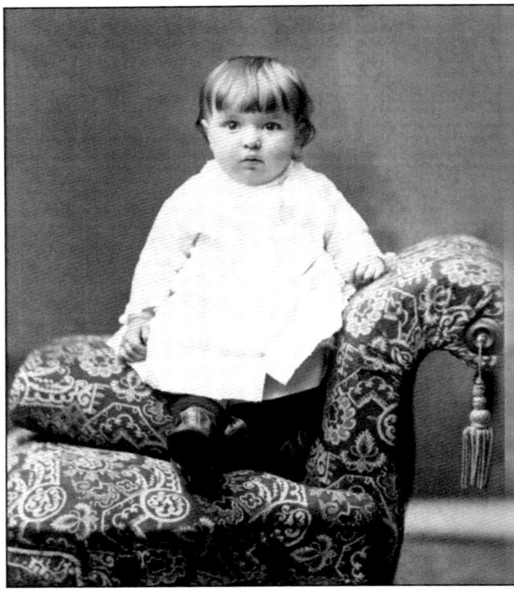
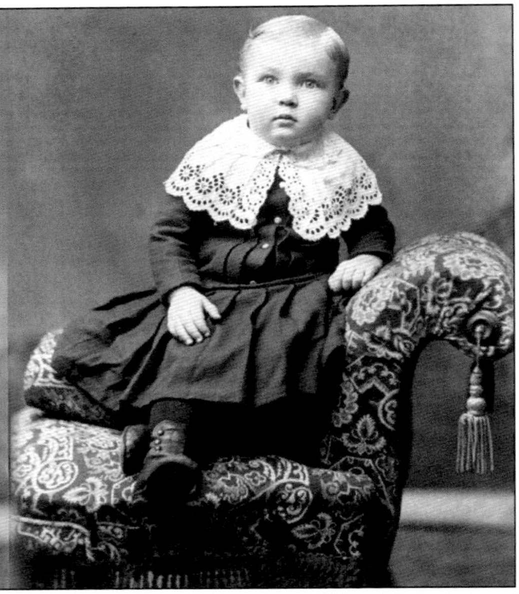

One day in 1886, Susan Edith Edwards and her sister-in-law Edith Gates Stowell had their babies' pictures taken. On the left is Frank Dexter Edwards (1885–1889), named for his uncle, Franklin King Dexter, and on the right is Arthur Stowell (1883–1957). While a childhood illness claimed Frank's life, Arthur grew up to preside over the world's largest spool-making company. (WWE.)

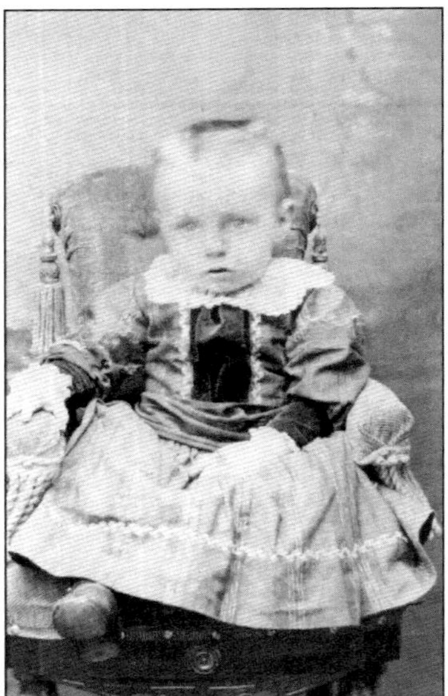
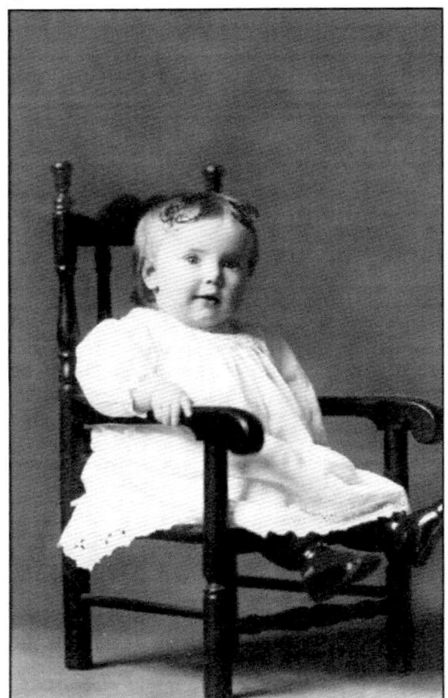

"Little Charlie" Knight is engraved into the Eustis Cemetery headstone of Charles Edwin Knight, less than three years old when he died on January 26, 1867, probably of typhoid fever. Born on February 27, 1864, he was the son of Edwin R. and Emily Barnard Knight. His father's death followed just four months later. Little Leila Holman happily enjoys her child's chair while having her picture taken in the 1890s. She would grow up to marry Ralph Walton and have four children, one of whom was Althea Walton Fish, librarian at the Ludden Library in Dixfield and local historian. (Both, DHS.)

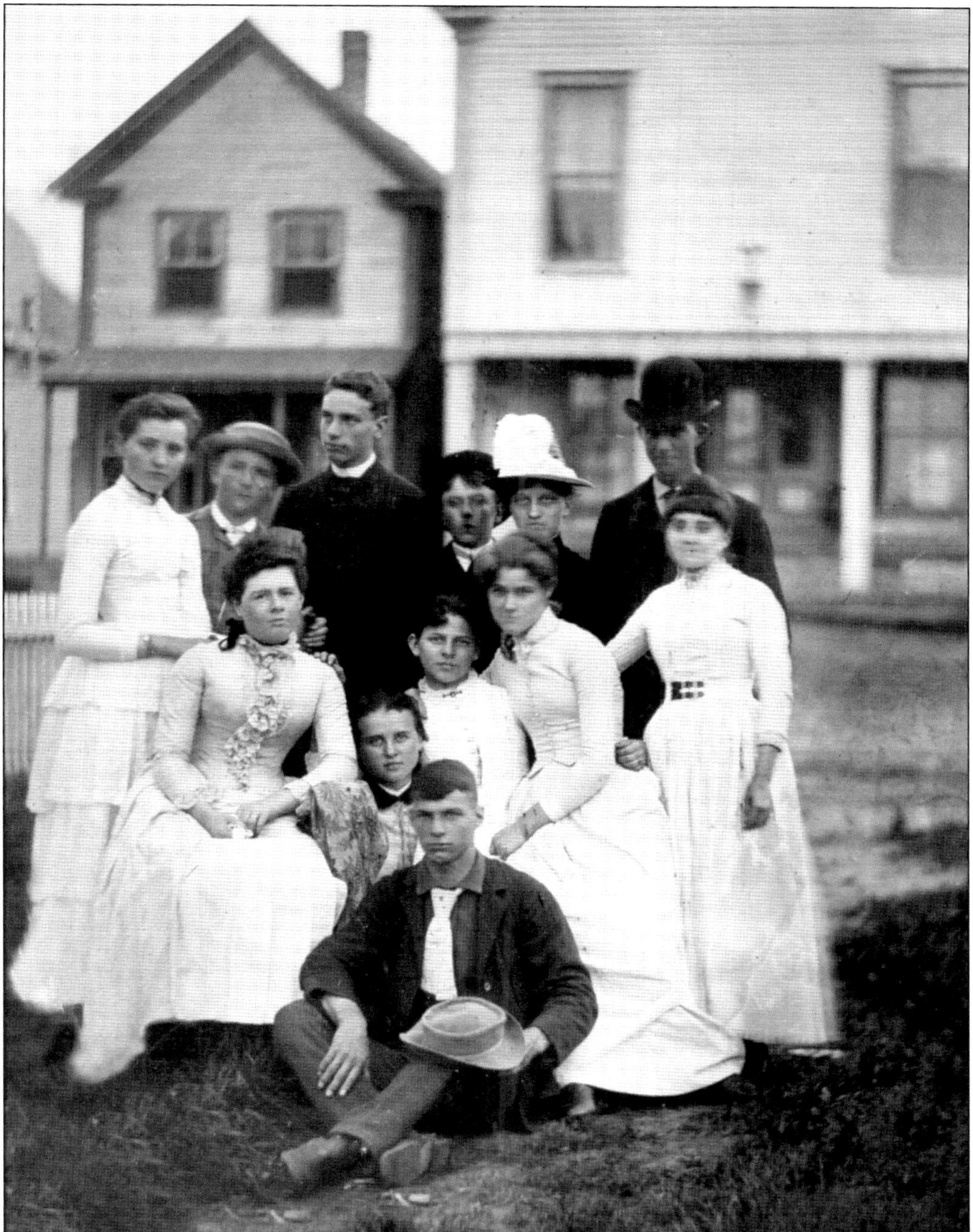

In July 1887, a group of young people has gathered in Dixfield Village for a photograph. Seated in front is E. Grant Harlow. Others pictured are, from left to right, (first row) Netta Marsh, Alfretta Whitman, Susie Stanley, Ione Harlow, and Addie Peck; (second row) Alice Cox, George Smith, Claude Griffith, Eustis (Mace) Greenleaf, Minnie Virgin, and Carroll Ellis. Ione was Grant Harlow's elder sister. He died in 1898, less than six months after his marriage to Caroline Prentice Thayer. (NDM.)

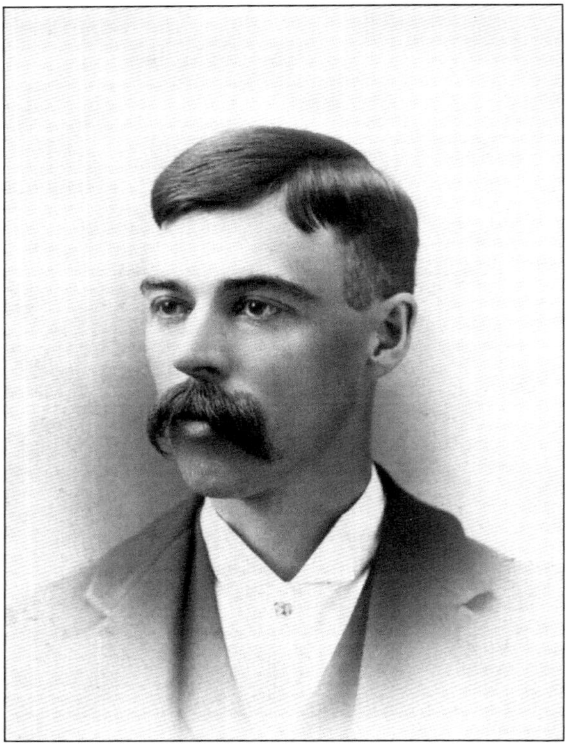

John S. Harlow (1859–1924), son of E.G. and Rosella Harlow, is shown in his graduation picture from law school in Minnesota about 1884. Both his father and mother had died less than two years before. Soon, Harlow would return to Dixfield and begin the practice of law. Opportunities beckoned in the toothpick and spool business and Harlow responded, building his first spool mill in the 1890s. Just a few years later, he was in the toothpick business as well. (ATK.)

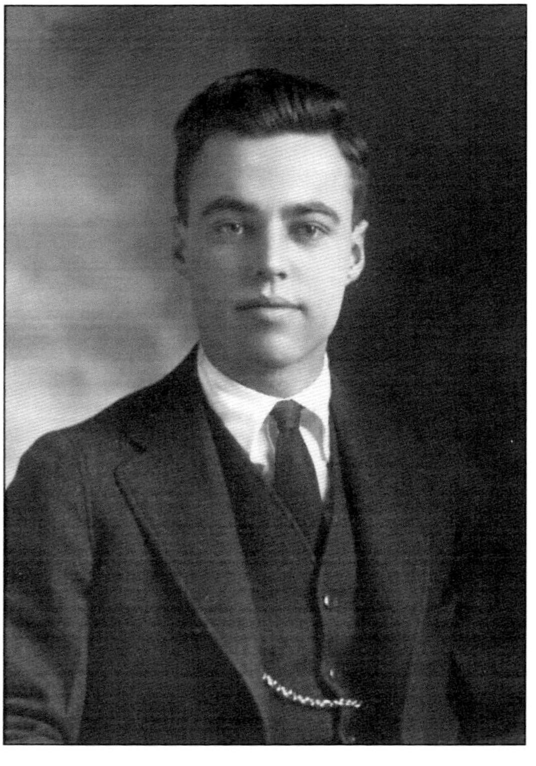

John S. Harlow Jr. (1896–1953) was a 1912 graduate of Dixfield High School, one of only a handful of classes to complete their educations in the new school on High Street before it burned in 1915 after only five years in existence. Harlow disappointed his father with his complete lack of interest in his father's business empire. Instead, he graduated from Harvard Medical School and served in the Ambulance Corps in World War I. (ATK.)

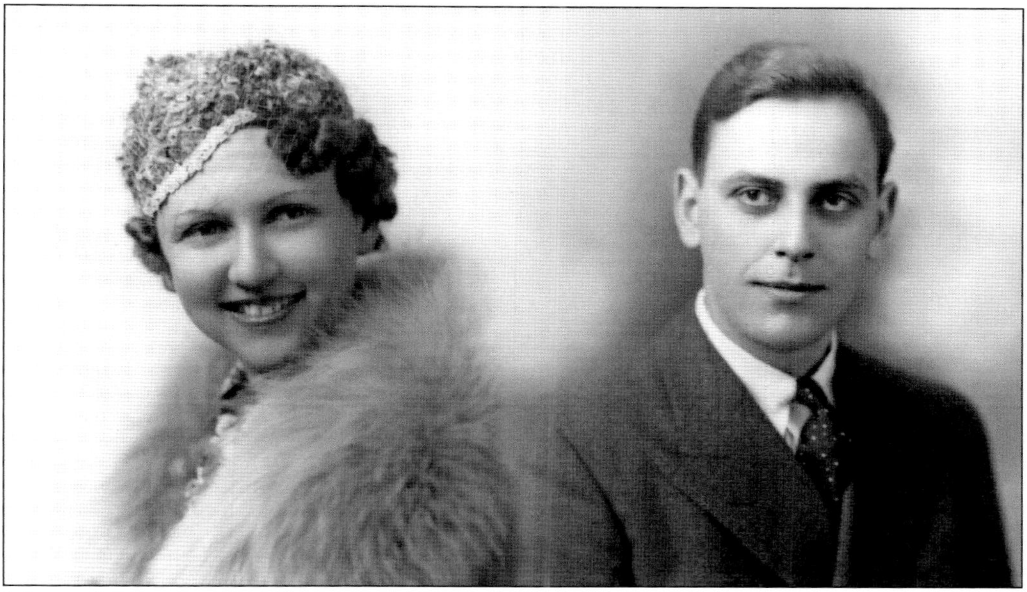

John and Betty Towle took over Towle's Hardware following Charles Towle's retirement. John added several product lines, expanded sales and storage space, and modernized the buildings. The old store was finally razed in 2008, making way for a modern facility. Betty did the bookkeeping, raised the children, and managed the stock on special occasions, such as Christmas. She often drove a truck as far as Lewiston and Portland to pick up supplies. (DCT.)

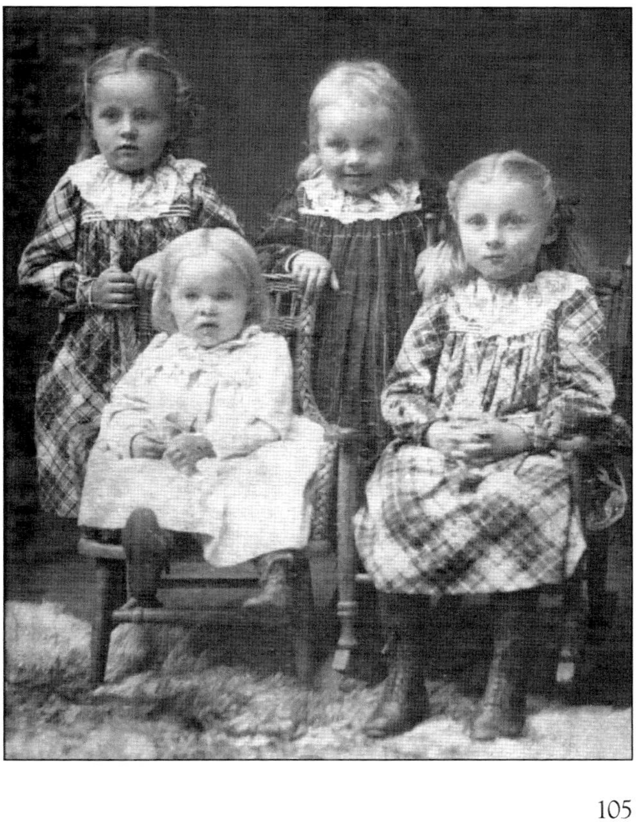

The children pictured here are the grandchildren of Sgt. Henry McIntire of the 1st Maine Cavalry and the children of Ambrose and Flora Knox McIntire. They are, from left to right, (sitting) Verna Ethel McIntire Holt and Charlotte Bailey McIntire Haley; (standing) Mary Ellen McIntire Holman and Bernice May McIntire Davenport. These children and three other siblings grew up on the poor farm but emerged to become the ancestors of many proud Dixfield families. (CC.)

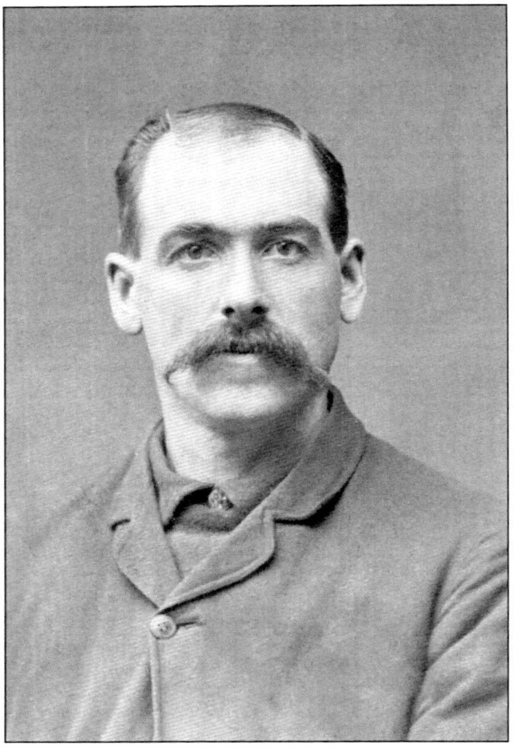

Thaxter P. Houston (1851–1905) was born in Roxbury, Maine, and married Fluella Louise Stockbridge. They lived in Dixfield Village on upper Main Street, neighbors to Joseph P. and Emma Edmunds. Fluella was the daughter of Isaacher and Lydia Newton Stockbridge. Her son Thomas stayed with her after Thaxter died and worked at the N.S. Stowell & Co. spool mill. (MB.)

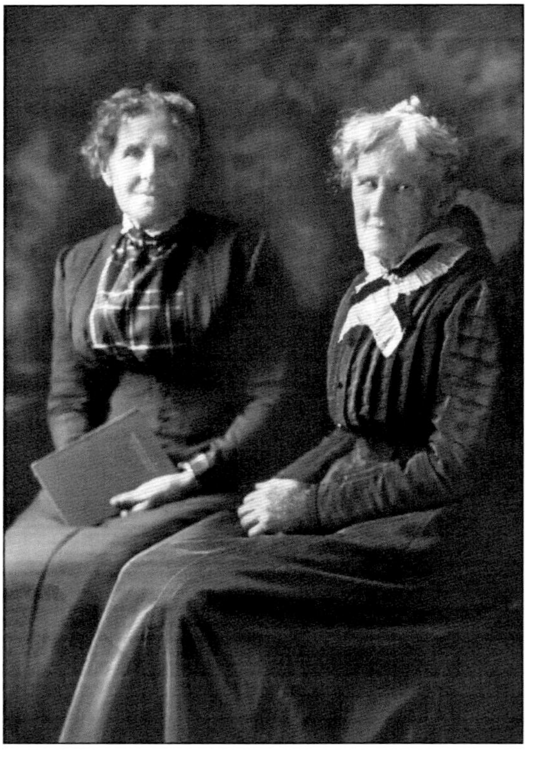

Emily Knight (left) and Delphine Barnard Root were the daughters of Silas and Lucy Barnard. Emily was born on September 12, 1838, in Dixfield; her sister was born June 5, 1833—both births occurring in the 1820 House on Weld Street. Once Dellie's husband, Daniel, left her and Emily's three-year-old son Edwin died, followed by her husband four months later, the sisters shared housekeeping in Dixfield, raising Dellie's son Albert. Dellie died in 1923; Emily died in 1935. (KRG.)

One of the early tavern keepers in the village, Samuel P. Morrill was also a teacher, a minister, and a congressman. For a time, the village school was conducted in his tavern, called Morrill's Tavern and located on upper Main Street next to the opera house. In 1836, he was among a party of men organized to kill a bear wandering through Dixfield Village. (DHS.)

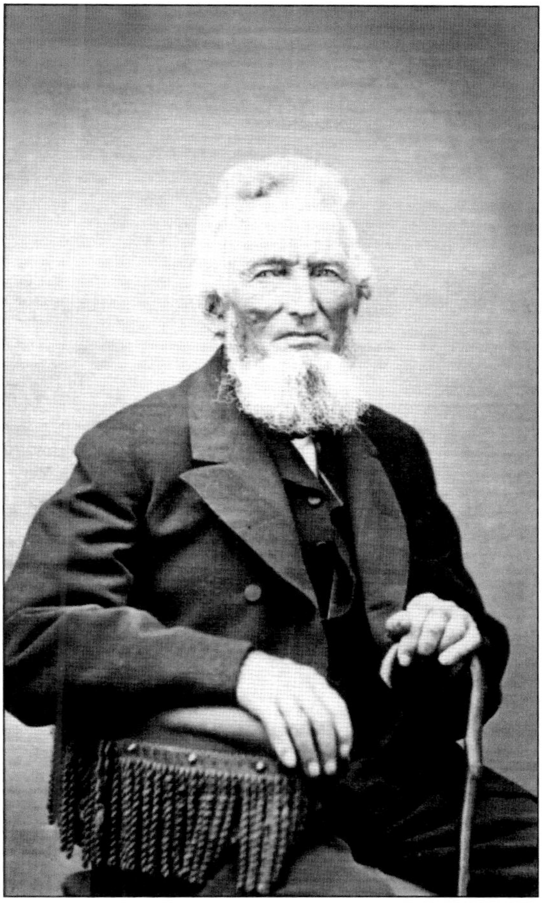

Anna Harlow (1861–1935), a daughter of E.G. and Rosella Harlow, moved with her family from Canton to Dixfield in the early 1860s. She likely attended the red schoolhouse on Weld Street near her home and married George M. Atwood (1860–1948), an ambitious attorney educated at Hebron Academy and Columbia Law School. He became a publisher of the *Oxford Democrat*, county treasurer, and director of the Atwood Grapefruit Company of New York City. (WWE.)

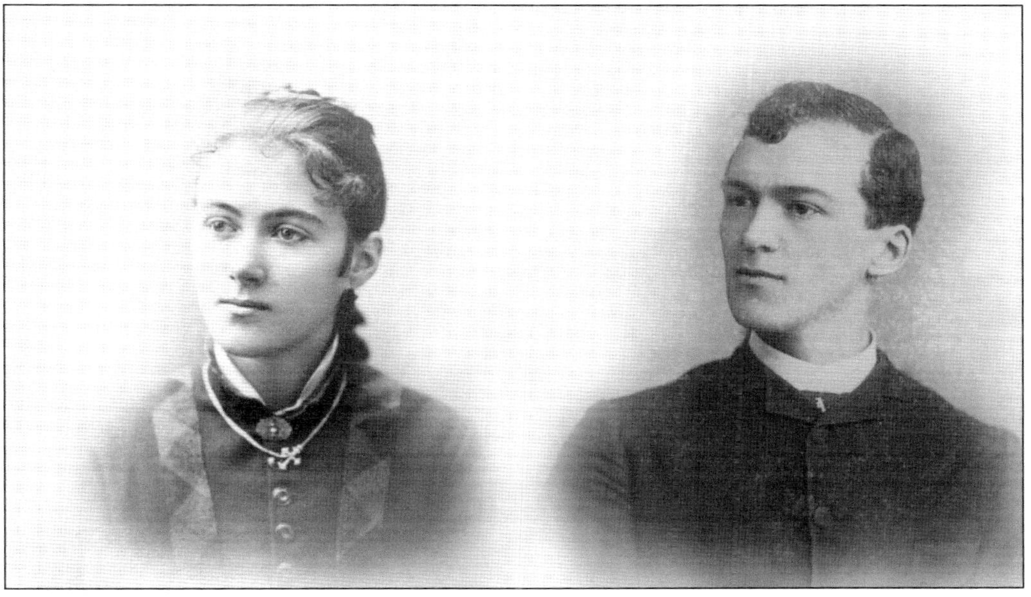

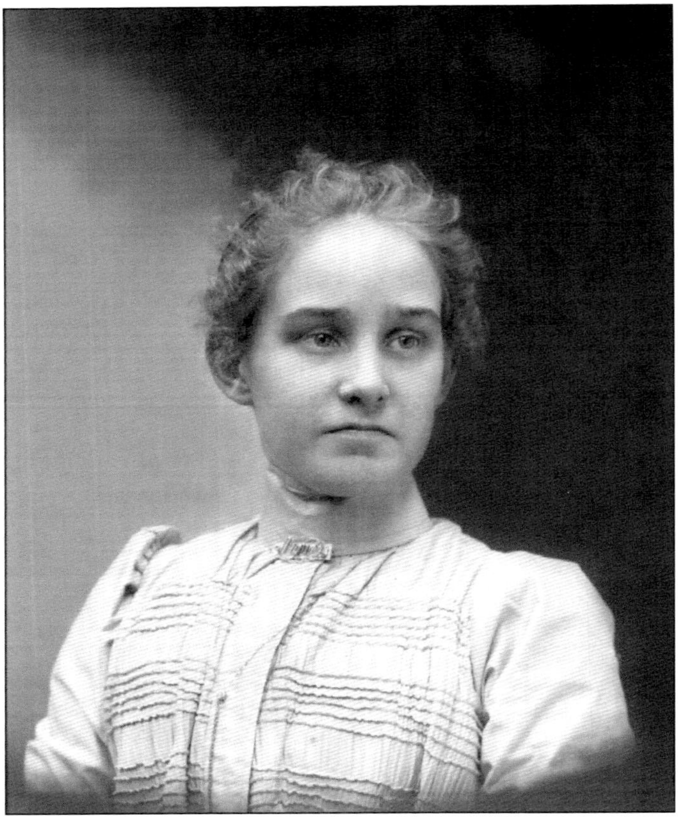

Mamie Holman (1883–1965) was a great-granddaughter of Col. Jonathan Holman and lived on the family farm at Dixfield Common. She married Jesse Adams of Wilton, Maine, and had three children, one of whom died at birth—and legend is the infant was buried in the snow by her father and then reburied in the spring at a location never revealed by the grieving parents. This picture was taken in 1889 when Mamie was only 16 years old. (DHS.)

Mamie and Jesse worked their farm diligently most of their lives. They are shown here in their wagon in 1955 preparing for a trip to the fields to fill the wagon with a load of hay. (LAH.)

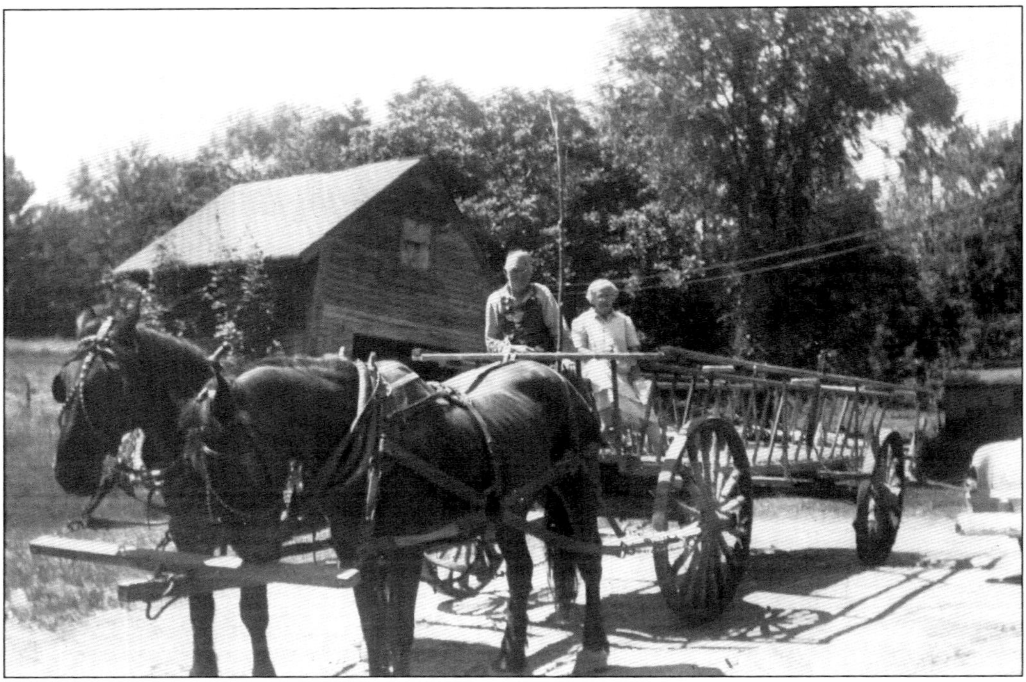

Anne Eustis was the eldest of Col. William Tappan Eustis and Elizabeth Stowell Eustis's two daughters. Anne lost her hearing following a bout with scarlet fever; however, her younger sister Augusta was born deaf. The entire family moved to Portland to take advantage of services for people with hearing problems, moving back to Dixfield after several years. (WWE.)

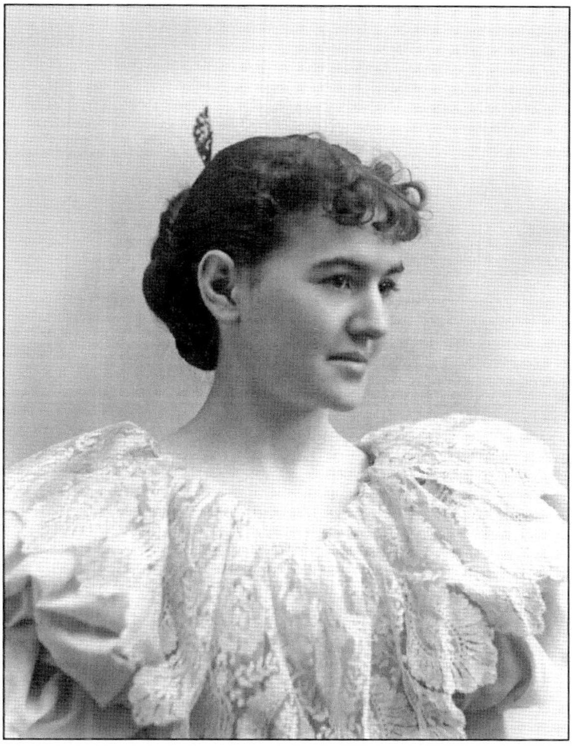

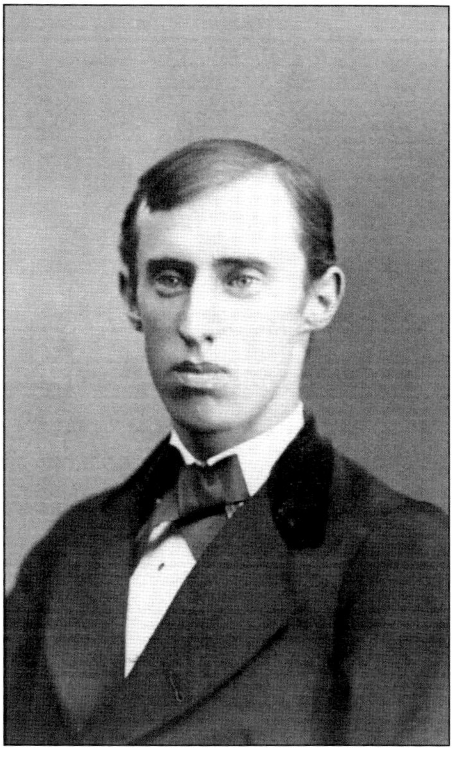

John Rolfe Trask (1853–1935) was the son of Peter Trask of Leavitt Street in Mexico. He enjoyed a long career as an attorney in Dixfield and sold insurance as well. He never married and died tragically in 1935, along with three other Dixfield men, all in their eighties, when the car he was riding in flipped over into Crooked River in Albany, Maine, as the men were on their way to the Waterford World's Fair. (DHS.)

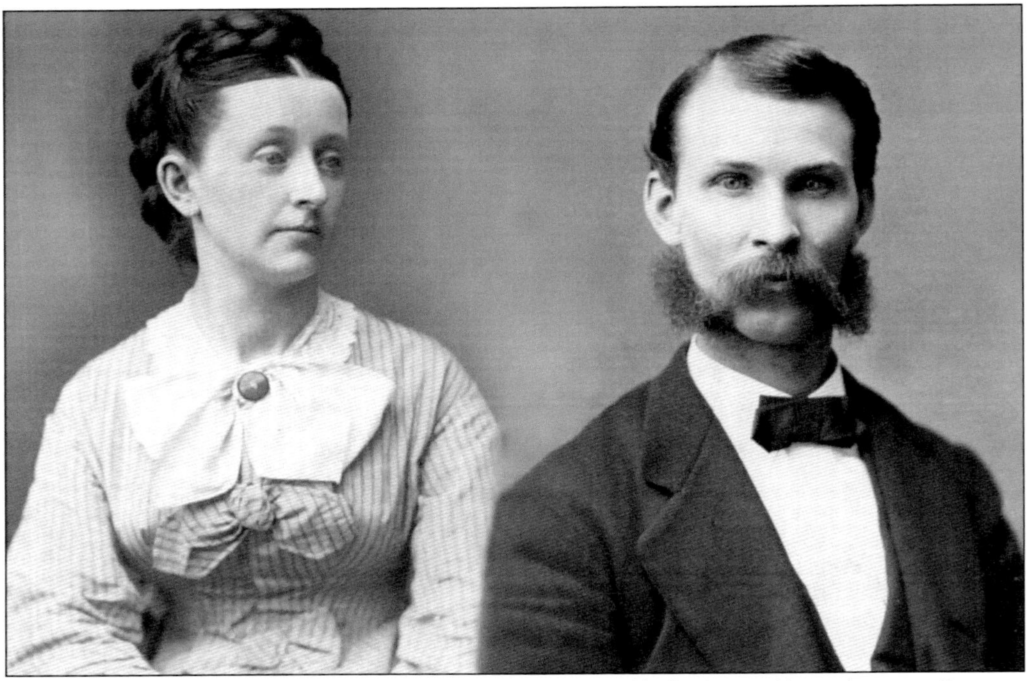

The daughter of Ira and Nancy Reynolds, Mary C. Reynolds (1851–1940) was born in Canton, Maine. She married Dixfield Civil War veteran Frank Stanley (1848–1935) in 1868. They had two daughters, Josephine, who died at 18 months, and Susie, who married Willis Bailey of Winthrop. The Baileys lived on High Street in Dixfield, where Willis continued his jewelry business. Mary Stanley's brother Ephraim Reynolds was a founding partner with Frank Stanley in the Dixfield Spool Mill in 1887. (WWE.)

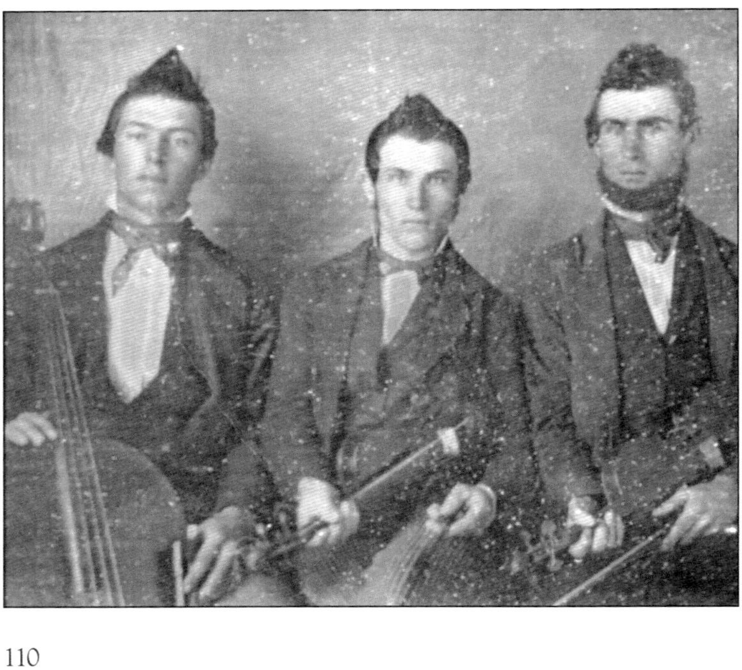

Three Dixfield Village fiddlers are shown together in this c. 1860 image. They are, from left to right, Charles Greenleaf, Walter Scott Chase, and Henry O. Stanley. Music was an important source of entertainment for Dixfield's people. Many bands were formed in Dixfield for marches, parades, dances, and civic functions. James Yeaton played fife while William Brock played the drum to recruit enlistments during the Civil War. (NDM.)

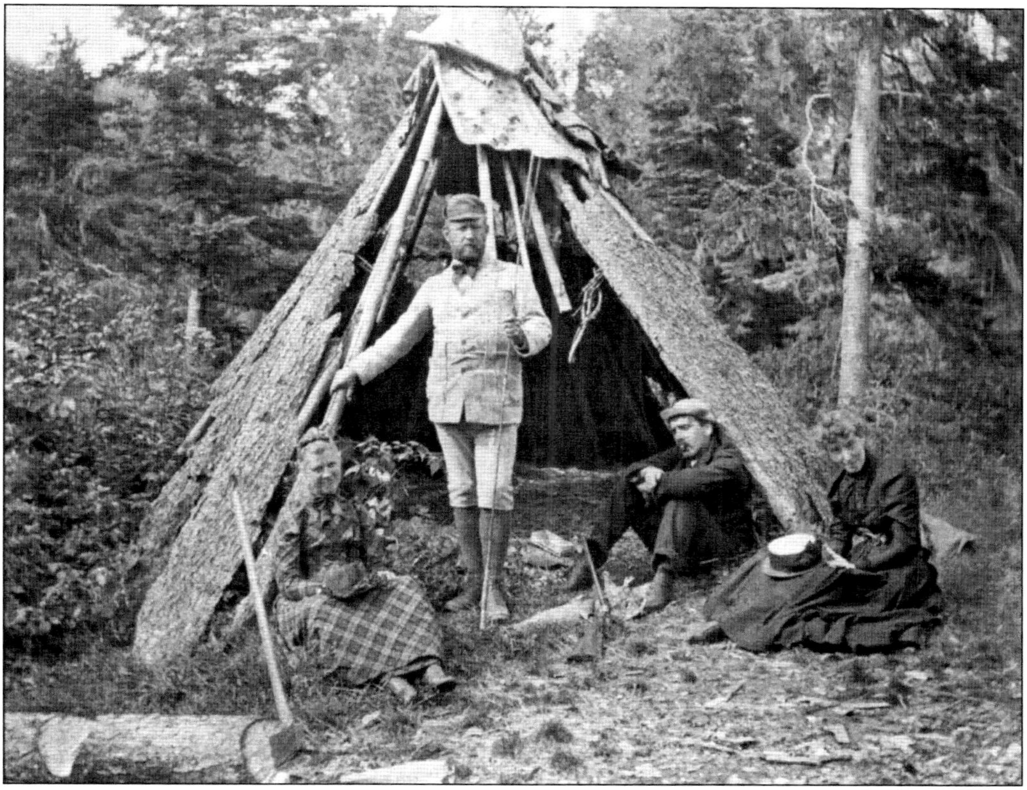

Pictured from left to right, Franklin King Dexter, his wife, Mary Dexter, William Tappan Eustis, and his wife, Elizabeth Eustis, enjoy an outing together. The makeshift nature of the teepee and the relaxed style of dress of the principals suggest that this most likely was a posed picture taken at Lake Webb, where the Dexters had property. (WWE.)

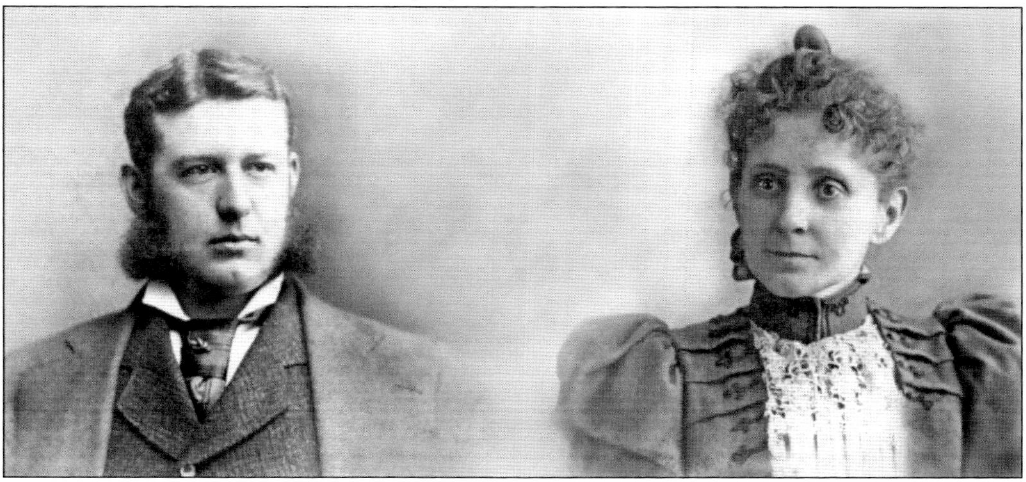

Franklin King Dexter and Mary Stowell Dexter were married on November 18, 1880, and lived in Boston, Massachusetts, and Weld, Maine, near Lake Webb, where they purchased the farm known as Mary Lea. Both the Kings were noted fishermen of their time, earning mention in a fishing magazine of the day. (WWE.)

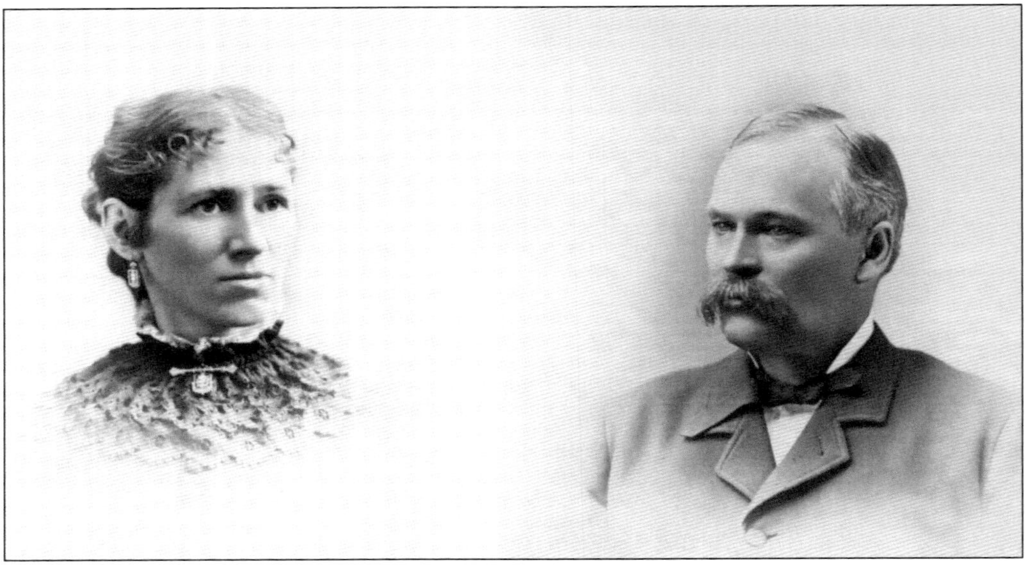

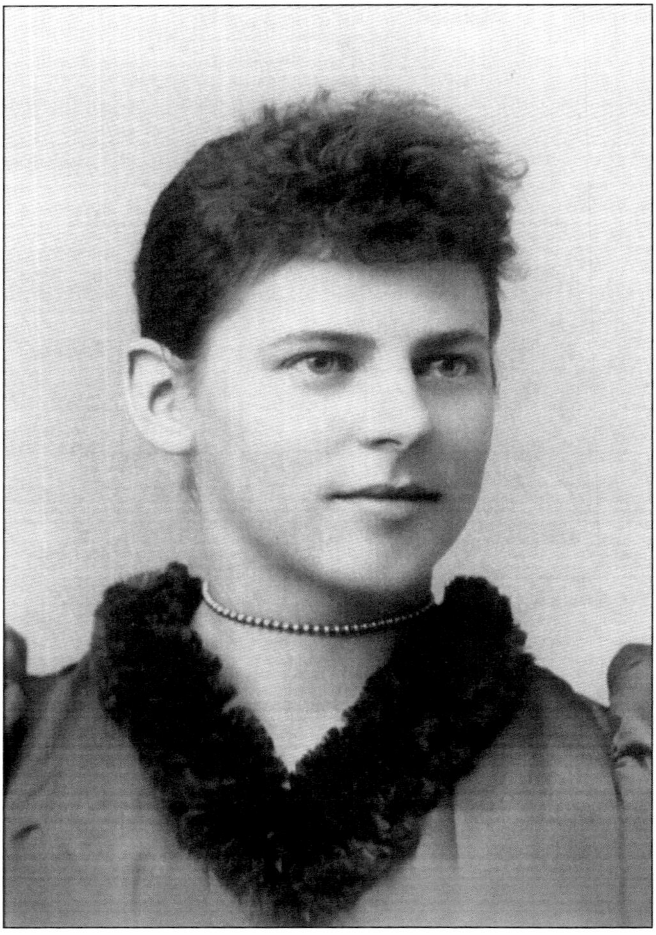

Pictured here are Louisa Ann Stanley (1843–1934), the youngest daughter of Isaac Newton and Susan Trask Stanley, and her husband, Civil War hero George Dana Bisbee (1841–1918). Louise, as she was called, was first married to Ezra Barden. The Bisbees lived at 39 Franklin Street in Rumford, Maine, and were instrumental in forming the local Baptist church. Lieutenant Bisbee was a prisoner of war at the notorious Libby Prison in Richmond, Virginia. Their grandson Col. Spaulding Bisbee worked in the administrations of Maine governors Percival Baxter and Frederick G. Payne. (WWE.)

Susie Stanley (1870–1972) is pictured here, probably when she was a student at the Westbrook Seminary in Portland, Maine. Stanley was the daughter of Frank and Mary Stanley of Dixfield. (WWE.)

This is a picture of Lucie Reynolds, daughter of Ephraim Reynolds and Abigail Edmunds Reynolds. Lucie attended the Dixfield schools and was close to her family. Although she lived in Massachusetts much of her life, she returned to Dixfield for family gatherings. Her father was a founding member of the Dixfield Spool Company in 1887 and moved to Boston with his family in 1896. Her brother Howard was sports editor of the *Boston Post*. (DHS.)

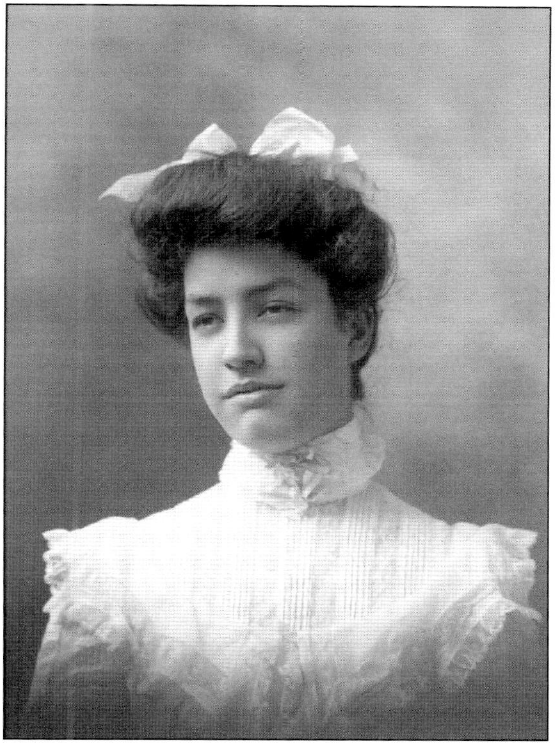

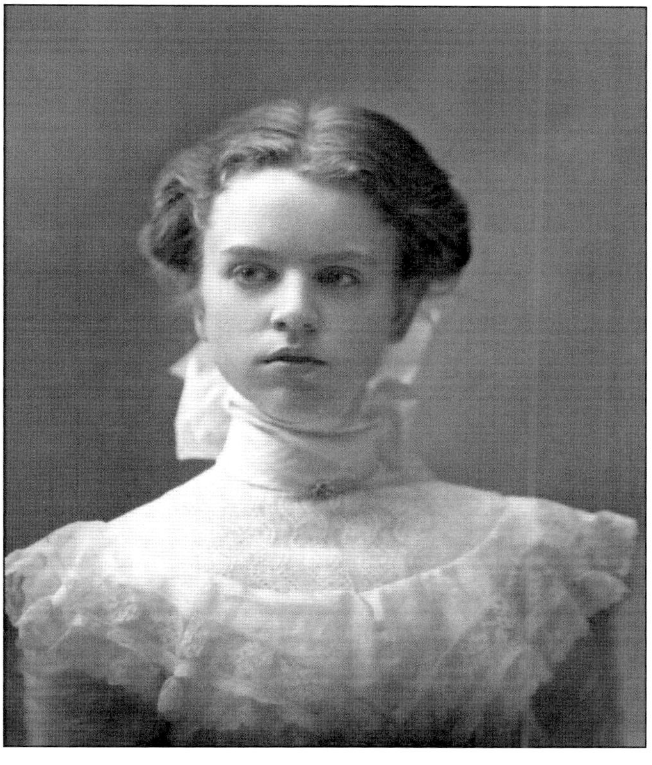

The daughter of Joseph P. and Emma Edmunds, Ina Elteen Edmunds (1885–1943) was born in Dixfield. She attended Grinnell College in Iowa and became director of the YWCA in Detroit, Michigan. Nonetheless, she annually returned to Dixfield, often stopping to visit her aunt Lucy Edmunds Brown, who lived in the upstairs apartment in the Klaus and Melissa Brackett home, which later became the home of the Dixfield Historical Society. Ina was a first cousin to Lucie Reynolds. (WWE.)

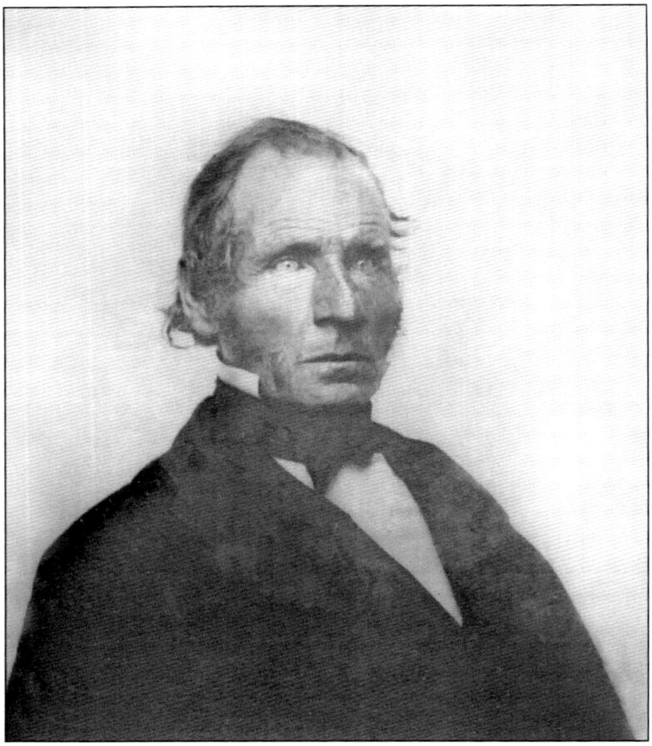

Silas Barnard (1795–1873) came to Dixfield from Massachusetts in 1803 with his parents. At a young age, he built a shingle mill on the Webb River. A veteran of the War of 1812, he also served in the Maine legislature. Maine often called upon his surveying skills to establish town and state boundaries. He worked in northern Maine in the 1830s to help determine the international border with Canada. Later, with his son Albion, he helped lay out the city of Minneapolis, Minnesota. (KRG.)

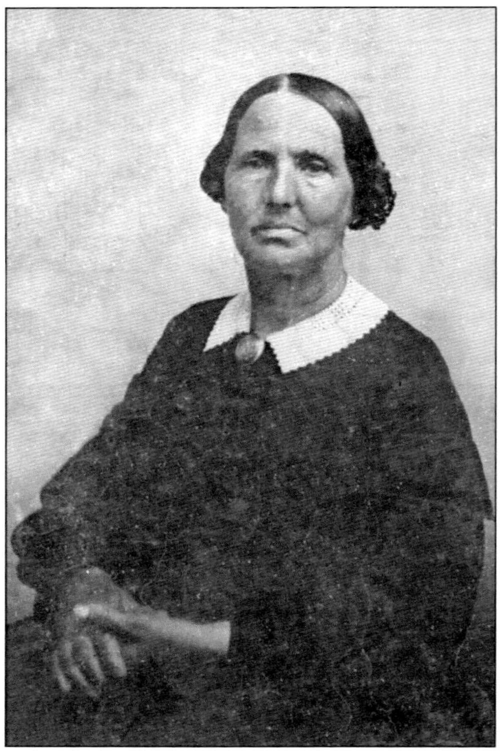

Lucy Trask Barnard (1800–1896) was the eldest daughter of Amos Trask. She married Silas Barnard, who built the first shingle mill on the Webb River in 1810. Known as Aunt Lucy, she was often a midwife, lending assistance. In 1850, she won a prize for her hooked rug, but she could not have foreseen that, years later, her rugs would grace the collections of famous museums. (KRG.)

Samuel Walker of East Dixfield was the grandson of Osgood Walker, the first settler on what was known as Walker Hill. He was the father of Zerua and Myrtie Walker. Zerua married Henry Babb of Dixfield, a lumber dealer, a 75-year member of the Mystic Valley Grange in East Dixfield, and once a member of the Williamson Lodge of the Independent Order of Odd Fellows. Myrtie married Warren Look and then Philetus Torrey. (JMB.)

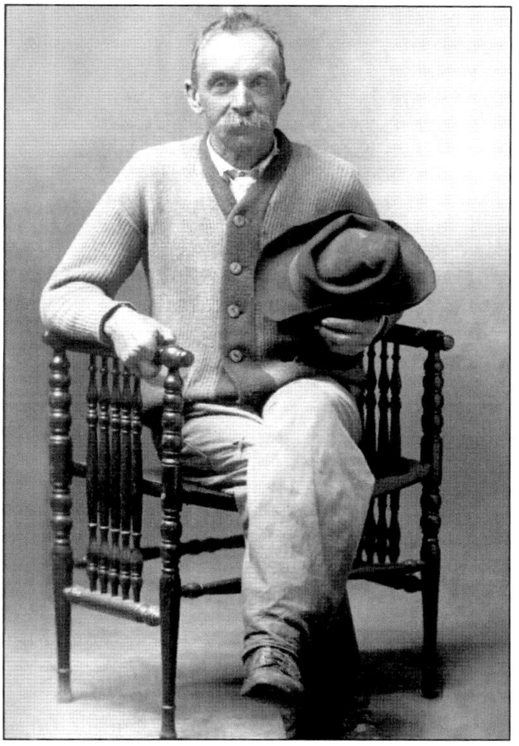

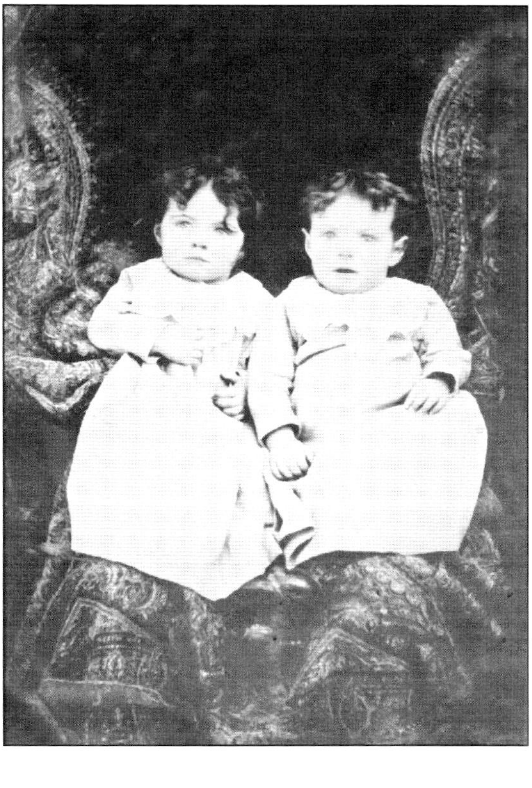

This 1876 photograph shows the youngest two daughters of E.G. and Rosella Harlow, with Ethel Grace on the left and Edith Gertrude on the right. They were born on November 25, 1875. Grace married Clayton Brooks and lived on Paris Hill in South Paris, Maine. Ethel married Frank Owen and lived in Dixfield. (WWE.)

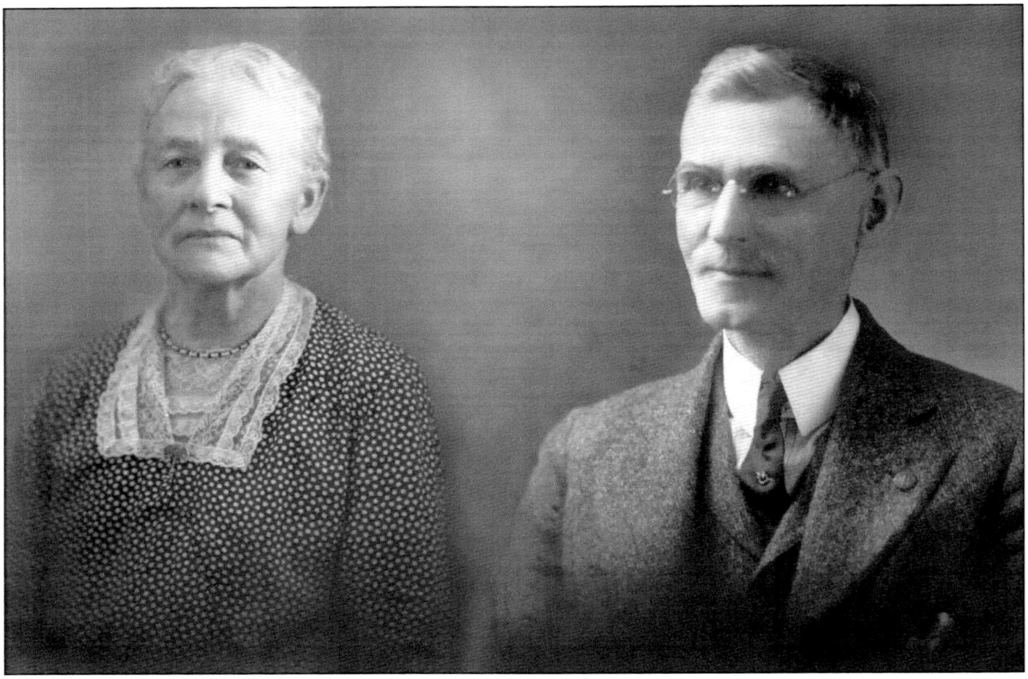

Mary C. Stanley and her husband, Frank Stanley, are shown here in their later years around 1910. Mary was active in civic organizations and women's groups. Civil War veteran Frank was elected to the Maine legislature. As World War I approached, Stanley said, "I was old enough to go to war at 15 years of age, and I am young enough to go again if needed." He was nearly 70 years old. (WWE.)

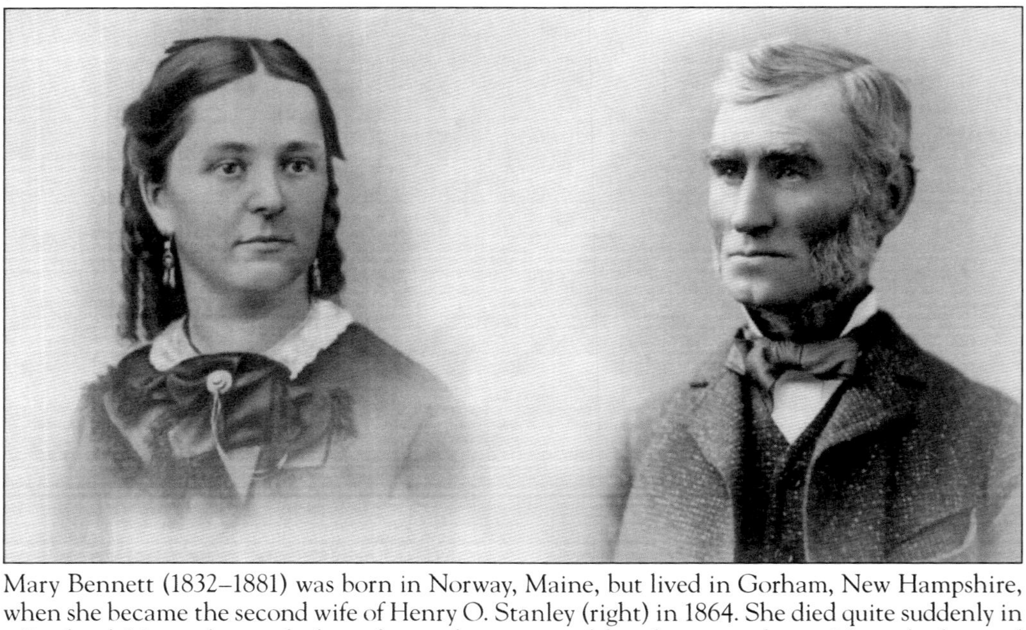

Mary Bennett (1832–1881) was born in Norway, Maine, but lived in Gorham, New Hampshire, when she became the second wife of Henry O. Stanley (right) in 1864. She died quite suddenly in a Portland, Maine, hospital where she was being treated for a heart condition. Henry had visited her the day before but was in Wiscasset, Maine, on business when she died. (NDM.)

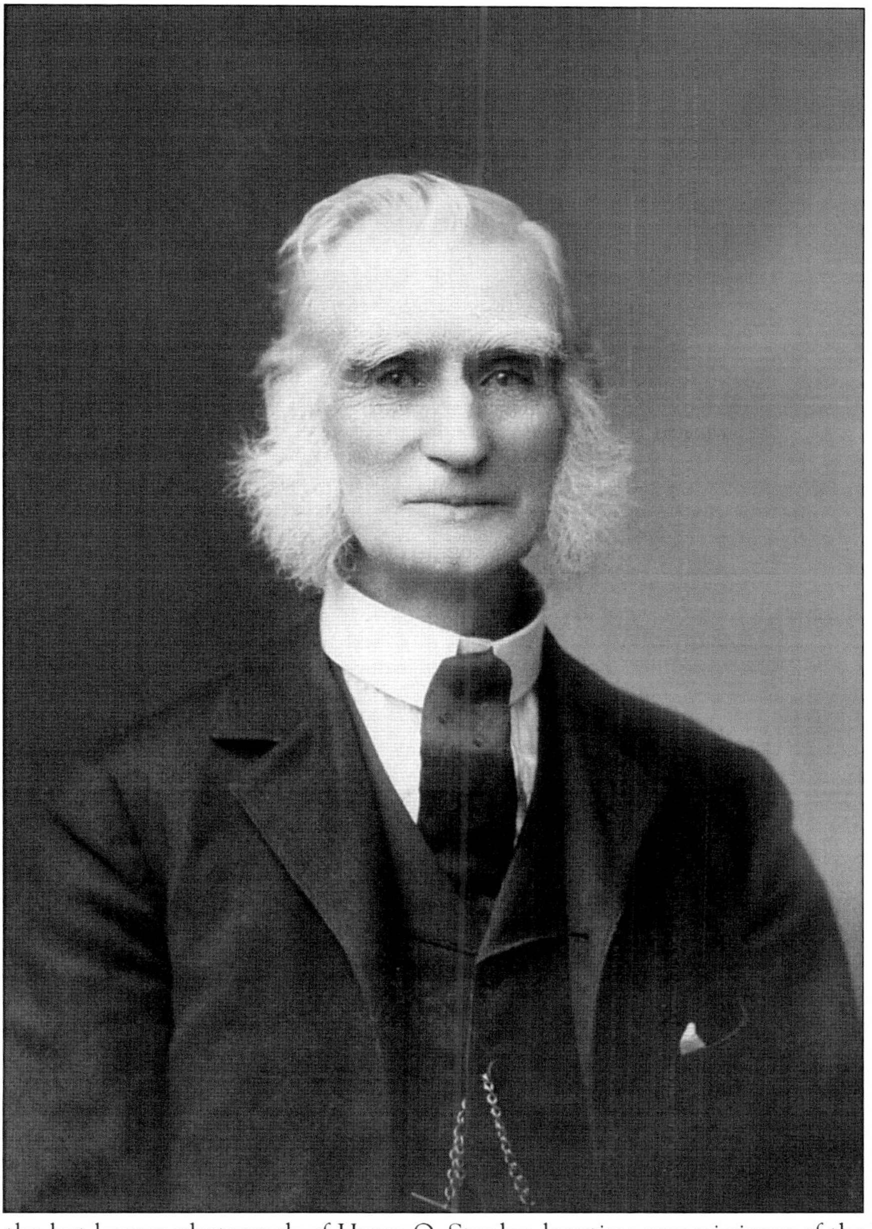

This is the last known photograph of Henry O. Stanley, longtime commissioner of the Maine fisheries and game department. At one time, he was a brigadier general in the state militia. He was a fiddler, as his father and grandfather had been before him. Henry O. built one of the first fish hatcheries in Maine in the neighboring town of Mexico, Maine. Widowed for the second time at age 52, he never again married. First appointed a commissioner by Gov. Sidney Perham, Stanley served more than 30 years in that capacity. In 1885, he constructed a cottage on Lake Webb for use by the East Oxford Angling Association and began keeping a register of visitors. Gov. Sebastian S. Marble was among them, as were his fellow commissioners from as far away as Bangor, Maine. Henry O. operated a sporting goods store in the 1890s and sold fishing tackle that bore his name as the inventor. He also sold bicycles there. (NDM.)

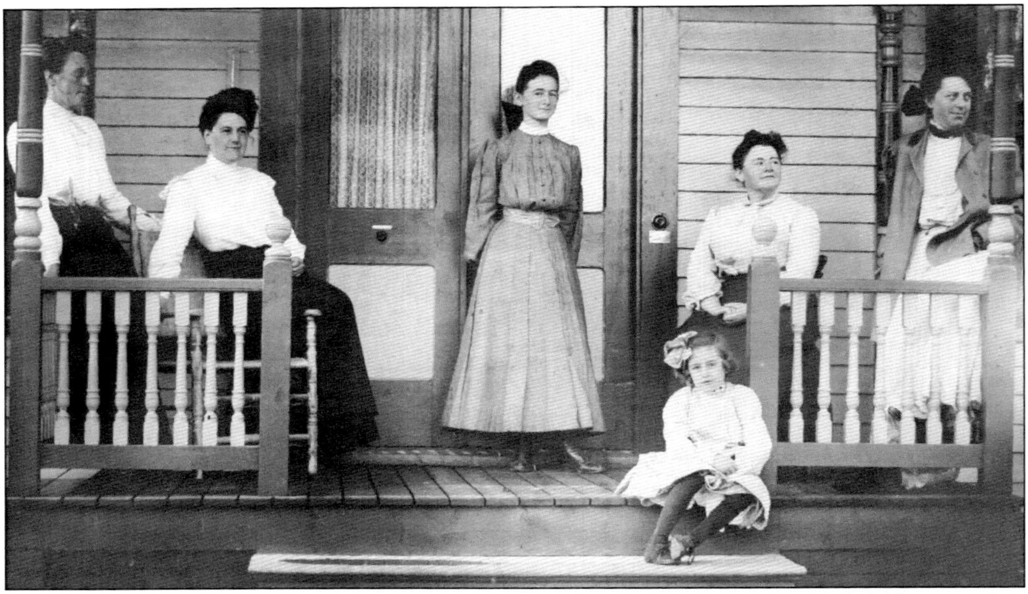

This 1907 photograph shows several women socializing on the porch of a Dixfield home. They are, from left to right, Gertrude Ladd; Alice Keith; 16-year-old Josie Stanley; her mother, Netta Stanley; and Sadie Ladd, Gertrude's sister. Seated on the steps is Thelma Keith, daughter of Alice Marsh and Maurice Keith. (NDM.)

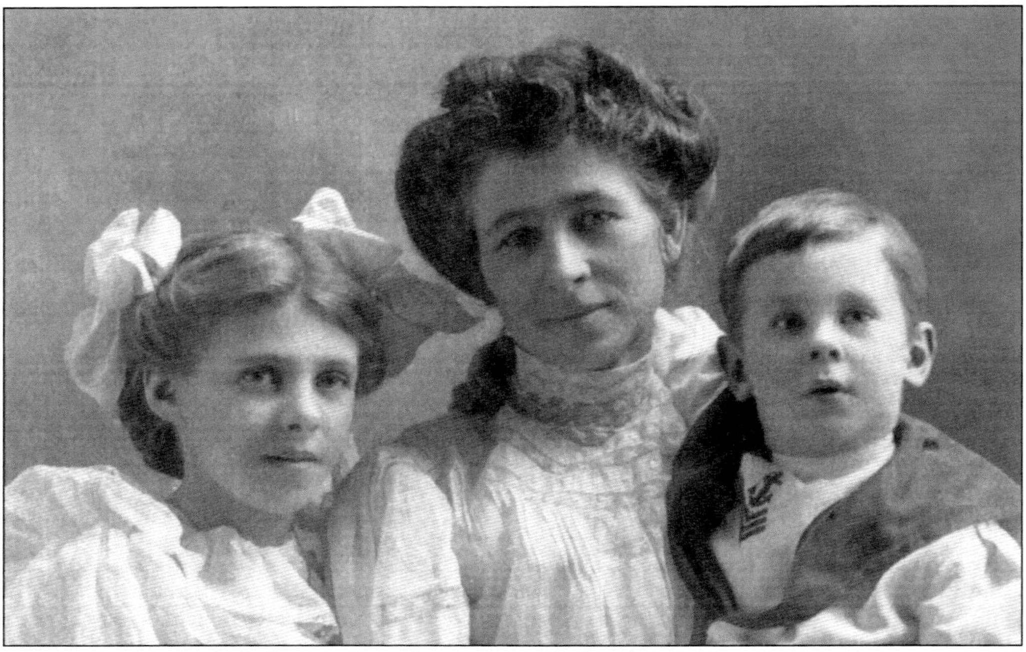

Nellie Stanley Kimball (born in 1865) was the only daughter of Henry O. and Mary Stanley. She married Reuben "Dick" Kimball and lived in Dorchester, Massachusetts, much of her life, returning often to the Dixfield area. Locals remember her in her eighties, climbing up a ladder to shingle the roof of her cottage on Lake Webb. She is shown here with her children Mary and Stanley. (NDM.)

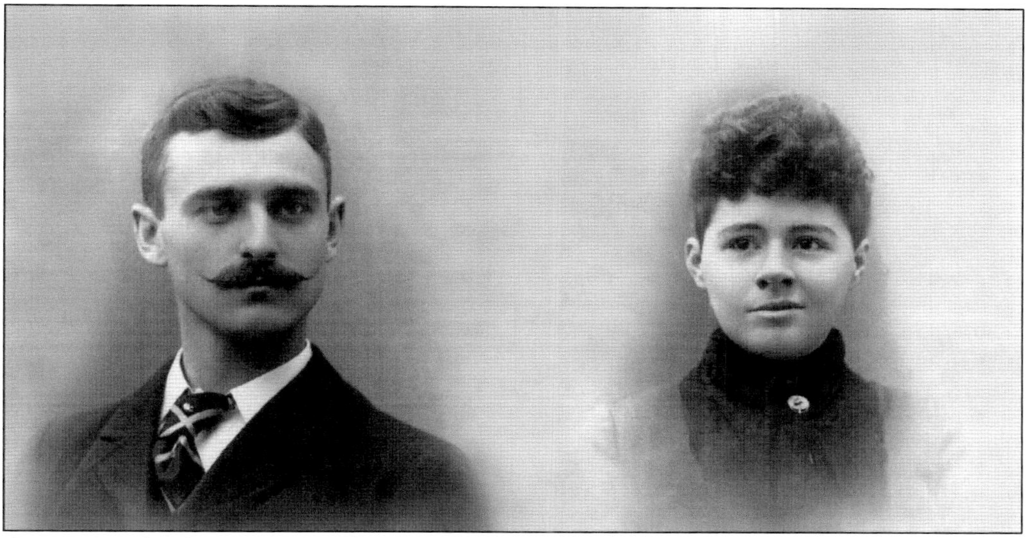

George Stanley (1869–1955) and his wife, Netta Louise Marsh (1870–1969), lived in Dixfield their entire married lives. Upon his death, Netta wrote, "On June 4th, 1955, George Page Stanley passed on to a higher life—a loving husband and father and a true friend to all who knew him. He gave so much and asked for so little. He loved all nature and through that love was very close to God. By his loving wife, Netta L. Stanley." (NDM.)

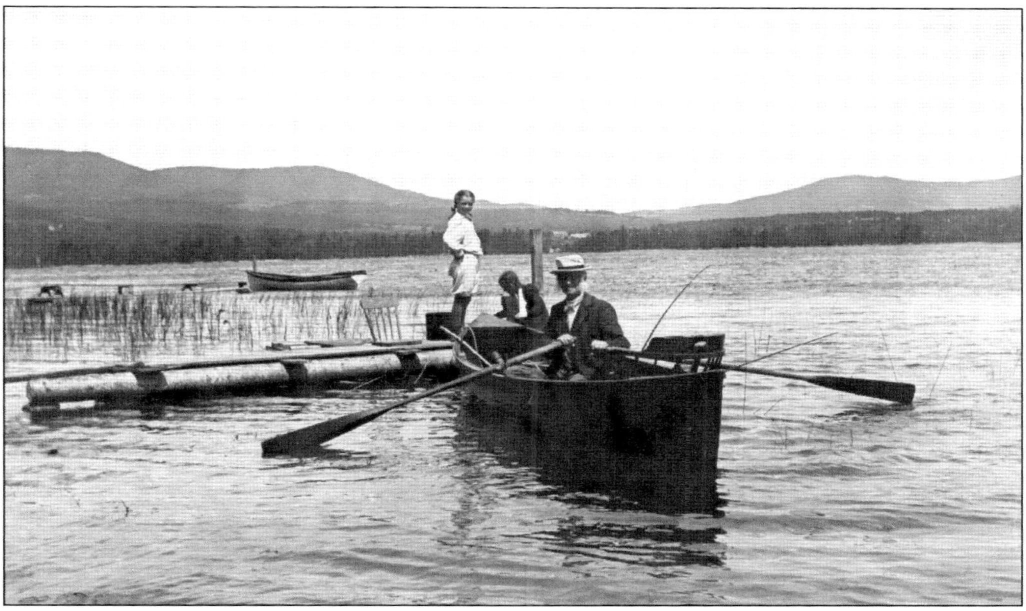

Taken in the 1890s at Lake Webb, this photograph shows fisheries commissioner Henry O. Stanley fishing in the lake with two young friends Edith Younkin (standing) and his granddaughter Josie Stanley. Beginning in the 1880s, many Dixfield residents built family cottages on the lakeshore. Many of them remain with the original families. (NDM.)

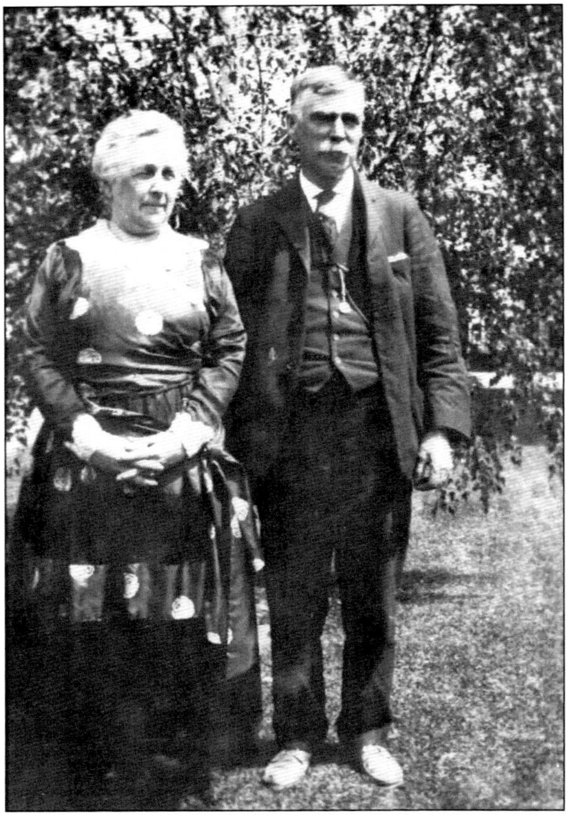

John S. Harlow and his wife, Agnes Doe Harlow, are shown in this c. 1920 picture. Harlow was instrumental in forming the Berst-Forster-Dixfield Corporation, which consolidated the operations of Dixfield's toothpick mills with mills in Minnesota. Later, the company headquarters was moved to Oakland, Maine. (ATK.)

This is a rare portrait of the four children of John S. and Agnes Doe Harlow taken in Dixfield around 1906. The children are, from left to right, Roselle, Marion, Kermit, and John Jr. Roselle married Carroll Marble of Dixfield, while Marion married Earle Tribou. Kermit died at age 15, and John served in World War I and became a medical doctor. (ATK.)

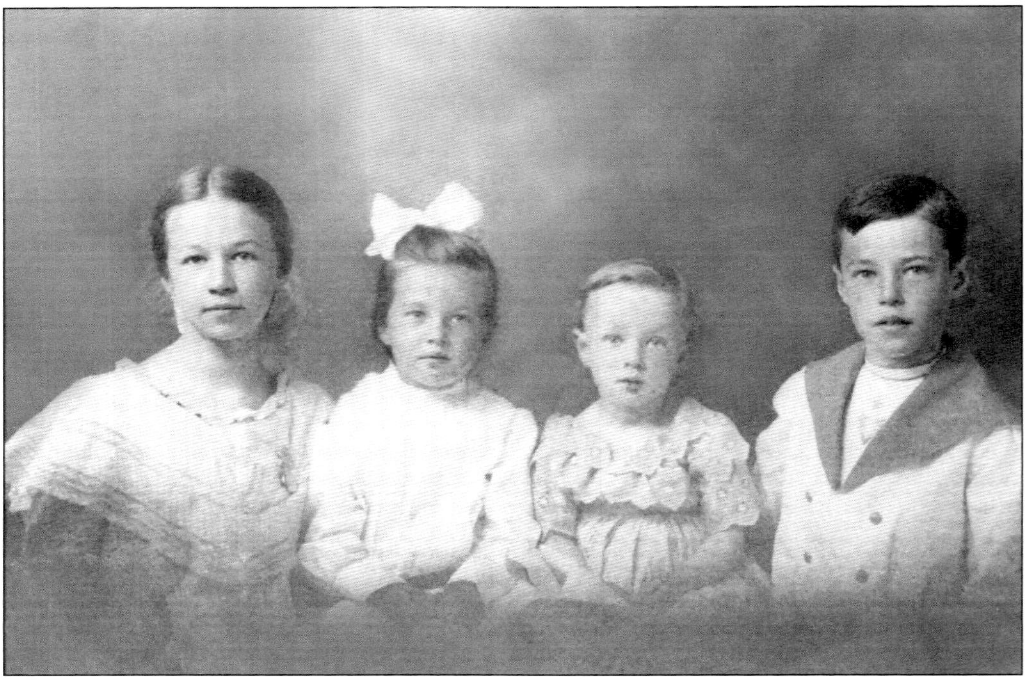

Clara Stetson (1909–2008), the daughter of Elisha and Lucy Stetson, graduated from Dixfield High School in 1926 and then married Raymond Howard. For many years, they operated Howard's Store in the Hotel Stanley, where they sold dry goods and furnishings. (DHS.)

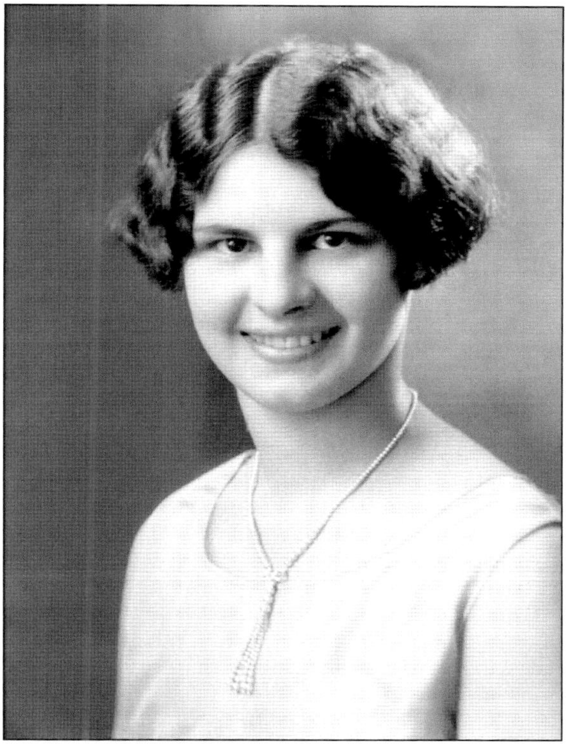

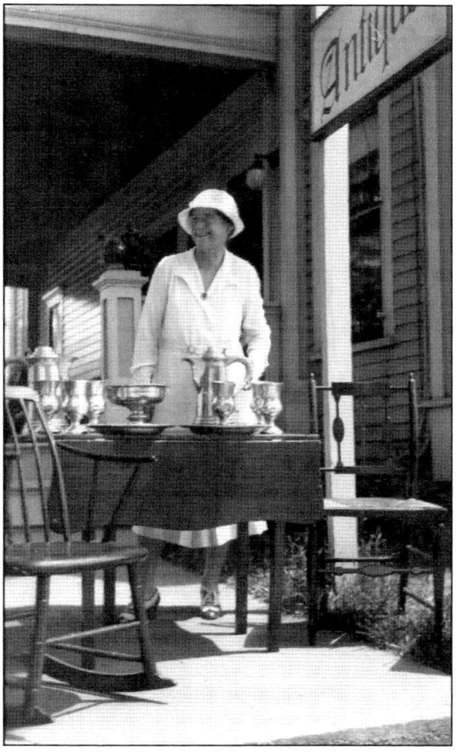

Ione Harlow is shown here at her antiques shop at the rear of the Ione Harlow Building at the corner of Main and Weld Streets. She quietly amassed a fortune during her lifetime, leaving much of it to the citizens of Dixfield. (ATK.)

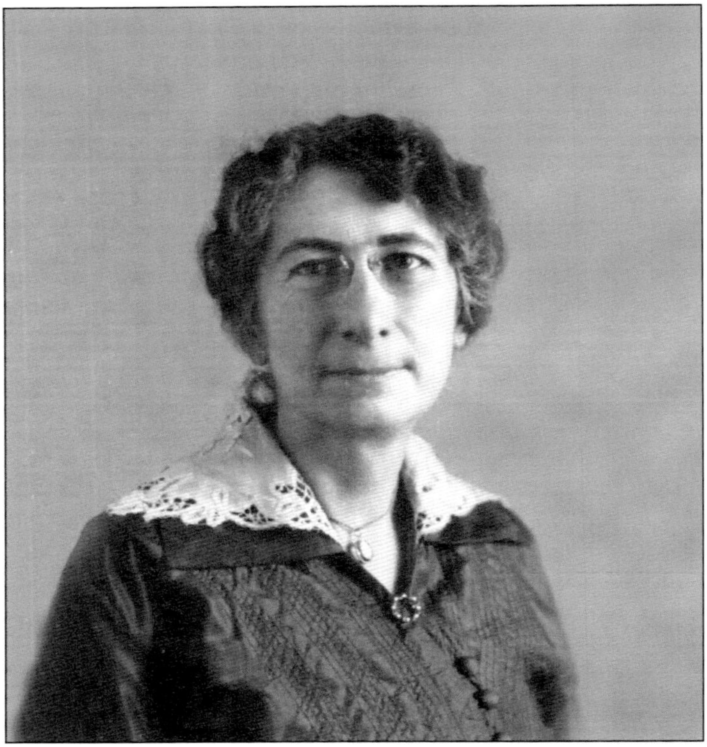

Anna May Mitchell was born in Dixfield in 1862. She was the daughter of Sarah Eustis and William Wallace Mitchell. She married the Rev. Cyrus Lorenzo Dow Younkin of Boston, who was a social reformer and ran a home for children. They had two children—Edith Younkin, who visited her Dixfield relatives often, and Kenneth, who died quite young. (WWE.)

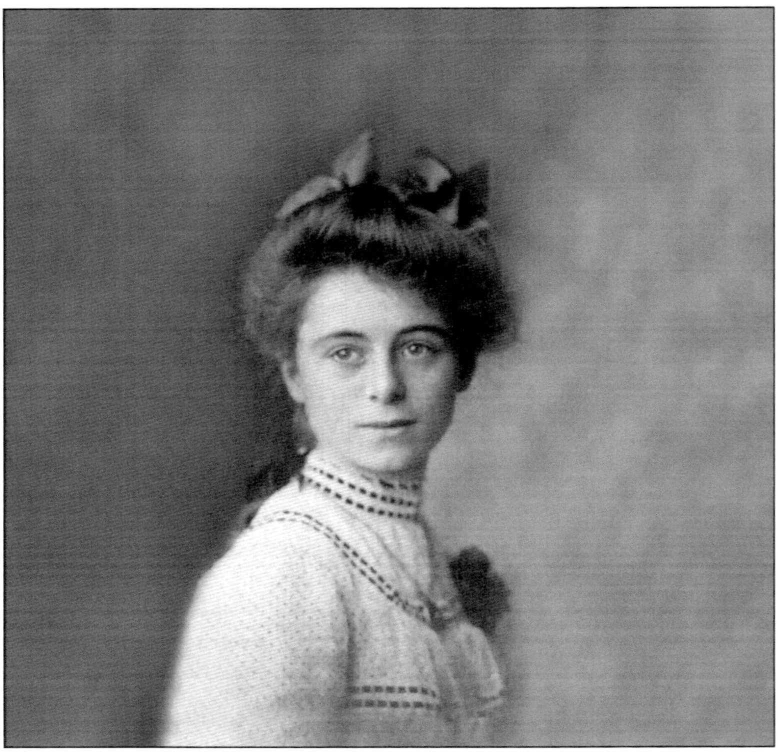

Edith Younkin was the only surviving child of the Rev. C.L.D. Younkin and Anna Mitchell. She lived in Boston first and then Iowa but returned to Dixfield in the summers to spend time at Lake Webb with the Roots, Mitchells, and the Stanleys. (WWE.)

Ebridge Gerry Harlow is pictured here in the prime of his life about 1870. At one time, he represented Dixfield in the Maine legislature, served on the governor's executive council, and served as a special commissioner on prison reform in 1870. He also taught high school in Dixfield. (ATK.)

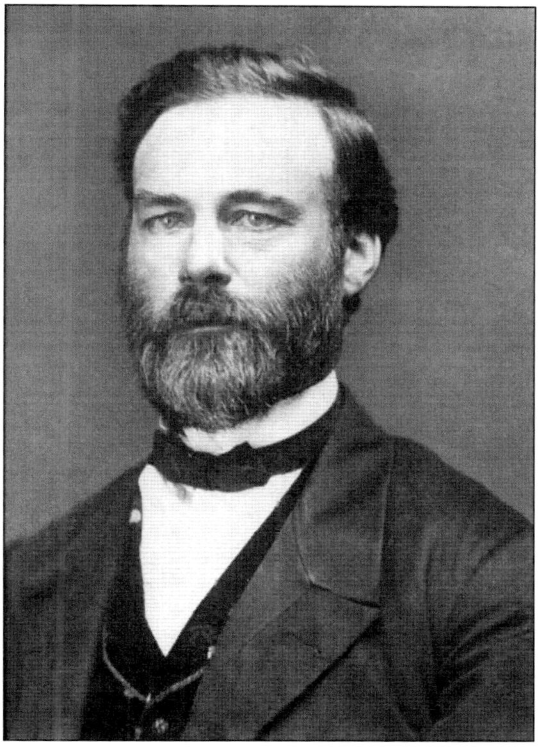

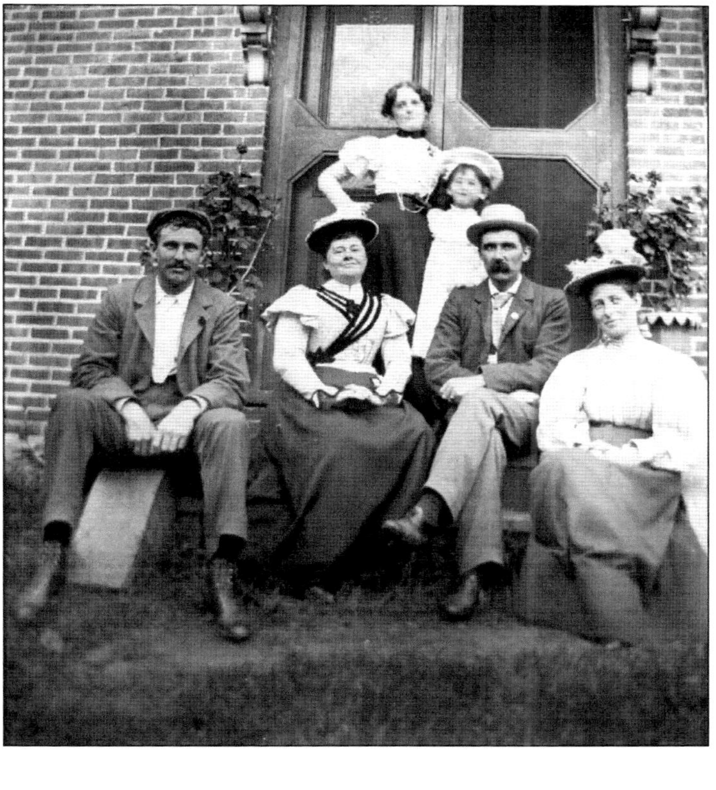

This picture shows a family gathering on Main Street in Dixfield at the George Marsh home. Shown are, from left to right, (first row) Reuben Kimball, Netta Stanley, Maurice Keith, and Nellie Kimball; (second row) Josie Walters and Josie Stanley. (NDM.)

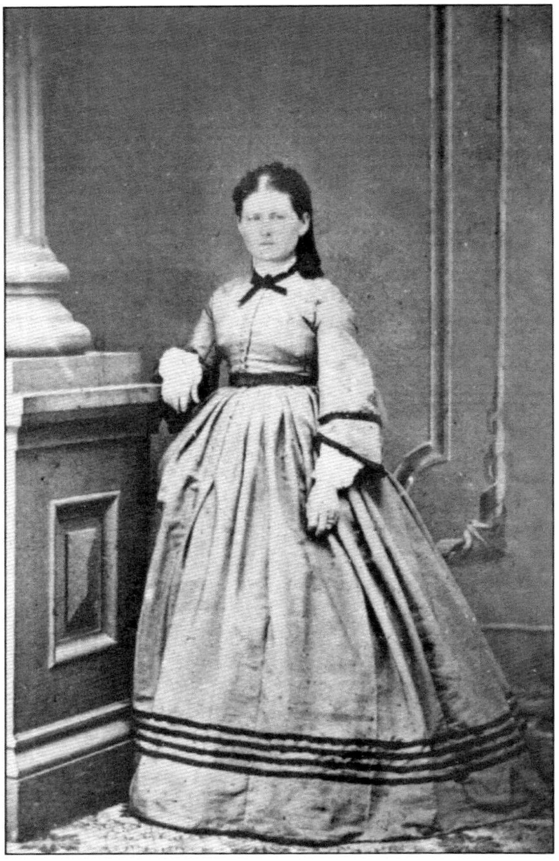

Taken in the 1850s, this is the earliest known photograph of Susan Trask Stanley, wife of early Dixfield settler Isaac Newton Stanley and mother of seven children. Three of her four daughters—Sophronia, Rosella, and Anna Louisa—married attorneys; the fourth, Mary, died at age three. Her three sons—Henry O., John, and Frank—all contributed to developing Dixfield's manufacturing and economic base. (WWE.)

John Hosley and his wife, Lucinda, were both born about 1815. They are shown in photographs taken in the 1870s. Their daughter Olive married Milan Morrison from Alstead, New Hampshire, who became the ancestors of the Dixfield Morrisons, including the founders of Morrison Motors. (JMB.)

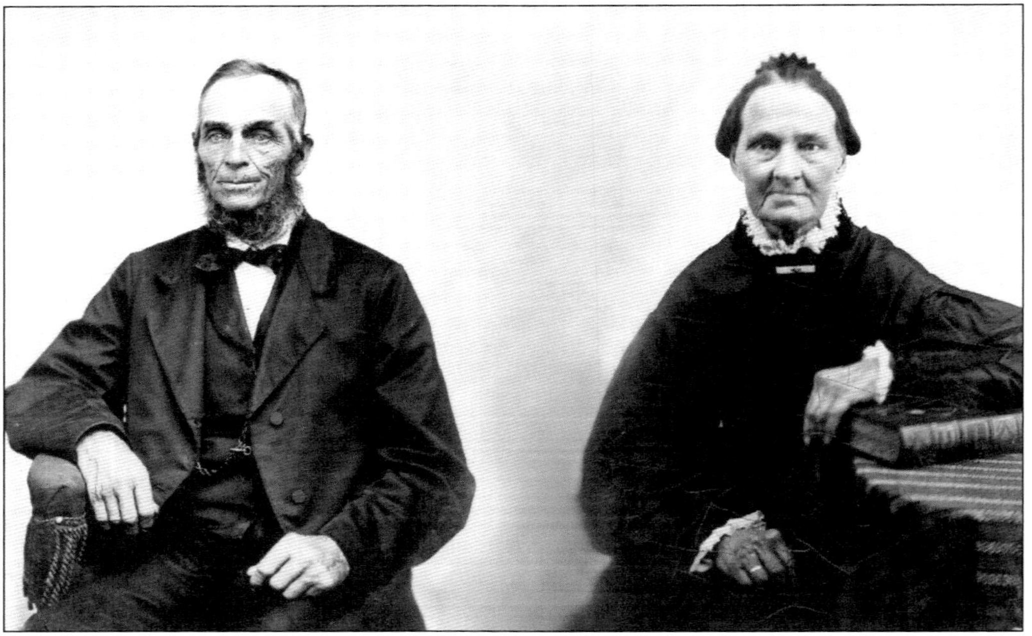

James P. Johnston was a druggist for many years, having a store on Dixfield's Main Street. In the 1890s, he began to take orders for photographic prints from glass-plate negatives. Several decades later, many of these negatives were preserved by Dale R. Harris of Dixfield, who bought them at auction in the 1960s. In 1903, Guy O. Gardner, another Dixfield druggist, moved to Dixfield and worked in Johnston's drugstore. (DHS.)

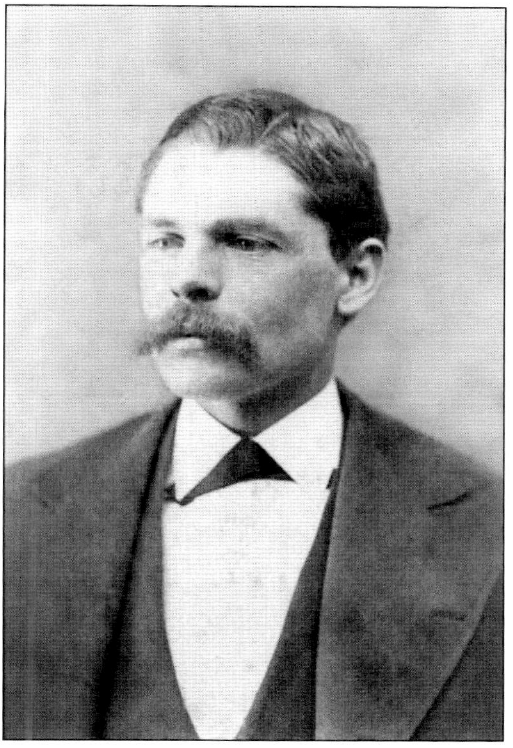

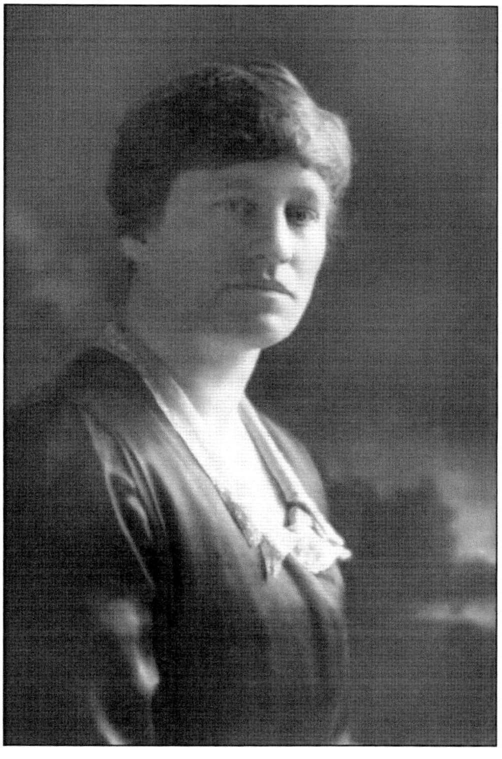

Lelia Randall Forster (died 1928) was a direct descendant of Dixfield Village founder Amos Trask and a granddaughter of attorney Isaac Randall. She married Maurice Forster, the toothpick mill partner of John S. Harlow. When both Harlow and Forster died in 1924, Lelia inherited much of the Forster estate. Alas, her time to enjoy it was brief as she survived her husband by only four years. (DHS.)

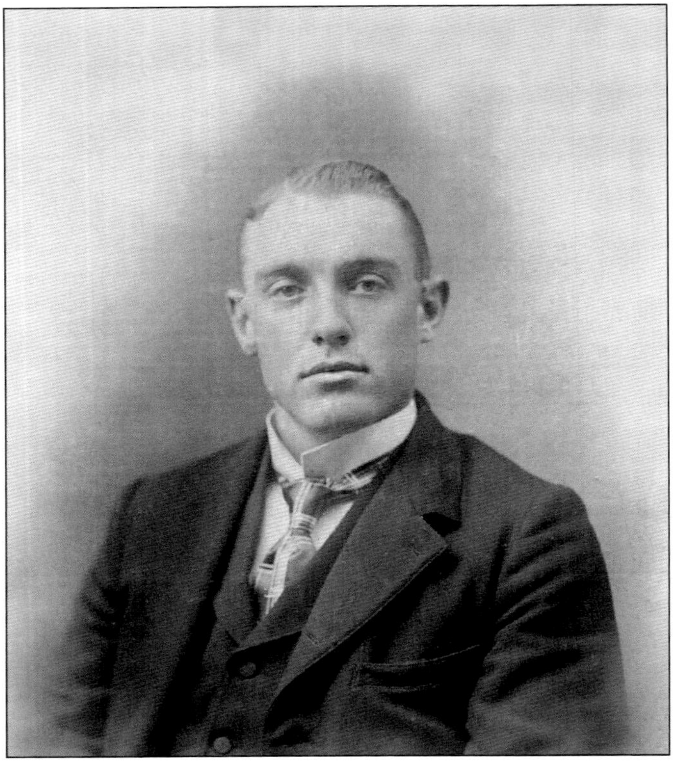

Olie Payne served the town of Dixfield for 50 years in the fire department, attaining the rank of captain and receiving a 50-year pin in recognition of his achievement. His wife, Mae Fogg Payne, was an ardent photographer and took hundreds of snapshots, preserving a glimpse of the way things were back in the 1920s and 1930s. (DHS.)

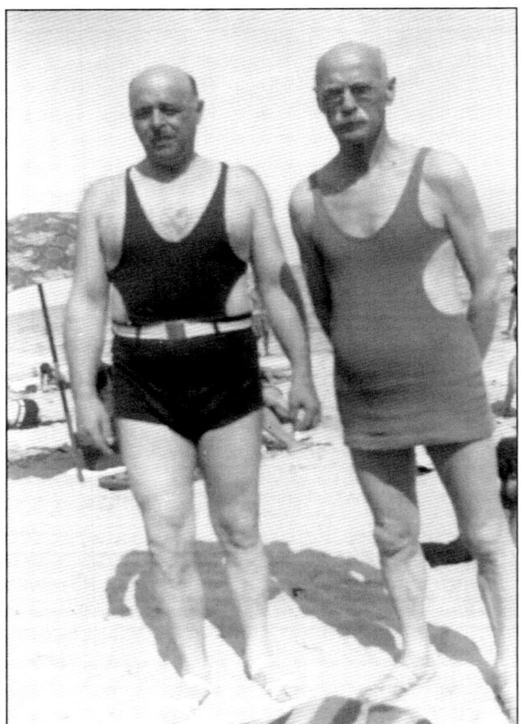

Shown here in the swimming attire of the day are the son-and-father team of Hamilton Harlow (left) and Frank S. Harlow (1865–1965), who, at one time, was the law partner of his brother attorney John S. Harlow in Dixfield. Hamilton was an architect in Cambridge, Massachusetts, and received the Navy Cross in World War I for his 1917 action in boarding a torpedoed steamship and bringing it safely into port. (ATK.)

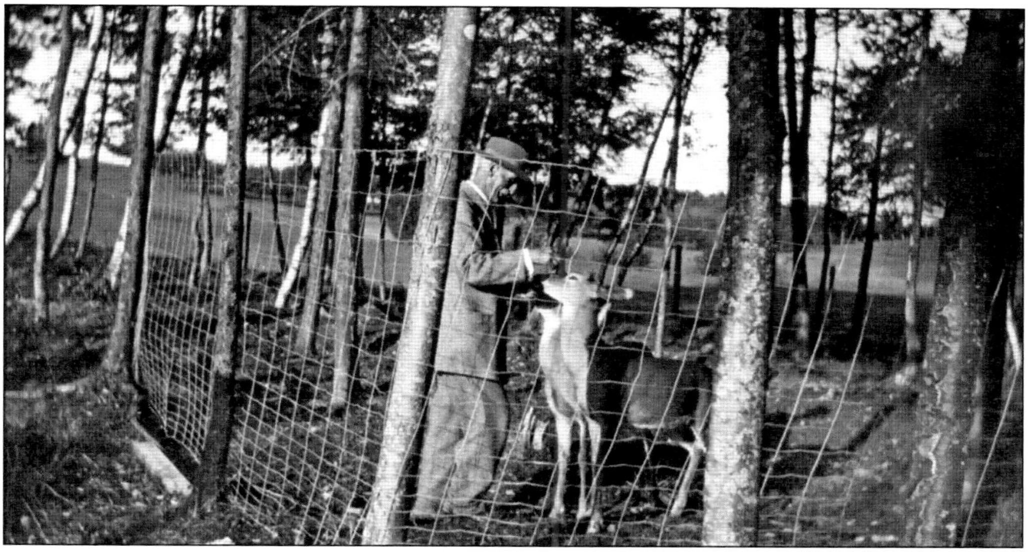

John F. Stanley (1839–1916) was a brother to Henry O. and Frank Stanley of Dixfield. He managed a fish hatchery in Auburn, Maine, from 1896 until his death, which was caused by a buck deer that attacked him while he was feeding it. The deer pushed him into a stream, causing him to develop pneumonia. (DHS.)

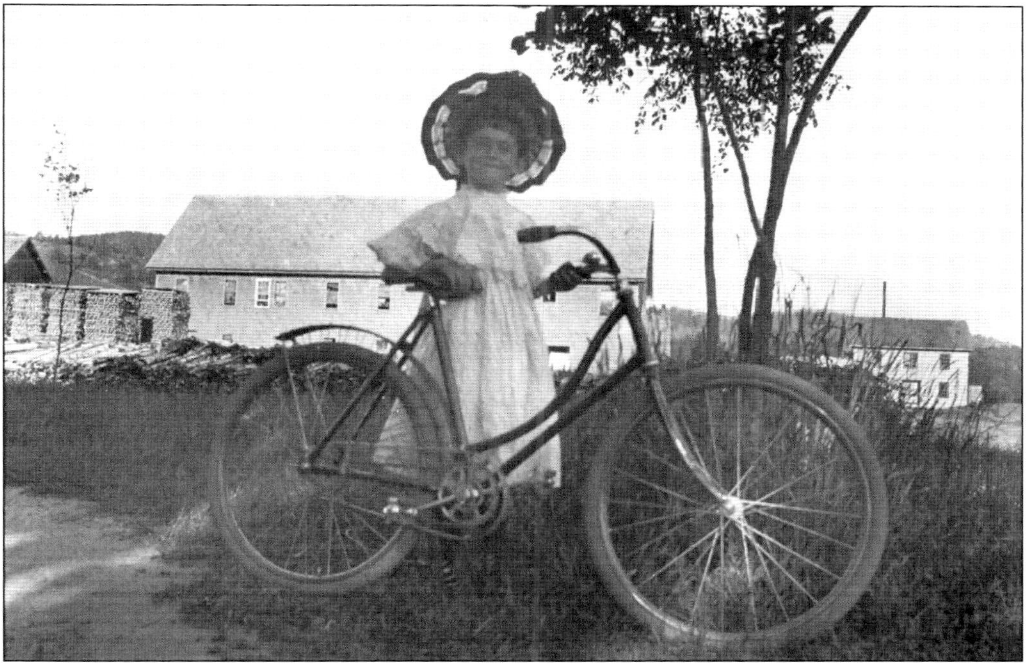

Josie Stanley's father, George, and her grandfather Henry O. Stanley were partners in a bicycle and sporting goods store on Weld. Street. This c. 1900 photograph shows her grandfather George A. Marsh's box factory in the right background and her cousin Newton S. Stowell's spool mill on Mill Street behind her. (NDM.)

Consistent with our mission to preserve history on a local level, this book was printed in South Carolina on American-made paper and manufactured entirely in the United States. Products carrying the accredited Forest Stewardship Council (FSC) label are printed on 100 percent FSC-certified paper.

MADE IN THE USA